DATE DUE

D1201084

Dynamic Assessment of
Young Children

Plenum Series on Human Exceptionality

SERIES EDITORS:
Donald H. Saklofske, *University of Saskatchewan, Saskatoon, Saskatchewan, Canada*
Moshe Zeidner, *University of Haifa, Mount Carmel, Israel*

ASSOCIATE EDITOR:
Vicki L. Schwean, *University of Saskatchewan, Saskatoon, Saskatchewan, Canada*

DYNAMIC ASSESSMENT OF YOUNG CHILDREN
David Tzuriel

HANDBOOK OF PSYCHOSOCIAL CHARACTERISTICS OF
EXCEPTIONAL CHILDREN
Edited by Vicki L. Schwean and Donald H. Saklofske

Dynamic Assessment of Young Children

David Tzuriel
Bar-Ilan University
Ramat Gan, Israel

Kluwer Academic / Plenum Publishers
New York, Boston, Dordrecht, London, Moscow

Library of Congress Cataloging-in-Publication Data

Tzuriel, David.
    Dynamic assessment of young children/David Tzuriel.
        p.   cm. — (Plenum series on human exceptionality)
    Includes bibliographical references and index.
    ISBN 0-306-46510-8
        1. Behavioral assessment.   2. Psychological tests.   I. Title.   II. Series.

BF176.5 .T98 2001
155.4'1393—dc21

00-067110

ISBN: 0-306-46510-8

©2001 Kluwer Academic/Plenum Publishers, New York
233 Spring Street, New York, N.Y. 10013

http:/www.wkap.nl/

10 9 8 7 6 5 4 3 2 1

A C.I.P. record for this book is available from the Library of Congress

Printed in the United States of America

To the blessed memory
of my beloved father, Yitzchack Subeiri,
a man of faith, ardent student of the *Mishnah*,
who always praised God in verse and song

Foreword

Dynamic/interactive assessment has been a long time coming! It has been almost a century since Alfred Binet suggested that assessment of the processes of learning should constitute a priority in the mental testing movement, and over 60 years since André Rey made the same suggestion. An important model that supports many contemporary approaches to "flexible" or "process" assessment was offered by Vygotsky in the 1920s. The ground breaking work by Reuven Feuerstein and his Swiss colleagues on process assessment of North African Jewish children was done in the early 1950s. In the intervening years almost every serious psychometrist has, at one time or another, called for emphasis on assessment of the processes of learning, rather than an exclusive emphasis on assessment of the products of prior opportunities to learn. One has to wonder why we have had to wait so long for formalization and instrumentation of the methods for doing just that! Of course, we psychologists like to do what we do well, and we have learned to do static, normative assessment, especially of "intelligence," very well indeed. Unfortunately, it is also true that dynamic/interactive assessment has not attracted or fueled the volume of high-quality research that is still going to be necessary if it is to survive as a widely used supplement to static, normative testing. This volume, incorporating a strong research base, goes a long way toward remediation of that situation.

In the 20 years since publication of Feuerstein, Rand, and Hoffman's *The Dynamic Assessment of Retarded Performers*, a rich variety of specific dynamic approaches, as well as an encouraging array of assessment instruments, has appeared. Most of the work has been done with school-age children, adolescents, and adults. It is high time we had a systematic approach to dynamic assessment designed specifically for young children.

Many years ago, I asked Feuerstein why he had begun his work on dynamic assessment (and on cognitive education as well) with older children and adolescents. His quite convincing reply was essentially this: In the new state of Israel and in post-World War II Europe, a vast number of persons were in great need of help with their learning abilities and—because of the disruptions of war and cultural transplantation—were about to enter adulthood and thus "disappear" from the reach of schools, guidance clinics, and child welfare agencies. Resources were very limited, so it was necessary to expend those resources first on persons with the most urgent need, and thereby to try to prevent their establishing life-long patterns of failure academically, vocationally, and socially. In other words, it was necessary to catch these young persons and give them essential help just before they vanished into an adult world where it would be much more difficult to reach them. One could have a bit longer time to reach children who were then in their early childhood. These were, of course, valid and sensible arguments for their time. Over the ensuing years it has become more and more obvious that if dynamic assessment is a good thing for older children, adolescents, and adults (and the evidence mounts that it is), then it would be an even better thing for young children. It would therefore be tempting to characterize this book as "timely." In fact, it is not. It is overdue!

Dynamic/interactive approaches to psychoeducational assessment continue to grow and to be elaborated by a diverse group of researchers and clinicians. It is important that their growth take place within a firm and clearly communicated theoretical context, that the most important questions about these approaches be examined in a thoroughly scientific manner, and that useful and "teachable" instruments be developed and made available to practitioners. Attention to those aspects is undoubtedly the most important contribution of this volume. It is also noteworthy that Tzuriel's approach has grown up, as did Binet's, in an educational context. The procedures described in this volume help us to make and to maintain the essential connections between psychoeducational assessment and the vital business of teaching and learning.

Often, new clinical instruments are constructed on the basis of testing experience, and then are submitted to some field testing—with or without having found a conceptual context within which to place them. By contrast, Tzuriel started with a theoretical orientation, both about cognitive development (what kinds of operations are important to learning and social adjustment) and about assessment (a "dynamic" approach is superior to a static, normative one). He then developed eight novel dynamic assessment tasks while simultaneously conducting research, so the assessment instruments are both the products of his research and the instruments for doing his research—at different stages of their development, of course. All eight tasks have been used extensively, both in clinical practice and in research, with diverse and interesting groups of children (immigrants, low-SES children, language-different children, children with learning disabilities, mental retardation, and hearing impairments, for example). Their metric characteristics have been established and reported.

Demonstrating the utility of dynamic assessment as an instrument of research, Tzuriel has used this method to investigate both educational and developmental questions that could not have been investigated so thoroughly with the use of more traditional methods. The combination of dynamic assessment with sophisticated research design and statistical analytic procedures has yielded inferences, for example, about the relation between parents' mediational behavior to their children and the children's subsequent cognitive modifiability. This same combination has made it possible to ask—and to answer—such questions as how to assess changes in children's ability to benefit from different interventions, especially from "mediated learning experiences." In that context, it is notable that the Tzuriel instruments have been used as primary criterion variables in the evaluation of the effectiveness of such cognitive education programs as Bright Start, Cognitive Modifiability Battery, and new models of intervention by peer mediation. One happy aspect of the use of these assessment instruments with children is the observation that dynamic assessment changes the children's functioning (albeit perhaps temporarily) as well as their motivation to engage in challenging mental tasks.

The modern history of psychometrics is spotted with frequent attempts to get rid of the cultural influences on intelligence test performance. These efforts lead to one of my all-time favorite psychology stories. The "draw-a-man" test was being used widely to assess intelligence in children from different cultural settings, and was thought to be relatively "culture free" or at least "culture fair." It was then found that some subcultural groups in the United States performed quite poorly on this test, including Hopi children in the American Southwest. Wayne Dennis then discovered that drawing persons was frowned on in Hopi society, so he quite ingeniously presented Hopi children with the "draw-a-horse" test—and found that estimates of their intelligence rose substantially, to levels that often exceeded those of American dominant-culture children on the same task!

Tzuriel's reliance in this volume on Vygotsky's "social-historical" cognitive psychology goes a long way toward putting the culture back into intelligence, and intelligence back into the culture. It now seems quite possible that if we had ever been successful in stripping away the cultural components of intelligence we would have found rather little remaining!

I congratulate David Tzuriel also on his refusal to suggest that we throw out static, normative tests and replace them entirely with dynamic methods. He recognizes that assessment is a much broader enterprise than testing. It is an enterprise that demands the gathering of information from a variety of sources, including social history, static test performance, achievement in academic and other settings, and cognitive modifiability inferences derived from dynamic/interactive assessment.

One of the most persistent problems in the dissemination of dynamic/interactive assessment is the reluctance of practicing psychologists to give it a try, to step beyond the familiar and the comfortable, to take additional training, and to invest the time and effort necessary to master these exciting methods. This volume makes the whole enterprise much more accessible, much less novel or alien, and ultimately more applicable.

H. Carl Haywood
Vanderbilt University

Preface

The development of dynamic assessment (DA) in general and particularly for young children has evolved mainly because standard psychometric measures were not designed to provide information about individual's learning potential, learning processes of the child, mediation strategies, and specific cognitive functions. Understanding of these factors is crucial not only for advancement of theory but also for improvement of intervention procedures with a variety of children with learning difficulties. Previous research has shown that standardized IQ scores explain about 50 percent of the variance in academic achievements. The questions that still remain are what are the factors that predict the other 50 percent? What type of intervention is necessary to defeat the existing prediction?

The use of norms in standardized testing is based on the assumption (usually implicit but sometimes explicit) that all persons of a given age had been exposed to equal learning opportunities. Clinical experience and research findings however indicate clearly that poor school performance and inadequate cognitive development reflect deficient cognitive processes, rather than low IQ. In regard to these issues some theoreticians and investigators raised the concept of *learning potential*. This concept, while being vague, has been developed out of necessity to explain that part of the variance in learning and academic achievement that is not associated with IQ scores.

In spite of awareness about the importance of DA for both theory development and practice, it has not been prevalent among psychologists and educators. The reasons might be related to theoretical fixation and perception of human beings' intellect as relatively stable. The traditional methods of measuring mental ability were intimately related to the conceptualization of intelligence, which can be tracked down to one's philosophical approach about the nature of the human being.

In this book I tried to establish DA as a useful and rich complementary approach that together with the standardized, normative assessment portray a holistic and accurate picture of cognitive functioning. DA appears to offer a more adequate assessment of handicapped persons (e.g., MR, sensory impaired, emotionally disturbed) and persons with learning disabilities, than do standardized, normative tests because of several reasons. First, they appear to reflect accurately individuals' learning capacity and relate closely to developmental variables such as the mediation patterns within the family. Second, they appear to offer specific and accurate intervention processes rather than vague and general recommendations about treatment procedures.

The focus of this book is on DA of young children. The reason is that early decisions about treatment procedures are much more crucial at an early age than later. I tried in this book to approach both practitioners who cope with learning disabled children on a day-to-day basis and researchers who grapple with theoretical issues. My belief though is that both target groups need to develop their theoretical, as well as their experiential, knowledge. Thus, establishing the theoretical and scientific foundations of the DA approach throughout the book is integrated with practical guidance as to how to intervene with a variety of children.

In the first part of the book, I describe the two major theories of Vygotsky and Feuerstein and their applications to DA. In the middle part, I describe the DA approach and more specifically the DA measures developed for young children in the last two decades. The last part of the book describes three major areas of research in which DA has been applied: developmental, educational, and cognitive intervention programs. The last chapter of the book—the epilogue—deals with some unresolved problems and open issues and suggestions for future developments.

David Tzuriel
April 2001

Contents

1

Dynamic–Interactive Approaches to Assessment of Learning Potential

INTRODUCTION

In the last two decades there has been a proliferation of research dealing with dynamic—interactive assessment (DA) as an alternative approach to the conventional psychometric measures. This proliferation has paralleled dissatisfaction with the static test approaches. The term *static test* refers to a test where the examiner presents items to the child and records his or her response without any attempt to intervene in order to change, guide, or improve the child's performance. Many psychologists and educators have pointed out static tests' inadequacy in revealing the learning potential of minority students or of students with varied types of learning disabilities (e.g., Budoff, 1987; Carlson & Wiedl, 1992; Feuerstein, Rand, & Hoffman, 1979; Guthke & Wingenfeld, 1992; Haywood, 1997; Lidz, 1991; Tzuriel & Haywood, 1992). This has been amplified by their inadequacy in indicating specific learning processes and in providing prescriptive teaching. DA, with all its limitations (i.e., time consuming, subjectivity of observation, and requirement of trained examiners), has been suggested as a more accurate procedure than the static testing approach in revealing individuals' learning potential.

CRITICISM OF STANDARDIZED TESTING

The main argument against standardized (conventional) static tests is that they are inadequate in revealing children's cognitive capacities, especially those

1

of children who come from culturally different populations and/or children with learning difficulties (Guthke & Al-Zoubi, 1987; Guthke & Wingenfeld, 1992; Feuerstein et al., 1979; Haywood & Tzuriel, 1992b; Hessels & Hamers, 1993; Lidz, 1987a, 1991, 1995; Lidz & Elliott, 2000; Skuy, Visser, Hoffenberg, & Fridjohn, 1990; Tzuriel, 1992a, 1997a, 1998, 2000c; Vygotsky, 1978). In Haywood's (1997) words, "the most frequent complaint is that they are not uniformly valid across ability levels, ages, and ethnic groups" (p. 103).

Four major criticisms have been raised with respect to the use of static tests:

(1.) The standard psychometric measures do not provide important information about learning processes, deficient cognitive functions that are responsible for learning difficulties, and teaching strategies that would facilitate learning (Feuerstein et al., 1979; Guthke & Stein, 1996; Haywood, 1988, 1997; Tzuriel & Haywood, 1992). The static measures provide important information on children's intellectual performance, but they were not designed to provide the type of information given in DA procedures. Of most importance, psychologists and educational practitioners need to know not only about the actual level of performance, but also what a child might achieve with an adult's guidance or a peer's help, the nature of learning processes, specific deficient cognitive functions, and specific strategies that could facilitate learning.

(2.) The low level of performance of many children, as revealed in standard testing as well as in academic achievement, very frequently falls short of revealing the learning potential of children, especially of those identified as coming from disadvantaged social backgrounds, or having some sort of learning difficulty. Many children fail on static tests because of lack of opportunity for learning experiences, or cultural difference, or specific learning difficulties, or traumatic life experiences that have acted as barriers to their cognitive development. Support for this was found by Rogoff and Chavajay's (1995) review on the effect of schooling on performance of Piagetian-type tasks in different cultures. The high variability found in Piagetian tasks has been attributed to familiarity with materials and concepts, rather than to ability. Cole (1990) also reached a similar conclusion "that concrete operational thinking is not influenced by schooling; what is influenced is the subjects' ability to understand the language of testing and the presuppositions of the testing situation itself" (p. 99). Many times psychologists and educators confuse *ability* and *efficiency* in observing or diagnosing children. Children might have a high level of intelligence and abstract ability, as evidenced by their problem-solving behavior, but they perform rather inefficiently on different cognitive tasks, especially on those involving time limits. For example, many of the WISC-R subtests are based on performance within a time limit. For many children a time limit is a constricting factor that is not necessarily related to their high-level mental skills.

(3.) Many standardized tests describe children in general terms, mostly in relation to their relative position in their peer group. They do not provide clear descriptions of the *cognitive processes* involved in learning and recommendations for prescriptive teaching and remedial learning strategies. This often creates a communication gap between psychologists and teachers who have incongruent expectations about testing goals. For example, in many psychological reports the gap between the verbal and performance subscales of the WISC-R is emphasized, but no specific recommendation is given about what exactly to do about it. Should the child be given more training in one of the domains? How exactly should one teach it? In what way can we ensure transfer training from that cognitive domain to classroom performance? In many psychological reports the emphasis is on the psychometric properties of the individual's functioning, whereas the learning processes that are required to bring about change are ignored.

Utley, Haywood, and Masters (1992) have remarked in regard to this point that the principal use of a psychometric intelligence test is *classification*, with the aim of giving differential treatment for individuals differing in level and/or pattern of intelligence. Such a classification not only has limited value, but also may have negative effects. First, the *manifest* cognitive performance shown by the IQ does not necessarily reflect individual differences in *latent* intelligence. Second, even if it does, it is highly questionable whether individuals with the same IQ have similar characteristics and needs that would necessitate similar treatment. On the contrary, practical experience shows that even children who are virtually identical in terms of age, gender, and IQ show markedly different behavior, cognitive or affective, and therefore require different teaching approaches.

The problems of psychometric static tests are magnified when applied with mentally retarded (MR) individuals. These individuals have difficulty understanding the nature and requirements of the standard tasks; therefore, their performance on those tasks does not necessarily reflect inability. In some cases, removal of some obstacles to conceptualizing the nature of the tasks improves their performance significantly (Haywood, 1997). Haywood has already made it clear that the validity of standardized tests for MR persons does not lie in what these persons can do but in identifying what they presumably cannot do. Empirical support has been found in studies showing lower prediction of school achievement by standardized tests in the case of persons with MR than those without MR. Furthermore, DA procedures, although not designed primarily for prediction, have been found to be better predictors of school achievement among persons with MR than those without MR (Budoff, 1987; Guthke, 1992; Haywood, 1997; Tzuriel, 2000c).

(4.) Another criticism of psychometric tests is that they do not relate to these nonintellective factors, which can influence individuals' cognitive performance. Nonintellective factors such as intrinsic motivation, need for mastery, locus of control, anxiety, frustration tolerance, self confidence, and accessibility to mediation (Tzuriel, Samuels, & Feuerstein, 1988) are no less important in determining children's intellectual achievements than are the "pure" cognitive factors. This is especially true with MR individuals whose personality or motivational problems interfere with their cognitive performance on conventional static tests (e.g., Haywood, 1992b; Haywood & Switzky, 1986; Paour, 1992; Zigler, Abelson, & Seitz, 1973; Zigler & Butterfield, 1968). Many investigators regard cognitive functioning and motivational—affective factors as inseparable, representing two sides of the same coin (Haywood, 1992b; Tzuriel, 1991a). As will be seen later, DA is conceived as a holistic assessment approach that permits observation of individuals on cognitive, affective, and behavioral levels as well as the interrelation among these levels of functioning.

It is interesting to note that in spite of the proliferation of criticism and allegations against conventional psychometric tests, Utley et al. (1992) did not find empirical support for most of them. No support was found for allegations of test bias with minority groups, of differential predictive validity, or differential construct validity. The only acknowledgment was that minority children are represented in special education classes far out of proportion to their number in the population and that assignment to special education classes has been based mainly on standardized tests. Haywood (1997) argued however, that one should bear in mind that placement decisions are made by persons, not by tests.

Haywood (1993, 1997) proposed very eloquently that "the problem lies not in what standardized tests do, which they do very well, but instead in what they do not do" (p. 104). Haywood (1993) noted the following:

> Based as they are on achievement itself, they [standardized tests] certainly do a good job of predicting achievement. They are not good indicators of learning potential, because individual differences in achievement are products not only of differential aptitude but of a host of other influencing variables as well, including language proficiency, cultural relevance and sophistication, attitudes toward learning, motivation to learn, and, perhaps most important, differential development of the cognitive tools of learning. Since it is so much easier to get into categories than to get out of them, I suggest that the objective of classification has outlived its usefulness and should be abandoned except for such purposes as the planning and distribution of the resources of whole school districts or even states. Prediction never was a particularly defensible objective. I could never understand what makes psychologists want to be fortune tellers! There should be scant satisfaction in knowing that our tests have accurately predicted that a particular child will fail in school. There are many sources of such predictor information. What we need is instruments and approaches that can tell us *how to defeat those very predictions!* So, I conclude that whereas standardized normative tests do their job very well indeed, a job that is not worth doing is not worth doing well! (pp. 5–6)

HISTORICAL AND SOCIAL BACKGROUND

Psychologists have suggested the idea of assessment of processes rather than the end products of learning since the beginning of the twentieth century. Alfred Binet (Binet & Simon, 1921) himself advocated assessment of processes but eventually developed static instruments. Other investigators such as Buckingham (1921), Dearborn (1921), Kern (1930), Penrose (1934), Rey (1934), and Thorndike (1924) all suggested measurement of the ability to learn as part of intelligence and as an ideal methodology for testing mental abilities. The interest, elaboration, and spread of the idea of DA occurred only in the 1970s with the introduction of Vygotsky's theory by Brown and colleagues (Brown & Ferrara, 1985), and Feuerstein's ideas by Haywood (1977) to modern psychology.

DA has emerged from both theoretical conceptions about human cognitive plasticity and practical needs to find novel diagnostic measures for children who for various reasons do not reveal their capacities in conventional static tests. The educational necessity for changes in assessment procedures can be explained on both *molar* and *molecular* levels (Tzuriel & Haywood, 1992).

Molar level. On a molar level, there have been social changes toward democratization of the educational system, and a realization that standardized tests do not provide answers for burning issues. These issues were related to questions such as: How much are human beings modifiable above and beyond their manifest level of performance? How is development and assessment of cognitive functioning is molded by sociocultural factors? What are the intervention procedures that are most efficient in bringing about cognitive changes? What are the basic preliminary factors that can explain human cognitive modifiability?

Molecular level. On a molecular level, DA has been motivated by conventional tests' inadequacy in providing precise information about individual differences of learning ability and specific learning processes, their operational translation into practice and prescriptive teaching, and the validity of individuals' assignment to special education settings. These issues are related in turn to such questions as: What are the specific cognitive processes that act as barriers for the actualization of learning potential? How is DA more efficient in directing the future treatment of individuals with learning difficulties?

The interest in DA has led to extensive research in Israel (Feuerstein et al., 1979; Tzuriel, 1989b, 1992a, 1997a, 1998, 1999b, 2000c), Europe (Elliott, 1993; Guthke, 1992; Hamers, Sijtsma, & Ruijssenaars, 1993), and the United States (Budoff, 1987; Campione & Brown, 1987; Carlson & Wiedl, 1992; Day & Hall, 1988; Haywood, 1988, 1997; Haywood & Tzuriel, 1992b; Lidz, 1987, 1991; Lidz & Elliott, 2000; Swanson, 1995). DA has been applied in a wide variety of testing contexts and populations as described in Table 1.1.

Table 1.1. Application of DA in Different Populations

Population	Studies
Socially disadvantaged children	Feuerstein et al., 1979; Luther & Wyatt, 1990; Tzuriel, 1989b; Tzuriel & Klein, 1985
Persons with mental retardation	Ashman, 1992; Buchel, Schlatter & Scharnhorst, 1997; Budoff, 1967, 1987; Paour, 1992
Deaf children	Katz & Bucholz, 1984; Keane, Tannenbaum & Krapf, 1992; Tzuriel & Caspi, 1992
Gifted disadvantaged children	Bolig & Day, 1993; Boreland & Wright, 1994; Hickson & Skuy, 1990; Lidz & Macrine, 2001; Skuy, Kaniel, & Tzuriel, 1988
Penitentiary inmates	Silverman & Waxman, 1992
Adults with learning difficulties	Barr & Samuels, 1988; Kaniel & Tzuriel, 1992
Children with learning difficulties	Missiuna & Samuels, 1989; Samuels, Tzuriel, & Malloy-Miller, 1989; Swanson, 1995
Patients with brain damage	Bates, Kuhl, & Sowarka, 1922
University students	Shochet, 1992
Preschool children	Burns, 1991; Gamlin, 1989; Hessels, 1997; Kahn & King, 1997; Lidz, 1991; Lidz & Thomas, 1987; Mearig, 1987; Tzuriel, 1989, 1995a, 1995b, 1997a, 1998, 1999b; Tzuriel & Klein, 1985; Tzuriel & Eran, 1990; Tzuriel & Ernst, 1990; Tzuriel & Weiss, 1988; Waters & Stringer, 1997
Ethnic Minorities	Hessels, 1997; Hessels & Hamers, 1993; Gupta & Coxhead, 1988; Pena & Gillam, 2000; Tzuriel & Kaufman, 1999

DEFINITION OF DYNAMIC ASSESSMENT (DA)

DA refers to *an assessment of thinking, perception, learning, and problem solving by an active teaching process aimed at modifying cognitive functioning.* DA differs from conventional static tests in regard to its goals, processes, instruments, test situation, and interpretation of results (Campione, 1989; Feuerstein et al., 1979; Feuerstein, Rand, Haywood, Kyram, & Hoffman, 1995; Grigorenko & Sternberg, 1998; Gupta & Coxhead, 1988; Guthke & Stein, 1996; Hamers et al., 1993; Haywood & Tzuriel, 1992b; Lidz, 1987, 1991, 1995; Lidz, Jepsen, & Miller, 1977; Tzuriel, 1996, 1997a, 1998, 2000c; Tzuriel & Haywood, 1992). These differences are listed in Table 1.2 and explained in detail in Chapter 4 (Distinctive Features of the Clinical DA Approach).

The main idea in DA is to use change criteria within the testing situation as predictors of future cognitive performance. The conceptualization behind using change criteria is that they are more closely related to teaching processes, by which the child is taught how to process information, than they are to static measures of intelligence. The mediational strategies used within the DA procedure

Table 1.2. Major Differences Between DA and Standardized Testing

Dimensions of comparison	Dynamic Assessment	Standardized Testing
Goals of testing	• Assessment of change • Assessment of mediation • Assessment of deficient cognitive functions • Assessment of Nonintellective factors	• Evaluation of static performance • Comparison with peers • Prediction of future success
Orientation	• Processes of learning • Metacognitive processes • Understanding of mistakes	• End products (static) • Objective scores • Profile of scores
Context of testing	• Dynamic, open, interactive • Guidance, help, and feedback • Feelings of competence • Parents and teachers can observe	• Standardized • Structured • Formal • Parents and teachers are not allowed to observe
Interpretation of results	• Subjective (mainly) • Peak performance • Cognitive modifiability • Deficient cognitive functions • Response to mediation	• Objective (mainly) • Average performance
Nature of tasks	• Constructed for learning • Graduated for teaching • Guarantee for success	• Based on psychometric properties • Termination after failures

correspond more naturally with learning processes in other life contexts than do conventional static methods and therefore give better indications about future changes of cognitive structures.

Vygotsky's (1978) zone of proximal development (ZPD) concept and Feuerstein's mediated learning experience (MLE) theory (Feuerstein et al., 1979), which serve as the conceptual bases of most DA elaboration, have emerged in response to needs to include sociocultural factors in the understanding of cognitive development and learning potential. These theories are described in detail in Chapters 2 and 3.

ISSUES RELATED TO DA

Comparison of DA to static testing was not limited to problems of theoretical nature. Such comparison also raises issues of applicative nature. Some of these issues are as follows:

- Prediction of school achievements by static-standardized versus DA measures (Embretson, 1992, Guthke, Beckmann, & Dobat, 1997; Lidz et al., 1997; Shochet, 1992; Tzuriel, 2000c)
- Evaluation of cognitive intervention programs aimed at developing learning potential (Rand, Tannenbaum, & Feuerstein, 1986; Tzuriel & Alfassi, 1994; Tzuriel, Kaniel, Kanner, & Haywood, 1999)
- The influence of cultural factors on individuals' performance in DA versus static tests (Guthke & Al-Zoubi, 1987; Hessels & Hamers, 1993; Skuy & Shmukler, 1987; Tzuriel & Kaufman, 1999; Vygotsky, 1978)
- The role of mediation within the family as a determinant of an individual's cognitive modifiability (Klein, 1988, 1996; Tzuriel, 1998, 1999b; Tzuriel & Ernst, 1990; Tzuriel & Weiss, 1998a,b)
- Internalization of novel "symbolic mental tools" with transition from one culture to another (Tzuriel & Kaufman, 1999).
- Creation of individualized teaching plans based on specific learning difficulties (Feuerstein et al., 1979; Tzuriel & Haywood, 1992).

The focus of this book is on DA of young children, mainly in kindergarten and the first grades of school, using Tzuriel's DA instruments. Most studies in which these instruments were used were carried out at Bar-Ilan University (Tzuriel, 1997a, b, 1998, 1999a, b, 2000a, b, c, d). It should be noted that several DA applications have been suggested with young children by other authors such as Gamlin (1989), Hessels (1997), Kahn and King (1997), Lidz (1991), Mearig (1987), Resing (1997), and Waters and Stringer (1997), most of which are based on Feuerstein's and/or Vygotsky's theories. These DA applications are discussed in relation to specific studies.

PURPOSES OF THE BOOK

The purposes of this book are manifold. First it is intended to provide a description of the social origins of cognitive modifiability and the development of learning potential, especially as related to the legacy of two theoreticians: Vygotsky and Feuerstein. The second purpose of this book is to describe and validate the MLE theory (Feuerstein et al., 1979), especially in relation to one of its applicative systems, the DA of learning potential. The third purpose is to present my own approach to assessment of young children, which is based on Vygotsky's ZPD concept and Feuerstein's MLE theory.

Vygotsky's concept of ZPD has inspired many researchers to investigate the learning potential of individuals and to focus on cognitive modifiability rather than on manifest performance. Feuerstein's approach, developed independently 30–40 years later, is in many respects similar to Vygotsky's approach but different in regard to conceptual elaboration, operational parameters, and the development of applied systems. These two key figures in the DA movement, Vygotsky and Feuerstein, who have played leading roles in changing the standard conventional testing approaches, developed their theories and techniques outside the psychological mainstream in the United States. Both developed their approaches independently as a response to the realities imposed by sociohistorical factors. Their theories emerged at times when large portions of the population with restricted backgrounds were required to confront sophisticated modern technologies coupled with social needs to integrate minorities and immigrants into the dominant culture. Both theorists criticized the existing normative static tests as measures that had been constructed in one social context and artificially transplanted into another. Both of them responded to sociocultural demands for a new perspective in assessment (and treatment) and looked to individuals' learning potential rather than their manifest or actual level of performance (Tzuriel & Haywood, 1992).

It should be noted that this book is focused on DA of young children and will not include detailed discussion of more general approaches to DA such as the *testing-the-limits* technique (Carlson & Wiedl, 1992), the *learntest* (Guthke, 1992), the *graduated prompt* (Campione & Brown, 1987), and the *learning potential testing* (Budoff, 1987). Because of space limitations they are not reviewed here and readers are referred to the appropriate literature. Readers are also referred to other DA techniques such as *induction of logic structures*, a neo-Piagetian approach developed in France by Paour (1992); the battery for assessment of learning potential developed in England by Gupta and Coxhead (1988); and the Preschool Learning Assessment Device developed by Lidz (1991).

In the following chapters the theoretical basis of the DA approach is presented. Vygotsky's theory as related to the DA approach and recent work on DA that has been carried out from a Vygotskian perspective are discussed in Chapter 2. Special emphasis is given to the neo-Vygotskian approaches of Campione and Brown (1987) and Guthke (1992). This is followed by a presentation of Feuerstein's theoretical perspective on structural cognitive modifiability and MLE (Chapter 3). A separate chapter deals with distinctive features of the clinical DA approach (Chapter 4). The basic principles of DA of young children have guided the development of seven DA instruments for young children. The principles that guide assessment of young children are presented in Chapter 5, followed by description of seven DA instruments developed for assessment and intervention with young children (Chapter 6). These chapters are followed by discussion of current research from three different perspectives. The research perspectives relate to educational/clinical issues (Chapter 7), developmental dimensions of parent–child interactions and their effect on children's cognitive modifiability (Chapter 8), and evaluation of cognitive education programs using DA criteria (Chapter 9). Special attention is given to use of DA within a developmental framework (e.g., effects of parent–child mediation on children's cognitive modifiability) and evaluation of cognitive education programs. In the last chapter of this book (Chapter 10) I will try to suggest some integration of the DA approach and outline directions for future research. In general, the theory and research findings suggest the DA approach is an efficient and accurate procedure for assessment of learning potential.

2

Vygotsky's Socio-Cultural Theory and Applications for Assessment

HISTORICAL BACKGROUND

Over the past two decades there has been a growing interest in the ideas of Vygotsky (1956, 1978, 1981). The major reason for this interest in Vygotsky's work in the West may be related to his contribution toward understanding of the social origins of cognitive processes and the conceptual foundation of dynamic/interactive assessment.

Vygotsky's Soviet colleagues received his ideas with enthusiasm initially and he was considered in his homeland to be the founder of the Cultural-Historical School. Later, however, his ideas were criticized because he neglected the role of "class conflict," and because he followed a sociological line of thinking without focusing enough on Soviet society. Vygotsky's ideas were equated with the questionable theories and practices of the "pedologists" (Guthke & Wingenfeld, 1992). "Pedology" had established itself in the Soviet Union, in the 1920s and early 1930s, as a science of child development the goal of which was to study child development from an interdisciplinary perspective. Pedologists practiced a sort of school psychology but without thorough education in psychology. In their practice, they adopted uncritically the standardized intelligence tests as well as the genetic interpretation of test results used in other countries. Because of these practices, many children were wrongly labeled "unintelligent" and incapable of learning. The unjustified labeling, which was especially applied to children from illiterate families or Asian backgrounds, led to protests by parents and educators. As a result of the criticism the Central

11

Committee of the Communist Party of the Soviet Union issued in 1936 the Pedology Decree in which pedology was strongly condemned. As a result many psychological and pedological journals in which Vygotsky had played a leading role as contributor were banned.

In defending Vygotsky's ideas neo-Vygotskian researchers (i.e., Guthke, Kozulin) explained that Vygotsky was by no means an uncritical supporter of traditional intelligence tests, nor an advocate of a fatalistic genetic position on child development. Contrary to criticisms, Vygotsky and his followers (e.g., Luria, Leont'ev) did not hold extreme positions on the nature—nurture issue. In fact, analysis of Vygotsky's theory as well as the ideas of Luria and Leont'ev shows that development of mental processes of children results from the *internalization* of the socially determined cultural heritage. The biological factors provide only the framework of the child's capacity for internalization. Vygotsky, who perceived the danger of the individualistic and reductionistic approach in traditional psychology, pleaded for a close relationship between the individual's internalization and the social origins of this psychological process. Vygotsky regarded internalization as a process during which *interpsychological* forms of higher mental functions are developed through adult—child interactions. These processes become *intrapsychological* as the child internalizes the socially formed external world (Wertsch, 1985).

THE CONCEPTS OF ZONE OF PROXIMAL DEVELOPMENT (ZPD) AND INTERNALIZATION

Vygotsky's concepts of the *ZPD* and *internalization* have captured the interest of many developmental psychologists and educators (Brown & Ferrara, 1985; Guthke, 1992; Kozulin, 1990; Moll, 1990; Rogoff, 1990; Tharp & Gallimore, 1988; Valsiner, 1984, 1987; van der Veer & Valsiner, 1993; van Geert, 1994; Wertsch, 1985; Wertsch & Tulviste, 1992). The ZPD was defined as the distance between a child's "actual developmental level as determined by independent problem solving" and the higher level of "potential development as determined through problem solving under adult guidance or in collaboration with more capable peers" (Vygotsky, 1978, p. 86).

The ZPD concept was developed originally to address the problems of measurement of mental age and the prediction of future learning and development (van Geert, 1994). These concepts however were applied also to explain developmental processes. According to Vygotsky, individuals' cognitive development can be understood only by considering the sociocultural aspects from which it derives. Vygotsky's claim about the social origins of cognitive development can be found in his "general genetic law of cultural development"

Any function in the child's cultural development appears twice, or on two planes. First it appears on the social plane, and then on the psychological plane. First it appears between people as an interpsychological category, and then within the child as an intrapsychological category. This is equally true with regard to voluntary attention, logical memory, the formation of concepts, and the development of volition. . . . [I]t goes without saying that internalization transforms the process itself and changes its structure and functions. Social relations or relations among people genetically underlie all higher functions and their relationships. (Vygotsky, 1981, p. 163)

In determining the child's cognitive development one should consider both the actual development level and the potential level. The actual level can be measured by observing the child's independent problem solving without any guidance or help, much like the static standardized testing approach, whereas the potential level can be observed after the child has been mediated on how to perform, as is done in DA.

The potential development becomes actual development through the internalization mechanism. In other words, the child's initial performance is an external operation, which is transformed and becomes internal after a process of guidance by a more competent individual. In Vygotsky's (1978) words:

An essential feature of learning is that it creates the zone of proximal development; that is, learning awakens a variety of internal developmental processes that are able to operate only when the child is interacting with people in his environment and in cooperation with his peers. Once these processes are internalized, they become part of the child's independent developmental achievement. (p. 90)

IMPLICATIONS OF THE ZPD CONCEPT

Vygotsky examined several implications of the ZPD concept in regard to instruction and assessment of intelligence. Instruction, for example, should correspond more closely to the potential development level than to the actual level of development. As for assessment Vygotsky used the following example to illustrate the ZPD concept. Suppose we tested two children of the same age and found that both have similar mental age. However, when attempts are made to teach these children to solve more advanced problems we might find an essential difference between them. One child might show higher performance on problems that are 2 years above his actual level of development when given help in the form of prompting, examples, and demonstration. The second child, given the same amount of help, might solve problems that are only a half-year above his level of actual development. In Vygotsky's view the cognitive development of these two children is sharply different. The first child demonstrates a much higher ZPD level than the second child. This means that with the ZPD method "we can take stock not only in today's completed process of development, not only the cycles that are already concluded and done, not only the processes of maturation that are completed; we can also take stock in processes that are now in a state of coming into being, that are only ripening, or only developing" (Vygotsky, 1956, pp. 447–448).

Vygotsky (1978) warned against estimation of the child's readiness for learning based on the child's "unaided" or manifested performance level. He criticized educational policy for mentally retarded children, which is based on the assumption that they are incapable of abstract thinking. As a matter of fact, these policies reinforce the concrete tendencies and suppress any rudiments for abstract thought that they still have.

Wertsch and Tulviste (1992) argue it is essential to bear in mind that the actual and potential levels of development respectively correspond to the individual's *intramental* and *intermental* functioning. In this way the ZPD will not be conceptualized simply as technique or a technical format for improvement of assessment. Instead it can be conceived as having powerful implications for mediation aimed at changing the individual's intermental functioning and, as a consequence, his or her intramental functioning.

These ideas have motivated several investigators to develop assessment techniques. The most known of Vygotsky's followers in DA are Campione and Brown (1987) and Guthke (1992, Guthke & Wingenfeld, 1992). These two approaches are described in the rest of this chapter.

THE "GRADUATED PROMPT" APPROACH

Inspired by the Soviet approach Campione, Brown, and their colleagues (Campione, 1989; Campione & Brown, 1987; Campione, Brown, Ferrara, Jones, & Steinberg, 1985; Ferrara, Brown, & Campione, 1986) have developed the *graduated prompt* procedure and carried out a series of studies to examine the reliability of DA measures. The principle behind the graduated prompt procedure is basically to help the child gradually until he or she solves the task. Mediation in this approach is delivered by predetermined hints that range from general to specific. The examiner stops providing hints when the child reaches the level of independent task solution predetermined for that task. The amount of aid needed in order to solve the problem is taken as an indication of the subject's ZPD. Resing (1997) commented that unlike other DA approaches (e.g., Budoff, Guthke, Hamers, Carlson) the outcome measure in the graduated prompt approach is not the amount of improvement in the child's performance, but rather the amount of help or mediation needed to reach a specified criterion. Consequently, one can infer how much additional help is needed to transfer the learned principles to novel situations. The outcome measures according to this approach are the sums of the total number of hints given at each of the testing phases (i.e., initial learning, maintenance, and transfer) and the total number of hints for the whole testing phases. A profile of the outcome measure is taken as an indication for the child's ZPD. The assumption is that a child with a broad ZPD profits more from the mediation and needs less help than a child with a narrow ZPD.

The procedure starts with introduction of an initial problem. Once this problem is solved another version of the problem is given and the number of prompts required to solve the new problem is taken as an indication for transfer of learning. The efficiency of learning is operationalized by the number of prompts and the breadth of transfer. The breadth of transfer is examined in terms of the degree of success with *maintenance* problems (i.e., problems that are parallel to the initial ones), *near transfer* problems (i.e., problems that are similar to the training problems contextually and formally), and *far transfer* problems (i.e., problems that are similar to the training problems contextually but incorporate a new relation).

Based on Vygotsky's theory, Brown and Ferrara (1985) argued that in addition to the importance of the graduated prompts, the assessment of ZPD should entail task analysis, and transfer of learning. These aspects coincide with contemporary theories of learning and cognition. Without these elements it would be difficult to select the series of graduated prompts and design appropriate methods for assessing efficiency of learning and transfer. Transfer of learning is considered to be especially important in academic situations, in which instruction is often incomplete and ambiguous. Campione and Brown suggested that the ratio of learning (i.e., number of graduated prompts) to transfer (i.e., the distance of application of knowledge from the original example) should be viewed as a measure of individual differences.

One of Campione and Brown's primary concerns was the relation between DA and standard IQ tests within the same domain. In other words they were interested in finding out whether learning and transfer are related to general ability differences and whether these measures provide information beyond that obtainable from the static tests. The type of tasks used within the graduated prompt framework included inductive reasoning problems (e.g., progressive matrices), series completion tasks (e.g., anagrams), mathematics problems, reading-comprehension tasks, and listening-comprehension tasks.

In their studies (i.e., Campione et al., 1985; Ferrara et al., 1986) they found that students of lower ability, as compared with higher ability students, require more instruction to reach the criterion and need more help to show transfer. In their first study, Brown and Ferrara (1985) used a letter completion task (alphabetical progression task) that required understanding of several rules (i.e., repetition of letters, occurrence of letters in forward or backward sequence). The problems were presented initially to a group of third and fifth graders to be solved independently much like a standard test. The next step included a set of standardized graduated prompts increasing in level of explicitness. The first prompt was a subtle hint whereas the final step was direct teaching of the problem's solution. The extent of the ZPD was empirically translated into the number of prompts needed to solve the first problem versus the second problem, and so on. A child revealing a wide ZPD was one who reduced the number of prompts needed from one trial to another, or in other words showed effective transfer of a new solution across similar problems. The findings showed, as expected, that the fifth graders learned more quickly than the third graders (needed less hints) and that high-IQ children required about three-fourths the number of hints needed by the average-IQ children to reach a criterion of learning. What is more important with regard to the difference between static and DA is that a good number of children (about a third) had a learning speed that was not predicted by their IQ level. The authors also reported that more prompts were needed to solve the far transfer problems than the maintenance and near transfer problems. Interactions of grade and IQ level with breadth of transfer showed that more prompts were needed for the third graders and for the low-IQ level than for the fifth graders and the high-IQ level, respectively. The IQ level did not predict the degree of transfer for about a third of the children. Comparison of speed of learning with degree of transfer showed that about a third of the subjects did not conform to the slow learning/low transfer and fast learning/high transfer patterns.

When learning speed and transfer level profiles were broken down by IQ level it was found that the IQ of almost 50% of the children did not predict learning speed and/or degree of transfer. The findings revealed several learning profiles such as: (1) *slow*: slow learners, narrow transferrers, low IQ, (2) *fast*: fast learners, wide transferrers, high IQ, (3) *reflective*: slow learners, wide transferrers, (4) *context-bound*: fast learners, narrow transferrers, and (5) *high scores*: fast learners, wide transferrers, low IQ.

In a second study Brown and Ferrara (1985) posed the question whether these profiles are consistent across domains. For this purpose they used the letter-completion task and a progressive matrices task, both of which involve inductive reasoning but were different in modality of presentation (verbal versus figural). The subjects were educable mentally retarded students (IQ = 70) who were classified according to the above learning profiles. The findings revealed that the correlation for number of hints required to reach learning criteria on both tasks was .66 ($p < .001$). The correlation for performance on maintenance/transfer tasks however was more domain-specific as reflected by the lower correlation of .39 ($p < .05$). Another finding was that for number of hints, 76% of the children displayed the same learning status on both tasks. On maintenance/transfer criteria, 43% were identical on both tasks but 52% shifted from one to the opposite status.

In two other studies (Campione & Brown, 1987), change scores on the Raven's matrices were predicted by ability (IQ) and dynamic (measures of learning and transfer) tests. The change scores were the residual gain calculated by the pre- to postteaching performance. The DA measures were simplified forms of the progressive matrices and a series completion task. The findings showed that the learning and transfer measures predicted the residual gain scores above and beyond the measures of ability.

Using the same approach Resing (1997) found that metacognitive training given to children in an experimental group improved their test scores more than those of children in a control group several months after training. Resing also reported that both posttest scores and learning-potential scores contributed significantly to the prediction of school achievement when compared with the pretest scores (the increase in explained variance was 4% to 40%, depending on the test).

The findings of Resing (1997) were also reported by other researchers (i.e., Day, Engelhardt, Maxwell, & Bolig, 1997; Speece, Cooper, & Kibler, 1990). Day et al. (1997) studied the prediction of posttest performance by pretest and learning tests with a sample of preschool children using structural equation modeling. The children were given pretests, training, and posttests on the *block design* and *similarities* tasks. The findings showed that the best-fit model was the one that included paths from both pretest and learning testing to posttest performances in block design and similarities.

Speece et al. (1990) studied the prediction of school achievement of first graders considered to be at risk for school failure (*n* = 104) versus controls with average ability (*n* = 83). Both groups were administered a dynamic test developed by Bryant (1982). The posttest results of the dynamic test were significantly predicted by measures of verbal intelligence, pretest knowledge, language variables, and number of prompts. These variables accounted for 48% of the posttest variance. What is important here was the finding that from the 48% of the explained variance, the graduated prompt measure accounted for a significant amount of variance beyond all other variables in the model. Another important finding was that while the at-risk and control groups could not be distinguished by standard achievement measures or the number of prompts, they could be distinguished by the posttest DA measure.

In conclusion the findings of studies based on the graduated prompt approach indicate that the ZPD has several advantages over the standardized IQ or achievement scores. The concept of ZPD within different domains allows differential diagnosis of competence areas, consideration of different learning parameters such as learning efficiency, and breadth of transfer within and across domains. A major conclusion of these studies is that the ZPD approach provides not only a more accurate diagnosis about an individual's learning potential but also a rich prescription for remediation.

THE LEARNTEST APPROACH

Guthke's learntest approach (Guthke, 1982, 1992; Guthke & Wingenfeld, 1992; Guthke et al., 1997) is based on Vygotsky's ideas and represents a myriad of testing procedures. Guthke regarded Vygotsky as the true creator of the learning test concept. According to Guthke, Vygotsky might have been able to go beyond just formulating that idea and succeeded in translating it into procedures applicable in practice but for his untimely death. Guthke tried to be faithful simultaneously both to the psychometric demands for objectivity and to measurement of the individual's ability to learn. The learntest is applied by a pretest–training–posttest paradigm. The intervention within the testing procedure is based on Gal'perin's (1966) theory of systematic formation of mental actions and concepts. According to Gal'perin teaching is perceived as a psychological experiment, the goal of which is to bring the student to a new, higher level of development.

Guthke's learning test methodology was also influenced by the theory of activity of Soviet psychology (Leont'ev & Luria, 1964). The activity theory grew out of the elaboration and continuation as well as criticism of Vygotsky's work (see, e.g., Rubinstein, 1958). According to the activity theory, mental processes and characteristics are conceived of as products of human activity with particular emphasis on the concept of age- and situation-specific dominant activity (Leont'ev & Luria, 1964). Examiners are required in their diagnostic procedures to include activities that predominate in a given age range and in everyday life situations—much like the principle of ecological validity in "Western psychology." The assessment of children therefore should be focused on learning as their dominant activity and not merely on the results of their learning.

Guthke and his colleagues distinguished several types of learning tests according to the length of the training phase (long- and short-term). They also developed procedures that are representative of each type. In general, the learning ability was measured by recording the effects of standardized cues incorporated into the test and the performance of children following teaching. An example of a long-term battery is the learning test consisting of a pretest, a training phase consisting of 7 days, and a posttest. The learning task is composed of reasoning problems in the three basic domains: verbal, numerical, and figural, with parallel items for pre- and posttests. In the training phase the students are taught cognitive and metacognitive strategies for problem solving. Guthke suggested rank ordering the children twice based on separate norm tables for pre- and post tests. The pretest score indicates the students' standing within their age group and with respect to their intellectual status in the domain examined (a standardized approach). The posttest score, on the other hand, characterizes the students' position relative to their potential for development (dynamic approach) after a controlled educational intervention.

In contrast to long-term learning tests, the short-term battery is designed so that the training phase is built directly into the test procedures. Short-term learning tests require only one testing session during which systematic feedback and assistance are given. Two types of short-term learning tests can be distinguished: (1) tests providing systematic feedback that are fairly limited and (2) tests providing extensive assistance in addition to simple feedback. Some of the tests are based on conventional tests such as the Raven's matrices whereas others include new items.

The short-term battery includes five learning-potential tests: Sequences of Sets (this is a series completion test designed to assess prerequisite skills for math in kindergarten and first grade), the Preschool Learning Potential Test (designed for 5- to 7-year olds), the Situation Learning Potential Test (designed for 7- to 9-year olds), the Speed and Recall test (designed for adults with functional brain disorder), and the Reasoning test.

Guthke and Stein (1996) suggested the Diagnostic Program, which is a variant of the short-term learning test. In the Diagnostic Program the authors tried to quantify both the learning gains and the learning process itself. In this assessment procedure, which is rather complex, the child is presented with a sequence of increasingly difficult figural items. In order to qualify for a next level of task complexity, the child has to solve a target item presented at the start and the end of each phase of the test. If the child makes mistakes, easier items are presented and the child has to work up to the point of his or her mistake. If the child still makes mistakes at this item, prompts are given until he or she is ready to move to the next level of complexity.

Findings from different studies showed an increase in performance on intelligence tests after training (Guthke & Wingenfeld, 1992). Moreover, the results strongly indicate that the training effects, as measured in the posttest or in learning gain indices, could not be significantly predicted from the pretest scores. In other words, the training effects provided additional diagnostic information. It is interesting to note that in some cases, there were major changes in the rank orders of subjects before and after the training. The importance of this finding is related to the previous findings (Meili, 1965) according to which diagnostically relevant changes in rank order after repeated administration of tests (with or without in-between training) occur only in very unreliable tests, not in highly reliable ones.

Validity studies showed that the learning test was a much better predictor of future scholastic progress of low-achieving students and children with learning disabilities than static tests (Guthke & Gitter, 1991). The validity of the learning test was investigated further by Guthke et al. (1997), using dynamic criterion variables rather than the static external criteria used in previous studies. They correlated students' performance in complex problem solving with their performance on conventional intelligence tests. These correlations then were compared with the correlations of the performance in complex problem solving with learning test versions. The findings showed that the conventional intelligence tests were not significantly correlated with knowledge acquisition but were correlated significantly with knowledge application. The learning tests, on the other hand, correlated at higher levels with both knowledge acquisition and knowledge applications.

A summary of several studies showed that learning tests (1) generally have higher factor validity than the corresponding static tests, (2) are less sensitive to environmental factors, (3) are more strongly related to the results of controlled learning experiments, (4) discriminate less strongly than do traditional tests between children taught by different kinds of instructional methods, (5) are more highly correlated with tests of creativity, and (6) partially reduce the effects of nonintellectual components (e.g., irritability, neuroticism) on the test result (Wiedl, 1984).

Longitudinal studies, covering a period of 7 years, using the Sequences of Sets Test and the Raven Short-Term Learning Test in groups of children with below-average intelligence revealed that the predictive validity of learning tests was clearly superior to static tests. The learning tests seem to be particularly suited for differential assessment of children with learning disabilities, handicaps, and irregular learning histories (Guthke et al., 1997).

Guthke, like other researchers (Feuerstein et al., 1979), concluded that learning tests are unlikely to predict the intellectual development of children better than conventional intelligence tests if the children continue to live in unfavorable social situations or will not receive some kind of intervention to change their cognitive functioning after the assessment. Based on findings from the learning test approach Guthke and Wingenfeld (1992) raised several questions that reflect basic unresolved issues awaiting more elaborate research:

(1.) Since most learning test items have been derived from conventional intelligence test items and assumptions of classical test theory, does current task construction satisfy the requirements for process-oriented tests that focus on enhancing thinking and learning ability? This question derives from Guthke's effort to overcome the procedural weaknesses of "conventional" learning tests and the conceptual shortcomings of conventional static intelligence tests. My answer to this question is that perhaps the time is ripe to develop novel tests that are not based on conventional tests. Since Guthke relied originally on conventional tasks and tried to integrate the conventional psychometric approach with a dynamic one, some conflicts are inevitable.

(2.) Guthke argues that many learning tests have been constructed to examine general, largely content, rather than domain-specific thinking ability. These tests are very similar to the general ability skills that characterize intelligence tests. The issue of general versus domain specific tests has been the subject of a controversial debate among diagnosticians and researchers for many years.

It seems that at present there is a synthetic position emphasizing the interaction of both general and specific abilities in problem solving. Guthke's question is, how can we derive specific suggestions for enhancing intellectual ability from test performance if learning tests are not domain and subject specific? My position regarding this question is that while we should make efforts to construct DA tests based on general skills, we should try to use complementary tasks that are specific-domain oriented. The basic conceptual framework, however, is general skills. Following Feuerstein's approach (see Chapter 3), I believe that we should assess *cognitive functions* or *deficient cognitive functions* characterized by their general nature. These cognitive functions can be applied to a variety of academic and nonacademic domains. Leont'ev (1968), an advocate of the activity-oriented approach to assessment, already stressed the importance of assessing general intellectual abilities besides knowledge of and abilities in special school subjects.

(3.) Another question raised by Guthke is related to the fact that the training phase in learning tests is relatively similar for all subjects to ensure standardization. Is the training phase sufficiently individualized to uncover individual process characteristics of learning? Guthke raised several other issues that are related to this basic question. For example, how does the match between personality traits and characteristics of the methods used affect the child's functioning? Should we describe, measure, and train not only task-specific cognitive strategies and operations but also an individual's orientational activity and non-intellective factors (i.e., metacognition, motivational and emotional factors, awareness, and learning strategies)? Although some empirical and theoretical work on these questions has been done (i.e., Guthke & Lehwald, 1984; Wiedl, 1984), most of them remain unanswered. Guthke mentions in this regard that the "quest for knowledge" (intrinsic motivation) influences the learning test posttest performance more strongly than the pretest performance whereas irritability, intolerance of frustration, and anxiety affect the pretest (conventional intelligence test) more strongly than the posttest.

Expanding on this, Guthke mentions that diagnosticians are caught between a rock and a hard place. On the one hand, a highly individualized training phase leads to subjective administration and scoring of the test. On the other hand, standardization and psychometric analysis of the test process and less individualized training makes the scores less meaningful. This unresolved problem could be partially solved by recording the type and amount of mediation given within the DA process.

Some of Guthke's questions are referred to in the following chapters especially in presenting the DA approach for young children (Chapters 5 and 6) and in the epilogue (Chapter 10). The following chapter examines MLE theory, which in many ways is similar to that of Vygotsky's but is considered to be more elaborated both conceptually and practically.

3

The Mediated Learning
Experience (MLE) Theory

THE BACKGROUND OF MLE THEORY DEVELOPMENT

Much like Vygotsky's development of the ZPD concept and its application to
DA, Feuerstein's MLE theory evolved within a historical, social, and cultural
perspective. It is my opinion that Feuerstein developed his theory independently,
about three decades after Vygotsky's theory was published in the Soviet Union,
without being familiar with Vygotsky's ideas. Feuerstein's theory was developed
after the establishment of the State of Israel, when a massive immigration of hundreds of thousands of Jews to Israel began from all over the world, but especially
from North Africa and Middle Eastern countries. Many of the immigrants had to
go through an accelerated process of integration, a process that required acquisition of sophisticated technology. The social pressures for integration and main-
streaming posed pressures for development of new assessment methods that
would take into account the immigrants' diverse cultures and allow the fulfillment of their learning potential, especially those who were "penalized" by the
conventional psychometric tests.

The MLE theory (Feuerstein, Klein, & Tannenbaum, 1991; Feuerstein,
Rand, Hoffman, & Miller, 1980; Feuerstein, Rand, & Rynders, 1988) evolved out
of many years of varied clinical experience with hundreds of cases representing
many different etiologic conditions, life histories, and prognoses. Many of the
cases diagnosed as mentally retarded or emotionally disturbed were assessed as
having much better prognoses by DA and consequently received a treatment that
eventually refuted the pessimistic prognosis suggested by the traditional assessment approaches. Later on the theory was extended toward normally developing
individuals and was applied with a variety of children.

This chapter will cover the basic assumptions of MLE theory and the concept of *cognitive modifiability*, the former theory including description of the main MLE criteria. Two sections will treat the use of MLE in DA, and the distinction between *cultural difference* and *cultural deprivation* made in regard to DA. Subsequently, the MLE theory is compared with those of Vygotsky and Piaget. Following that theoretical section is a description of the Learning Propensity Assessment Device (LPAD; Feuerstein et al., 1995) which is a DA approach based on MLE theory. Several instruments from the LPAD will be described. Finally, research aspects of the LPAD, including its reliability and validity, will be discussed.

BASIC ASSUMPTIONS OF THE MLE THEORY

The MLE theory is based on several assumptions. The first assumption is that human beings have a unique capacity to modify their cognitive functioning and cognitive structures and adapt to changing demands in the environment. Second, cognitive modifiability is possible irrespective of the barriers of age, etiology, and severity of condition. Third, MLE processes explain cognitive modifiability (see definition below) better than do direct unmediated experiences. These assumptions shift the responsibility for an individual's modifiability from the developing child or a person in treatment to the mediating adult.

THE CONCEPT OF COGNITIVE MODIFIABILITY

Cognitive modifiability is characterized by *permanence, pervasiveness*, and *centrality*. Permanence refers to the durability of the cognitive changes or their endurance over time. A process according to which changes in one part affect, through a "diffusion process," the whole is characterized by pervasiveness. Centrality reflects the self-perpetuating autonomous and self-regulating nature of cognitive modifiability.

DEFINITION OF MLE

MLE refers to an interactional process in which an adult interposes him- or herself between the child and a set of stimuli and modifies them by affecting their frequency, order, intensity, and context. The mediated child is aroused to a high level of curiosity, vigilance, and perceptual acuity. Both the child and the mediator interact to improve and/or create the cognitive functions required for temporal, spatial, and cause–effect relationships. The MLE processes are internalized by the child and gradually become an integrated mechanism of change within the child. Adequate parent–child MLE facilitates the development of various cognitive functions, learning sets, mental operations, and needs systems. The acquired and internalized MLE processes allow the child to use them independently, to benefit from learning experiences, and to modify his or her cognitive system. The more the child experiences MLE interactions, the more he or she is able to learn from direct exposure to formal and informal learning situations, regardless of the richness of stimuli they provide. Lack of MLE may represent two broad categories: (1) lack of environmental opportunities for mediation, and (2) inability of the child to benefit from mediational interactions, which are potentially available.

DISTAL AND PROXIMAL ETIOLOGY OF COGNITIVE DEVELOPMENT

Feuerstein has distinguished between two major etiological categories for cognitive development: *distal* and *proximal*. The distal factors, in spite of their importance, do not explain directly individual differences in learning, cognitive change, and cognitive development. Examples of distal factors include poverty, socioeconomic status, organic determinants, and emotional states. The distal factors might correlate with learning ability, but they affect learning ability only through the "prism" of the proximal factor of MLE. MLE processes are considered as proximal factors because they explain directly the development of cognitive processes.

CRITERIA OF MLE

Feuerstein has described 12 criteria of MLE, the first 3 being necessary and sufficient for any interaction to be classified as MLE: *Intentionality and Reciprocity, Transcendence*, and *Meaning*. These criteria, which are responsible for the individual's cognitive modifiability, are considered to be universal and can be found in all races, ethnic groups, and socioeconomic strata. Mediation does not depend on the language modality or content and can be carried out by gestures, mimicry, and verbal interaction, provided that the three major criteria are present.

The other MLE criteria are: Mediation for Feelings of Competence, Mediation for Self-Regulation, Mediation for Sharing Behavior, Mediation for Individuation and Psychological Differentiation, Mediation for Seeking of Goals, Mediation for Seeking of Challenge, Mediation for Change, Mediation for Search after Optimistic Alternatives, and Mediation for Feelings of Belonging. These criteria, which are explained in detail elsewhere (e.g., Feuerstein et al., 1988), are task dependent, strongly related to culture, and reflect variations in cognitive styles, motivation, type or content of skills mastered, and the structure of knowledge.

The first five MLE criteria were operationalized by Klein (1988, 1996) and used extensively in several studies with infants (e.g., Klein & Aloni, 1993; Klein, Weider, & Greenspan, 1987), preschool children (e.g., Tzuriel, 1996, 1998, 1999b, 2000c; Tzuriel & Ernst, 1990; Tzuriel & Hatzir, 1999), and school children (e.g., Shamir & Tzuriel, 1999; Tzuriel & Weiss, 1998a, b; Tzuriel & Weitz, 1998). The MLE criteria were validated in several cross-cultural studies (i.e., Klein, 1996, Tzuriel, Kaniel, & Yehudai, 1994). A detailed description of the observation model and technique will be given later critically with other methodological issues (see Chapter 7). In this chapter I will consider only the first five MLE criteria which are used mostly in the context of DA. These criteria were also operationalized for observation in many developmental studies (see Chapter 8).

Intentionality and Reciprocity refers to an interaction in which the mediator intentionally creates in the child a state of vigilance, in order to help him or her to register the information, process it, and/or respond to it. Reciprocity is observed when the child responds vocally, verbally, or nonverbally to the mediator's behavior. For example, Intentionality and Reciprocity is observed when a mediator intentionally focuses the child on a picture and the child responds overtly to that behavior. This criterion is considered essential for the development of basic feelings of competence and self-determination.

Mediation for Meaning refers to interactions in which the mediator attaches to the presented stimuli significance, affect, worth, and value. Nonverbally, this can be conveyed by facial expression, tone of voice, rituals, and repetitious actions. Verbally, it can be expressed by illuminating a current event, activity, or learned context relating them to past or current events and emphasizing their importance and value. Children who experience mediation of meaning will internalize this interaction and will later initiate attachment of meaning to new information rather than passively waiting for meaning to come.

Mediation for Transcendence refers to teaching of generalized cognitive principles and strategies. In Mediation for Transcendence the mediator goes beyond the concrete context or the immediate needs of the child, tries to expand them, and reach out for general principles and/or goals that are not bound to the "here and now" or the specific and concrete aspects of the situation. In mother— child interactions, for example, mothers might go beyond the children's concrete experience and teach strategies, rules, and principles in order to generalize to other situations (i.e., "this flower grows in the springtime"). In formal teaching situations, the teacher might mediate rules and principles that govern a problem or a learned subject and show how they are generalized to other school subjects or daily life situations. In a DA context the examiner mediates the rules and strategies for solving a specific problem and assesses the level of internalization of these rules and strategies to other problems of increased level of complexity, novelty, and abstraction. It should be noted that although Mediation for Transcendence depends on the first two criteria, the combination of all criteria becomes a powerful vehicle for the development of cognitive modifiability and the widening of the individual's need system.

In Mediation for Feelings of Competence the mediator conveys to the child that he or she is capable of functioning independently and successfully. This is done by organizing the environment, providing opportunities for success, and rewarding the child for attempts to master the situation and cope effectively with problems. The mediation provides feedback not only to successful performance but also to attempts for mastery.

In Mediation for Control of Behavior (or Self Regulation) the mediator regulates the child's responses either by inhibiting impulsivity or by accelerating the behavior, depending on the child's reactive style and the task demands. This mediation is of critical importance in order to bring the child to register the information. Mediation for Control of Behavior can be done in various ways such as analyzing the task components, inhibiting the child's acting out behavior, focusing on task characteristics, and eliciting metacognitive strategies.

USE OF MEDIATION IN DA PROCEDURES

It is important to understand the MLE processes because they are integrated in DA processes. Mediational strategies used within the DA procedure facilitate learning processes and give indications about future changes of cognitive structures, deficient cognitive functions, and academic performance. The changes in the cognitive structures are not automatic but depend on appropriate mediation to be given to the examinee as well as on environmental modifications following the assessment. The emphasis in DA is on "assessment" in the clinical sense rather than on "measurement," which is more applicable to the psychometric paradigm. It is also important to note, that the focus in DA is on ways to bring about change rather than on etiology of the manifest deficiency. The biological factors are not ignored, nor are their detrimental effects diminished. The argument is that in spite of their strength there are ways to overcome them—with some individuals more easily than with others.

The mediation process in DA is composed of a series of steps by which the examiner is leading the child to register the information systematically, understand the problem, use and internalize efficient cognitive strategies, self-regulate behavior, and use metacognitive strategies. The examiner is not supposed to provide the necessary information immediately after the child reveals a difficulty, but rather use mediation processes so that the child arrives independently at the solution. The examiner might focus the child on the dimensions of the problem, create associations with previously known concepts, connect past events to present experiences, emphasize efficient and inefficient behavior patterns, give feedback on the solution process and the quality of the answer, and encourage the child on successes even if they are partial. The mediation process includes the following points:

1. *Improvement of (deficient) cognitive functions.* The examiner should know how to identify the cognitive functions required for solution of a problem in the test and the mediation needed to improve the deficient cognitive functions.

2. *Preparing the child for complex tasks by establishing prerequired thinking behaviors.* Establishing prerequired thinking behaviors is carried out often by using mediation for transcendence and for self-regulation. Adequate initial investment in preparing the child brings about reduction of mediation efforts in later more abstract and complex problems. It is common to find children who solve difficult advanced problems much easier than the initial easy problems. Mediation of rules and principles (transcendence) has a motivational aspect as the child becomes independent of the examiner's mediation, and enhances the child's sense of self-control. Mediation for self-regulation is carried out by focusing on systematic sequencing processes especially in complex problems requiring an analytic approach. The examiner might ask the child to repeat the process of solution in order to crystallize the order of solution and to acquire feelings of mastery and efficiency.

3. *Self-regulation by planning and organization of the solution.* One of the most frequent deficiencies among low functioning children is impulsivity. Inhibition of impulsivity is done many times by decreasing the importance of time for performance. This is carried out by intentional delay of the child's response, longer exposure to the problem, systematic planning of the solution alternatives, verbalization of the problem, representation of the solution before pointing to the correct answer, and metacognitive analysis of the impulsive behavior. An efficient way of coping with impulsivity is by enriching the child's cognitive repertoire with thinking operations, comparative behavior, verbal tools, and hypothesis-testing techniques.

4. *Enhancement of reflective, insightful, and analytic processes.* Enhancement of reflective, insightful, and analytic processes is carried out by focusing the child on the relation between his or her own thinking processes and the consequential cognitive performance. The focus is not on the end product but rather on the thinking process in the context of the required operations, type of task, and situation. Creation of insight is important for generalization and transfer of learning. It can be done by a dialogue with the child before solving the problem ("What should we look at before we will start to solve this problem?") or after the solution ("Why did you succeed in solving the problem that was so difficult

for you to solve before?"). The most efficient way of enhancing reflective processes is by presenting the child with conflicts, incongruent information, intentional ambiguity, and absurd situations, which will bring about a need to close the cognitive gaps.

5. *Teaching of specific contents that are related to the task-specific context.* Teaching of specific contents (concepts, terms, relations) is not for the sake of language enrichment but for further use in problem-solving tasks. For example, the use of the terms up, down, vertical, horizontal, diagonal, similar, opposite, and different is necessary for performing the mental operation. The examiner can deviate for a short time from the task to teach and establish missing concepts and return later to the task to assess the performance efficiency and use of the newly acquired concepts.

6. *Feedback on success or failure in the learning process.* The feedback given, which is one of the cornerstones in DA, is mutual—from the child and the examiner sides. It is especially important with low performing children who are limited in their skills for giving feedback to themselves. This limitation is related to difficulties in self-correction and comparison of findings not only because of lack of knowledge and verbal tools of the children, but also because of lack of orientation to make comparisons. Many tests are based on the assumption that trial-and-error behaviors will eventually bring the child to learn the correct answer. This assumption is wrong with regard to low functioning children who are characterized by episodic grasp of reality. These children do not relate between their behavior and its consequences. A trial-and-error behavior blocks their learning rather than facilitates it. The importance of feedback in DA derives from the examiner's ability to focus the child on the relation between behavior and consequence. The feedback is given not only on wrong answers but also on correct or partially correct answers, in order to teach self-correction. The goal of the feedback is beyond teaching the child a specific response. The aim is to teach insight, lawfulness, and meaning in relation to both cognitive and emotional—motivational aspects.

7. *Development of basic communication skills and adequate response style.* The MLE model (S–h–O–h–R) includes the mediator (h) who interposes him- or herself between the child (O) and the response (R). The mediation here is aimed at changing the child's response style so that problem solution will find a proper and efficient external expression. The examiner teaches the child how to communicate efficiently by the use of clear and accepted terms and avoiding egocentric communication. The examiner also teaches the child how to communicate precisely, how to justify the answer using logical arguments, and use verbal "codes" of expression and abstract high-order concepts rather than body gestures and facial expressions. It should be emphasized that previous communication style is not taken away before establishing new response styles.

CULTURAL DIFFERENCE VERSUS
CULTURAL DEPRIVATION

Feuerstein has distinguished between two concepts with regard to MLE theory: *cultural difference* and *cultural deprivation* (Feuerstein & Feuerstein, 1991). Cultural difference occurs when an individual is exposed to MLE processes the content of which is different from that of the culture in which he or she is living. Cultural deprivation on the other hand, results when an individual lacks adequate MLE within his or her own culture. MLE, which explains the individual's development of cognitive modifiability, does not depend on the content embodied in the culture but on the quality of the interaction between mediators and learners. The distinction between these two terms provides the basis for observation of learning processes that go beyond cultural differences. In line with MLE theory, *culturally different* individuals are those who may manifest certain deficient cognitive functions, but are expected to overcome them rather quickly and/or with less mediational efforts. This occurs because the MLE they have received prepared them to be more modifiable. *Culturally deprived* individuals, on the other hand, have a relatively reduced modifiability, a result of insufficient mediation on a proximal level. Based on MLE theory we would hypothesize that culturally different children, as compared with children of mainstream culture, would show initial low performance on cognitive abstract tests but after a short intervention given within the DA situation they would improve their performance and narrow the gap with their counterparts of the mainstream culture. Previous findings with adolescents (Kaniel, Tzuriel, Feuerstein, Ben-Shachar, & Eitan, 1991; Luther & Wyatt, 1989) and young children (Tzuriel & Kaufman, 1999) support this hypothesis.

THE DIFFERENCES AMONG FEUERSTEIN, PIAGET, AND VYGOTSKY

Feuerstein uses some of Piaget's maturational terminology (e.g., structure) but this does not mean that he agrees with Piaget's whole maturational approach. For example, Feuerstein uses Piaget's concept of "cognitive structure" only to describe a certain functioning of an individual at a certain time but this structure serves as a basis for change rather than as a relatively stable condition. Piaget concentrated on describing the universal cognitive developmental stages and did not pay much attention to the role of caregivers or of culture in developing the individual as Vygotsky and Feuerstein did. According to Piaget's S–O–R model the organism (O) processes the impinging stimuli (S) and consequently produces a specific response (R). Feuerstein criticizes the S–O–R model for not taking into account individual differences deriving from factors that are related to parent–child mediations and interactional patterns in the family. Another difference supported by accumulating empirical evidence is that Piaget's developmental stages are not stable as Piaget described them (Case, 1993), and that there is much room for significantly higher performance above Piaget's "prescribed" stages. Feuerstein's and Vygotsky's contribution is in introducing human mediation as a critical factor that, together with other factors, determines intellectual development. Although both Vygotsky and Feuerstein agree with Piaget that spontaneous interaction of the child with the physical world is a precursor to development of schemes and symbolic operational thought, they argue that the activity is mediated (e.g., organized, regulated) by society.

The main differences between Vygotsky and Feuerstein relate to the level of theoretical elaboration and operationalization of the theoretical concepts into applied systems. Unlike Vygotsky, Feuerstein has developed the concept of MLE by suggesting an elaborated list of MLE criteria, a list of deficient cognitive functions that are partly the result of lack of or inadequate MLE, a "cognitive map" that specifies task dimensions analytically, and a conceptual framework that defines the role of *distal* and *proximal* factors as determinants of cognitive development.

Beyond the theoretical concepts, the MLE theory has produced practical tools for diagnostic and intervention processes such as the LPAD, the Instrumental Enrichment program (IE; Feuerstein et al., 1980), the Bright Start program (Haywood, Brooks, & Burns, 1986), the Cognitive Network program (COGNET; Greenberg, 1990), the Cognitive Modifiability Battery (CMB): Assessment and Intervention (Tzuriel, 1995a, 2000d), and the More Intelligent and Sensitive Child (MISC; Klein, 1996; Klein & Hundeide, 1989).

In discussing the similarities between Feuerstein and Vygotsky, Kozulin and Presseisen (1995) have argued that "Vygotsky made no attempt to elaborate the activities of human mediators beyond their function as vehicles of symbolic tools. This left considerable lacunae in Vygotsky's theory of mediation" (p. 69).

ASSESSMENT PROCEDURES OF THE LEARNING PROPENSITY ASSESSMENT DEVICE (LPAD)

The LPAD is a continuous teach–test procedure rather than a test–teach–test procedure. The examiner intervenes during both the teaching phase and the testing phase to assist the examinee to use effective cognitive strategies, rules, and behaviors to arrive at the correct response. This approach does not provide an objective baseline and hence necessitates expert clinical administration in which mediation is provided only when necessary and careful records are kept. The LPAD tasks are constructed to permit learning processes. The tasks do not tap specific contents but rather relate the general cognitive aspects (i.e., deficient cognitive functions) that are responsible for failure. Most tasks within the LPAD instruments (see below description of some instruments) are constructed to be sensitive to change through variation of task complexity and abstractness. In a typical task the examinee is taught a problem using a mediational style and the application and transfer of learning of rules, principles, and strategies to other problems are examined. A detailed description of the main characteristics can be found in Feuerstein et al. (1979, 1980, 1988, 1995).

The teach–test format maintains the mediational components throughout the assessment process so that the examinee is willing to risk and can perform optimally throughout.

THE LPAD INSTRUMENTS

In the following, eight of the LPAD instruments are presented. For a detailed description of the whole battery the reader is referred to Feuerstein et al. (1995).

Organization of Dots. The Organization of Dots test is often given as the first test in the LPAD as it is highly motivating and different from other tasks that examinees may have experienced failure on in the past. The Organization of Dots also permits assessment of a broad range of deficient cognitive functions that are required later in other more complex tasks (i.e., control of impulsivity, systematic exploratory behavior, need for precision, hypothetical thinking). This test was developed originally by Rey and Dupont (1953) and modified for DA by Feuerstein et al. (1979).

On the Organization of Dots, the examinee must find two or more figures in an amorphous cloud of dots and draw them accurately as in a model presented at the top of the page. To perform successfully, the examinee must be able to plan, use a specific strategy, compare drawn figures to the model, conserve shape and size constancy beyond changes in other parameters, and deal with spatial rotations and overlapping of the figures. The test is composed of two pages: *teaching* and *testing*. The examinee is first given a teaching page on which the examiner teaches the examinee how to solve problems. This is done by eliciting from the examinee a description of what he or she is required to do, defining the nature of the task, controlling for impulsivity, using appropriate concepts and terms, planning a strategy for solving the problems, comparing the task with the model, using several sources of information (i.e., size, form), and rejecting irrelevant data. On successful completion of the teaching page, composed of relatively easy problems, a test page with more complex problems is given. Mediation of items on the test page is provided only when the examinee has difficulty solving the problems. The responses and the type and amount of mediation are recorded on a special recording sheet. Previous research using this test is reported in Feuerstein et al. (1979), but no reliability is provided.

Raven's Colored Progressive Matrices (RCPM). The RCPM (Raven, 1956) is a static test, which was adapted as a DA instrument in the LPAD. The test consists of 36 problems divided into three sets, each containing 12 problems (A, AB, B). The examinee is required to complete a matrix by choosing the missing part from six alternatives. The examinee has to deduce a relationship on the completed part of the matrix, and then apply the relationship to the incomplete part. The test requires making comparisons, perception and organization of space, analytic perception of visual stimuli, and analogical thinking. The RCPM in its dynamic version is given at the beginning of the LPAD and is used for preparation for more complex tasks (SV-I and SV-II, see below). The goals of the RCPM are to assess the child's capacity to grasp a principle underlying a problem and apply a newly acquired principle to solve other problems. A difference between the standardized administration and the dynamic one is that in the latter, the examinee is focused on data gathering strategies and given feedback on each item. For example, the examiner is prompted on relevant information (e.g., "What is missing here?"), asked to justify correct answers (e.g., "Why is that answer the best one"?), and to reconsider and correct wrong ones (e.g., "There is a better answer; can you show it to me? Take a careful look").

Set Variations-I (SV-I). The SV-I is usually given after the RCPM. It is composed of 36 analogy problems based on items B8 to B12 of the RCPM. There are five sets of problems, each containing a prototype sample problem followed by six variations. The sample is used for intensive mediation, if required, while the other items are used as the test phase. Split-half reliabilities of SV-I and SV-II (see below) given in a group DA condition and with different ability groups ranged between .82 and .98 (Tzuriel & Feuerstein, 1992). No reliability data have been reported reported on individual clinical administration. Feuerstein et al. (1979) and Tzuriel and Feuerstein (1992) report validity data.

SV-II (SV-II). The SV-II is based on the C, D, and E Series of the Raven's Standard Progressive Matrices (Raven, 1956). Items are more complex and require a higher level of abstractions than the RCPM or SV-I. The examinee must abstract the rule or principle governing the problem, and select the solution from among eight alternatives that are given at the bottom of the page. There are five sets of tasks, each containing a prototype sample item (to mediate on, if necessary) and increasingly difficult items that can be solved by application of the same general rules and principles. Feuerstein et al. (1979), Tzuriel and Alfassi (1994), and Tzuriel and Feuerstein (1992) report validity and reliability data.

In all of the matrices (RCPM, SV-I, and SV-II), the examiner intervenes as necessary by focusing, prompting, teaching rules and strategies, controlling for impulsivity, overcoming blocking, motivating the examinee, and teaching specific concepts and terms that are necessary for solving the problems. The amount and type of mediation provided by the examiner are taken into account in analyzing the examinee's performance. For example, the examiner might attempt to reduce impulsivity by covering the responses until the examinee gives a verbal response. If the verbal response is correct and the item selected is correct, the item would be scored as correct. However, if the verbal response is incorrect, more mediation would be provided and the response would be scored as incorrect.

The Complex Figure (CF) Test. The CF test consists of a geometric figure structured around a base rectangle. The test was developed originally by Rey (1956) as a static test but modified as a DA measure by Feuerstein et al. (1979). The goal of the test is to assess the examinee's ability to plan and organize complex stimuli, his or her level of precision, memory of figural stimuli, and level of modifiability following a teaching phase. The test is composed of five phases: (1) In the first phase, the child is asked to copy the figure and then (2) to draw it from memory. (3) In a mediation phase, the child is taught how to gather the information systematically, to plan the construction (i.e., drawing first the major lines and then secondary lines, going in clockwise order), and pay attention to precision, proportions, and the quality of lines. (4) A second copy phase and (5) a second memory phase are administered exactly as in Phases 1 and 2. Comparison of copy and memory phases before and after mediation provides information about the modifiability of the child's performance. The CF has 18 components, each of which is given one point for accuracy and one for location, for a possible total score of 36. A third, qualitative, score, ranging from 1 to 7, is given for organization. The CF test has been developed for young children by Tzuriel and Eiboshitz (1992) and used with different groups of children with learning disabilities and with academically high-risk disadvantaged children (Tzuriel & Eiboshitz, 1992; Tzuriel et al., 1999) as well as with children aged 5–8 who were very low birth weight babies (Tzuriel & Weitz, 1998). It was found effective in predicting treatment effects of a program aimed at developing visual motor integration ability with these preschool children. The Post-Teaching scores were significantly predicted by mother—child MLE interactions (Tzuriel & Weitz, 1998). For a description of the CF young children version, including reliability data, see Chapter 6.

The Plateaux Test. The Plateaux test developed by Rey (1950) consists of four plates with nine buttons, arranged in a 3×3 matrix. On each plate there is one fixed button; all other buttons can be removed. The task is to search and find, in a series of trials, the fixed buttons on each plate. There are no visual clues for finding the fixed button and the examinee has to rely on visual memory of location. The objectives of the test are to assess the examinee's efficiency in positional learning through repeated exposures, the strategies used, planning behavior, level of impulsivity, transfer of learning from the three-dimensional to a two-dimensional schema, and internalization of learning as reflected in a rotation phase of the plates. The test procedure consists of three phases. In the first phase, the examinee is asked to find the fixed buttons. The number of errors (touching incorrect buttons) and number of trials to reach a learning criterion of three consecutive correct trials are recorded. In the second phase, the examinee is required to indicate the location of each button on a schematic drawing of the matrix. Performance on this phase indicates whether there is internalization of the learned position. In the third phase, the examinee is asked to find the location of the fixed button on each plate, after the plates are rotated first 90°, then 180°, and 270°. It should be emphasized that, unlike the other LPAD tests that are used, in general, the Plateaux test does not involve intensive mediation. The only mediation that is used is (1) focusing (e.g., "This is more difficult," "Pay attention as the plates are rotated," (2) restraint of impulsivity (e.g., "Don't rush, look carefully"), and (3) use of strategies to recall the locations ("How could we remember the location?" "Can you think of a label that might help?").

The Organizer Test. The Organizer consists of 5 teaching items and 20 test items. A series of statements or premises are presented within each task. Each statement provides part of the information required in organizing and placing objects in positions relative to one another. The location of each item is not precisely specified within any single statement and must be inferred from data presented about the position of other items or the position of a given item relative to others. Tasks vary in their level of complexity in terms of the number of items to be organized (from 3 to 8) and the level of inference required (e.g., negative statements, and number of eliminated objects). The strategies and rules required for solving these tasks remain constant. This test requires a moderate to high level of abstract representation and hypothetical-inferential thinking. Cronbach-alpha reliability coefficients received in a group DA for the pre- and postteaching phases were .73 and .87, respectively (Tzuriel & Alfassi, 1994).

Representational Stencil Design Test (RSDT). The RSDT is based on the Stencil Design Test (SDT)) developed by Arthur (1947). In the RSDT, the examinee must mentally construct a design from colored stencils that are printed on a gray poster. Unlike the original SDT where the stencils could be concretely manipulated to form the required design, in the RSDT the examinee is required to superimpose the stencil in a representational way in order to achieve the required design. The shape and color of the specific design determine the selection of the stencils to be used and the order of their placement one upon the other. This test requires representational thinking and is at a high level of both complexity and abstractness (Feuerstein et al., 1995). The RSDT is composed of teaching and testing sets, each containing 20 items increasing in level of complexity.

RELIABILITY OF THE LPAD

Reliability issues of individually administered LPAD have been addressed by both proponents (Haywood & Tzuriel, 1992b; Samuels et al., 1989; Tzuriel,

1992a; Tzuriel & Samuels, 2000; Vaught & Haywood, 1990); and opponents (e.g., Frisby & Braden, 1992) of this approach. The reliability of the LPAD is of critical importance as it is essentially an observational procedure, which requires inferences, based on complex information. Furthermore, on the LPAD, the examiner has a role not only as an observer but also as a mediator and an agent of change. The examiner-mediator is not only responsible for modifying the individual's performance during the assessment but also observes and records cognitive performance, behavioral characteristics, nonintellective factors, and his or her own mediational strategies that bring about change. Feuerstein et al. (1995) have mentioned that some degree of subjectivity is an essential feature of DA. Feuerstein, Rand, Jensen, Kaniel, and Tzuriel, (1987) have also argued that reliability measures are inappropriate for DA as the main goal is to modify the individual's functioning rather than to measure constant and static levels of performance. In other words, DA should not look for stability and consistency, which characterize reliability, but rather for change and inconsistency. One must interpret this argument as relating to within-subject reliability or interitem reliability, which, of course, is contradictory to the goal of change in the individual. Scientific criteria, however, require interrater reliability before inferences can be made about the individual. Interitem reliability, the individual's performance across test items, would be expected to be low, whereas interrater reliability, the level of agreement between two raters, assessing the same individual should be high.

The problem of DA reliability has been raised by several investigators many of who doubt whether the interpretation of the individual's performance during DA is indicative of the actual level of the tested individual or the subjective interpretation of the tester (Frisby & Braden, 1992). In spite of the importance of the reliability issue in DA, it is surprising to find that only a few studies have attempted to establish reliability (Samuels et al., 1989; Tzuriel & Samuels, 2000; Vaught & Haywood, 1990).

Vaught and Haywood (1990) investigated the interjudge agreement of DA using two instruments from the LPAD: RSDT and SV-I. The main rationale behind this study was that without demonstrating judge agreement, the validity and utility of DA is questionable. Two expert examiners administered the two LPAD tests to four adolescents. Videotapes of the assessment were given to 10 expert judges to be rated. Three dimensions were rated: (1) the list of 28 deficient cognitive functions (Feuerstein et al., 1995), (2) the amount and type of mediation required, and (3) mastery/transfer of learned processes (response to mediation). The overall results of this study were discouraging, as there was relatively low agreement among raters. Percentage agreement of the overall deficient cognitive functions was as follows: for Subjects 1 and 2, 57.1 and 50.0%, respectively, and for Subjects 3 and 4, 71.4 and 82.1%. Lidz (1991), however, perceived the results as encouraging when specific deficient cognitive functions were investigated rather than an overall agreement. Three categories were found to have an interrater agreement, for all four subjects, of 80% or above. These were *blurred and sweeping perception, episodic grasp of reality,* and *egocentric communicational modality.* These categories represent the *input, elaboration,* and *output* phases of the mental act, respectively. A level of 70% or above for all four subjects was found for four categories: *failure to perceive the existence of or define a problem, trial-and-error responses, impaired communicative verbal tools,* and *impulsive acting out behavior.* Nine more categories reached a 70% level of agreement or above for three of the subjects. Lidz (1991) concluded that a total of 16 deficiencies could be scored with at least questionable to high interrater agreement. The cognitive deficiencies observed on SV-I yielded much higher agreement (coefficient of .77) than ratings on the RSDT (.44). The findings also indicate very poor agreement on the type and intensity of mediation. Lidz commented that she participated as a rater and believes that this level of modest agreement is impressive in view of the fact that the definitions of the deficiencies were not standardized across raters.

From my experience as an observer and rater in the above study, I agree with Lidz's comment. Furthermore, a problem in Vaught and Haywood's (1989) study was that the raters were asked to view the video clips without perceiving the whole testing context and without being actively involved in the mediational process. Tzuriel (1992a), in his reply to Frisby and Braden's (1992) critique of Feuerstein's approach, has said that the lack of direct contact by the examiner and active attempts to modify the examinee makes it very difficult to rate cognitive functions, even for experts.

In another more sophisticated study, three changes from the previous study (Vaught & Haywood, 1990) were made. First, the raters were involved in the process of mediation and assessment as DA examiners. Second, testing was much more extensive and included the whole test and not only excerpts on video clips. Third, the assessment included a wide-ranging test battery rather than two tests (testing time was between 8 and 15 hours for each subject). Thirty-five children previously classified with learning disabilities ($n = 11$), learning disabilities with attention deficit disorder ($n = 10$), educable mentally handicapped ($n = 9$), and normally achieving children ($n = 5$) were assessed using eight tests from the LPAD (see earlier list). The subjects' pool represents a typical student population referred for DA for cognitive difficulties. All children were between the ages of 12 and 14; this particular age range was chosen because the LPAD tests are designed for children who have reached the formal operations stage (Piaget, 1952). Reliability was calculated by dividing the number of agreements by the total number of agreements and disagreements. An agreement was considered when the two raters had exactly the same rating or a rating that was off by one. One of the difficulties evident in the rating scale was the nonoccurrence category. *This category was designed to be used only when the task did not permit observation of a specific category* (e.g., on the Complex Figure there was no opportunity to observe expressive language). The overall agreements were calculated with and without the nonoccurrence category.

The findings from this study reveal that interrater reliability was relatively satisfactory (above 83%) only for the deficient cognitive functions that both observers agreed had occurred (the nonoccurrence category was excluded). The ratings on the nonintellective factors and on type of mediation categories were less satisfactory (between 66 and 73%). The higher ratings on deficient cognitive functions than on nonintellective factors may be due in part to the fact that Feuerstein and colleagues have written much more about the deficient cognitive functions than the nonintellective factors and hence the shared understanding is greater. Since the LPAD tests are designed primarily to tap deficient cognitive functions, accurate and sensitive observation of the nonintellective factors becomes secondary. There were also more attempts to operationalize the deficient cognitive functions in terms of their behavioral referents than the nonintellective factors. Emotional and motivational factors are also more difficult to assess as their presence is determined by observation over a series of tasks.

The separate analysis of the amount of agreement, with and without the *nonoccurrence rating*, revealed interesting findings. It was most evident for the deficient cognitive functions and nonintellective factors ratings and less so for the type of mediation ratings. It should be noted that although the inclusion of the nonoccurrence rating was problematic for the examiners in this study, it was nevertheless important as it raises some concerns and clarification about rating of LPAD tests. The nonoccurrence category was included in the first place because not all tests tap all cognitive behaviours. This is evident when examining the ratings on the Plateaux and the Complex Figure tests, which require a limited range of cognitive functions for solution and relatively limited possibilities for mediation and observation. The problem for examiners was deciding that if they did not observe a particular behavior, was it because the child has no difficulty (i.e., efficient cognitive functioning) or because the test did not require that specific cognitive function? Raters may have used the *nonoccurrence* when they felt that a cognitive function was very efficient and hence was difficult to observe occurring during the task. Agreements for relevant categories (when the nonoccurrence category was removed) generally were higher. This was likely to be because when the deficient cognitive function is clearly elicited then its severity can be observed and determined.

In conclusion the overall findings of Tzuriel and Samuels (2000) reveal much better reliabilities than those reported by Vaught and Haywood (1990). It is interesting to note that for two out of three categories reported by Vaught and Haywood (1990) as having high interrater agreement (80% or more) for all four subjects (i.e., Blurred and Sweeping Perception, and Episodic Grasp of Reality), there was also high agreement in Tzuriel and Samuel's (2000) study—87 and 88%, respectively. For the third category, Egocentric Communication, the findings in the present study were lower (69%) than in the previous study. Thus, Tzuriel and Samuels (2000) and Lidz (1991) agree that the relatively modest level of agreement found in Vaught and Haywood's study is impressive in view of the fact that definitions of the deficient cognitive functions were not standardized across raters.

Ratings for the *type of mediation* in Tzuriel and Samuel's (2000) study revealed a more inconsistent picture. In the teaching phase, the level of agreement was similar with or without the nonoccurrence category. This was probably because the situation required more mediation and enabled a clearer picture to emerge. However, in the testing phase, agreements decreased when the nonoccurrence category was excluded. This finding coincides with Vaught and Haywood's study, which reported lower levels of agreement on the type of mediation than on deficient cognitive functions categories. This result may be explained by considering the differences between rating the type of mediation and rating the deficient cognitive functions and nonintellective factors. When rating the type of mediation, the examiner's focus involves both observation of the examinee and observation of *his or her own* behavior. On the other hand, when rating the deficient cognitive functions and nonintellective factors, the examiner focuses on the examinee's behavior alone. For type of mediation, the nonoccurrence rating may have been problematic because the decision was not based on whether the test could reveal a specific behavior (as in the deficient cognitive functions and nonintellective factors), but rather whether the particular mediation was needed on that test. Thus, agreement in the testing phase may have been higher with the nonoccurrence rating because examiners did less mediation, and did so only when the examinee encountered difficulty. In the teaching phase, on the other hand, examiners provide mediation even without observing a difficulty, in order to clarify levels of knowledge and understanding, to crystallize learning, and to generally ensure optimum performance. Determining what is the mediation required for a particular deficiency (as related to a particular test) versus what is not required is difficult to determine, hence the lower level of agreement in the teaching than in the testing phase. This is supported by results from specific categories in which there was at least 10% or greater agreement on the testing phase than the teaching phase. Categories such as Questioning, Teaching Prerequisite Concepts, and Teaching Prerequisite Language are used much more frequently during teaching than testing. It may be hard to determine when they were necessary *during the teaching phase* and therefore agreement is relatively low. On the other hand, if that type of mediation is observed *during the testing phase*, it is more likely to be rated as needed as it normally would not be done, hence there was more agreement.

RESEARCH PERSPECTIVES OF THE LPAD

Feuerstein's LPAD approach, followed by others (i.e., Greenberg, 1990; Haywood, 1988, 1997; Haywood & Tzuriel, 1992b; Lidz, 1991; Samuels et al., 1989; Skuy & Shmukler, 1987; Tzuriel, 1998; Tzuriel & Samuels, 2000), has been found to be a productive and efficient approach in assessing children's learning potential (Feuerstein et al., 1980; Greenberg, 1990). In the rest of this chapter I will present some of the research findings concerning the LPAD.

The LPAD has been used with deaf children (i.e., Keane & Kretschmer, 1987), learning-disabled children (Samuels et al., 1989), penitentiary inmates (Silverman & Waxman, 1991), vocational school and English as a Second Language students (Luther & Wyatt, 1989), adults with learning difficulties (Samuels, Lamb, & Oberholtzer, 1992), disadvantaged black undergraduate students in South Africa (Shochet, 1992), disadvantaged gifted children (Skuy et al., 1989), and Ethiopian immigrants to Israel (Kaniel et al., 1991).

Much of the research carried out on the LPAD has been related to case studies (e.g., Haywood & Menal, 1992; Kaniel & Tzuriel, 1992) or group DA (Rand & Kaniel, 1987; Tzuriel & Feuerstein, 1992). In the following, I will present two studies aimed at showing the reliability of the LPAD, DA in a group situation, examples from clinical–educational research, and finally research related to the use of the LPAD in cognitive education programs.

GROUP DYNAMIC ASSESSMENT

The advantage of using group DA over individual DA is that group DA is economical, allowing examination of many children in a relatively short time. Group DA can be used to analyze the learning processes of groups and later on to prescribe specific treatments designed for remedial of deficient learning processes. Another use is to identify children who need further procedures such as in-depth individual assessment or group assignment to an enrichment program. The utility of group DA was investigated by Tzuriel and Feuerstein (1992) with the SV-II instrument administered as a group DA test. There were three experimental conditions: High Teaching (HT), Low Teaching (LT), and No Teaching (NT). It should be noted that Jensen (1969) considers tasks such as those in SV-II, as tapping Level II of thinking, and therefore essentially untrainable.

The SV-II was administered to advantaged and disadvantaged students ($n = 749$) in Grades 7–9, following a teaching condition (except the NT). The Raven Standard Progressive Matrices (RSPM) was administered as a static test to all groups twice, before and 2 weeks after the treatment. The initial scores on this test were used to classify subjects to three levels of initial performance.

Analysis of the SV-II scores showed significant effects of Treatment ($F(1, 488) = 47.47$, $p < .001$), Type of School ($F(1, 488) = 29.74$, $p < .001$), and Initial Performance Level ($F(2, 488) = 8.20$, $p < .001$). Performance on the SV-II was higher (1) for subjects who received the higher level of teaching, (2) for subjects who had initially high performance (based on first Raven's initial score), and (3) for socially advantaged subjects as compared with those from disadvantaged families. A Treatment by Type of School interaction ($F(1, 488) = 10.81$, $p < .001$), however, indicated that the difference between advantaged and disadvantaged children was much lower in the HT condition than in the LT condition. The results of this study indicate, in general, the invalidity of the RSPM, as a static test, in representing the individual's "psychometric intelligence," especially for low-performing groups, and that with the relatively short intervention procedure given in group LPAD situations one can achieve much higher performance. The fact that the second administration of the RSPM was 2 weeks after the intervention strengthens the argument that the changes were not superficial or temporary but represented a solid phenomenon.

Task analysis of the Raven's items, especially of Sets C–E and the SV-II items based on these Sets, revealed that the items require rather abstract reasoning and high analytical skills. Modifiability in these kinds of items reflects a basic cognitive change (for some individuals even structural) and not merely changes in attitudes and motivation.

In an intriguing educational study carried out by Shochet (1992), the role of DA in predicting the success of black undergraduate students in South Africa was investigated. Shochet used the Deductive Reasoning Test (Verster, 1973) as a DA measure to tap syllogistic reasoning. The criterion measures were the number of credits and the average grade achieved at the end of the first year. In the next step students were divided into less or more modifiable groups on the basis of the Deductive Reasoning Test; in each group the Deductive Reasoning Test scores predicted the criterion measures. The results revealed significant prediction of the criterion measures among the less modifiable students ($r = .55$, $p < .01$ for Credits) as compared with negative prediction among the more modifiable students ($r = -.22$, $p = $ ns). The explanation of this finding is that the less modifiable students were less susceptible to being modified during a period of 1 year, hence the higher correlation between the modifiability measure and the achievement criterion. The more modifiable students showed, on the other hand, that what was being measured in the static test was not a reflection of their skills in the range of the cognitive area being tested. Shochet concluded that it is not only unfair to rely on static measures but also inaccurate, in that the test was invalid for predicting achievement of the more modifiable disadvantaged students. This study raises the issue of the construct validity of the SAT as an aptitude test rather than as an achievement test (see also Jencks & Crouse, 1982).

CLINICAL–EDUCATIONAL RESEARCH

This type of research is scarce and composed mainly of case studies (i.e., Haywood & Menal, 1992; Kaniel & Tzuriel, 1992). Haywood and Menal reported on a developmental cognitive psychotherapeutic procedure based on Feuerstein's theory. Using the LPAD with a 16-year-old mentally retarded girl, they demonstrated an accurate estimation of her learning potential, identification of specific cognitive deficiencies, and the type and amount of mediation required for improving her performance. Samuels et al., (1989) carried out an extensive DA clinical study. In this study, a battery of eight tests from the LPAD was administered individually to teach learning-disabled children (LD), learning disabled with attention deficit disorder children (LD/ADD), educable mentally handicapped children (EMH), and children with no diagnosed difficulty. Three types of data were collected: *performance scores*, *deficient cognitive functions* as rated during the training and testing phases, and *type and amount of mediation* required during the training and testing phases. All of the testing interactions were videotaped and rated later on a list of deficient cognitive functions (i.e., deficient spatial orientation, deficient comparative behavior) and type and amount of mediation (i.e., restraint of impulsivity, metacognitive questioning). Two performance scores were computed for each child: *Correct without Intervention* and *Correct with Intervention Prior to Response*. The findings showed that the performance scores (with intervention and without intervention) of the normally achieving children and LD children were similar. Both groups did not have difficulties on the LPAD tests. The LD/ADD group, however, had significantly lower scores than the normally achieving children and the LD children on all tests. The EMH group showed the poorest performance on all tests *but also showed significant gains on every test when mediation prior to response was computed.* Group differences were reduced when a score of correct answers with mediation prior to response was computed. On three tests there were no differences and on the other five tests the differences were much lower.

The findings on the deficient cognitive functions showed that a higher percentage of LD/ADD children were rated with deficient cognitive functions than the LD children. This finding was consistent across all categories. The highest percentage of children rated as deficient was found in the EMH group. Interestingly, the group differences are primarily in degree of deficiency rather than in kind. Comparison of training to testing phase showed, as expected, a consistent drop in the percentage of children rated as deficient, with the exception of language and communication categories, which remain high for all three groups.

The findings on type and amount of mediation showed that the EMH group required the greatest amount of mediation followed by the LD/ADD group. The LD group required less mediation than the LD/ADD or EMH groups, except mediation for competence, which was given more extensively to the EMH group than to the other groups. The categories of prompting, focusing, promoting metacognitive awareness, teaching rules and strategies, and mediation of competence, were the most frequently required mediations for the EMH group and the LD/ADD and LD groups to a lesser degree. The normal achieving group required minimal mediation.

Of most importance are the findings showing that the gains of the EMH group, following mediation, as well as their ability to deal with abstract formal operational tasks, could not have been predicted by their standard WISC-R scores. The authors also reported that, while the WISC-R scores could have predicted the general performance pattern among the groups across all LPAD tests, this was not the case for the LD and LD/ADD groups. Both groups showed similar performance on the WISC-R but demonstrated consistent differences in performance on the LPAD tests. The LD/ADD group consistently made more errors, exhibited more deficient cognitive functions, and required more mediation to perform effectively. The authors concluded that the LPAD provides useful information about children with LD that is not readily apparent from static assessment and that it can change clinicians' and teachers' views about children's learning potential.

USE OF THE LPAD IN COGNITIVE EDUCATION PROGRAMS

One of the most important uses of DA is the evaluation of the effects of cognitive education programs. A major problem in such an evaluation is choosing the criteria of evaluation and the methods for assessing individual differences on those criteria. At the most obvious level, one might assume that programs should be evaluated according to their own stated goals. Thus, if a program is designed to enhance "learning how to learn" processes, it appears to be of critical importance to assess precisely this ability as the primary criterion for evaluation. It is therefore surprising that so many intervention programs designed to develop learning abilities do not use the DA approach to tap "learning how to learn" capacities (Tzuriel, 1992b). One exception is Tzuriel and Alfassi's (1994) work in which the effects of the Instrumental Enrichment (IE) program (Feuerstein et al., 1980) were investigated using a DA procedure. The major objective of IE is to enhance the capacity of the individual, via the mediation of a supportive teacher, to become modified as a result of exposure to new experiences. In other words, the principal aim is to teach individuals how to learn and be independent in developing their learning potential. According to the MLE theory on which the IE program is based, enhancing a child's learning potential via mediation allows the child to learn additional and even more complex cognitive operations and strategies. The child's potential for such enhancement may be measured by the DA of his or her learning potential (Haywood & Tzuriel, 1992).

Tzuriel and Alfassi (1994) used the IE as a cognitive intervention program designed to change cognitive and motivational functioning, and LPAD to evaluate the effectiveness of the IE program. The advantage of using both applied systems (IE and LPAD) within the same theoretical framework is that there is a conceptual continuity between the assessment process and the intervention procedures. An experimental group of seventh-grade students ($n = 93$) of low-SES background participated in the IE program for 2 years and were compared with a nonprogram group ($n = 98$) of similar social and academic background. Three tests from the LPAD were administered: the Organizer, RSDT, and SV-II (Feuerstein et al., 1995). The Organizer test, which is considered to be among the most difficult of the LPAD tests, contains 10 items in the preteaching test and 20 items in the postteaching tests. In each item, a series of statements or premises is presented. Each statement provides part of the information required for organizing and placing objects in required positions relative to one another. The location of objects is not precisely specified within any single statement but must be inferred from successive clues about the position of the objects in relation to each other. Tasks vary as to their level of complexity, in terms of the number of objects to be organized, and the level of abstraction and inference required (i.e., some items contain negative statements such as "the Lion is not beside the Bear"). The strategies and rules required for solving the tasks, however, remain constant. The cognitive functions required to perform the tasks include precise and systematic gathering of data, discovery of spatial relations among objects, simultaneous consideration of several sources of information, inferential deductive reasoning, use of logical evidence, and control of trial-and-error behavior. The mental operations required to perform the tasks are related to encoding and decoding, representation, transitive and inferential thinking, negation and propositional thinking. A multivariate analysis of variance carried out on the cognitive measures indicated that the IE program group showed higher gain scores than did the nonprogram group on the LPAD Organizer. Higher gain scores on the Organizer were also found for the IE program participants who obtained the lowest scores on an initial indicator of cognitive modifiability. In other words, the IE program was found to be more effective for those who initially demonstrated low cognitive modifiability than for those who showed medium or high levels of initial cognitive modifiability. This result suggests that the IE program is most effective for individuals who are in need of a cognitive remedial program and supports the divergent effects hypothesis of IE, according to which IE is most effective with low performing individuals (Ruiz, 1985). Further research demonstrating the use of DA within cognitive education programs is presented later in relation to DA of preschool.

4

Distinctive Features of the Clinical DA Approach

IMPULSIVITY AND TEST PERFORMANCE: A CASE STUDY

The distinctive features of DA can be presented using the following example of Jacob, an adolescent boy who was referred for dynamic assessment in 1989 after a failure in a standardized group-test and subsequent enrollment in a secondary high school. Jacob, a sensitive 14-year-old, was referred by his parents with the aim of finding an appropriate educational setting after his 6 years in a primary school. The family was of medium socioeconomic status and lived in a developing town in northern Israel. The parents tried to enroll Jacob in a prestigious high school in a neighboring town but were informed that Jacob would have to be tested by a conventional group test administered at a well-known institute for vocational counseling in Jerusalem. The conventional group test is required by all candidates as part of the registration requirements.

The test findings showed that Jacob was in the 4th to 6th percentile across several domains of the test profile. As a result, Jacob was rejected, but the school counselor suggested to the parents that they consider a less demanding and less prestigious school. Based on the group-test findings, Jacob was also rejected by the second school and referred to a vocational school considered to be appropriate for children functioning on a low intellectual level. At this point, the parents as well as Jacob were frustrated and confused. First, Jacob was regarded to be a bright resourceful boy, full of initiative activities around the house, a rich social life, and creative in daily life problem solving. Second, his academic achievements, although not superior, were adequate indicating an appropriate level of understanding. All of these factors did not justify the level of education assigned to him by others.

The parents, following friends' advice, approached a psychologist who began to test him using the WISC-R. However, after 15 minutes Jacob showed signs of stress and anger and complained about the need to be tested. He finally decided to walk out of the test and refused to come back. Following this session, the psychologist met with Jacob's parents and diagnosed him as having an emotional instability problem and referred the parents to a psychiatrist. In a later interview, the parents reported deep despair because of their impression that from one helping agent to another their child's situation had become worse. The father complained sarcastically, "I guess that the next step is to hospitalize the child." Following the advice of another psychologist, who applied a cognitive education intervention project in their town, the parents decided to bring Jacob to me for DA.

During the first DA session, which took about 2 hours, Jacob was very suspicious and depressed but within 30 minutes he felt more confidence and his overall emotional mood changed. Jacob was given several tests from the Learning Potential Assessment Device (LPAD, Feuerstein et al., 1979). It was clear that Jacob is intelligent and a fast learner. He could immediately grasp new cognitive principles, work systematically to gather information, and apply the newly acquired principles to novel problems. The main deficient cognitive functions revealed were impulsivity in gathering the information (input phase), impulsivity in pointing to the right answer after correct verbal anticipation (output phase), deficient verbal tools that help to register information, and deficient need for accuracy in data gathering. These deficiencies were significantly improved after an intervention aimed at enhancement of self-regulated behavior, learning a few task-specific concepts and terms, and developing awareness of the importance of accuracy and precision. These deficiencies could easily explain his failure in the first group-test administered at the vocational counseling institute. That test was composed of a set of multiple-choice questions. The nature of the task requires fine distinctions among several alternatives, paying attention to specific verbal terms that provide cues about the correct answer, and choice of the best answer after considering very similar alternatives. For children who have these kinds of cognitive deficiencies, the multiple-choice type of test is disastrous. The multiple-choice task requires exactly the cognitive functions that are deficient. It should be noted that these cognitive functions are not indicative of the child's ability for abstraction and understanding but rather of poor learning habits, behavioral tendencies, and attitudes toward learning. It seems that the low score achieved by Jacob on the group test did not reflect his true level of functioning, but rather a behavioral tendency to react impulsively, lack of learning opportunities to learn verbal tools, and poor mediation in the family for accuracy and precision.

As a result of the DA testing Jacob was referred for cognitive intervention aimed at remediation of the specific deficiencies. In the psychological report sent to the school it was strongly recommended that Jacob be accepted, on the premise that by the time that school starts (6 months from the testing date) a cognitive intervention program would have been implemented to prepare Jacob for school activities. Jacob received the planned intervention for 6 months (3 hours a week) and made significant progress. He was eventually accepted by the secondary high school, continued after that in a high school, and graduated successfully. Today, 10 years after the testing, Jacob is serving in the army in a responsible job and planning to attend college. It should be noted that acceptance to the secondary high school was not automatic on receiving the psychological report. There was a need for a special meeting with school staff to explain the DA results and the prognosis based on it, as well as to negotiate the terms for acceptance.

Jacob's case exemplifies many of the problems and difficulties psychologists and educators face when dealing with DA findings. The difficulties lie in understanding the goals of DA, the specific diagnostic procedures, the translation of findings into intervention processes, and the educational and socioemotional implications of the assessment. In the following sections of this chapter the goals of DA are identified followed by discussion of one of the key factors in DA—the concept of *cognitive functions*. In turn, I discuss four shifts to DA from the conventional psychometric model of testing, a triadic mediator–task–child model, the taxonomy of DA approaches, and the conditions that necessitate the use of DA.

GOALS OF DA

The goals of DA are remarkably different from the static conventional approach. The following goals are based on Feuerstein et al. (1979):

(1.) *Initial performance level.* According to this goal the examiner assesses the capacity of the child to grasp the principle underlying an initial problem and to solve it. This goal is also common with the conventional approach.

(2.) *Nature and amount of mediation.* An important aspect of the DA process is to assess the nature and amount of investment (mediation) that is required to teach a child a given rule or principle. Mediation may be given after each item and not only in sample or initial practice items. Moreover, mediation may be given frequently for correctly solved items to ensure success in the following items, create insight, and facilitate generalized processes that are applied to further problems. Repetition of a response or performance is also used to crystallize the acquired strategy or operation. The examiner, however, must be very sensitive regarding when to intervene and when to withdraw; when to "press mediation" intensively and/or repeatedly and when to refrain from mediation; when to be firm and demanding and when to be soft and appeasing. The specific approach depends on the child's responses, deficient cognitive functions, mental set, accessibility to mediation, level of competence, type of cognitive and motivational orientation, circumstantial factors, and individual history.

It should be noted in this regard that several attempts have been made by conventional test constructors to include some kind of teaching within the testing procedure. This was done mainly as a result of the realization that the child's manifest performance does not reflect his or her potential. It is my opinion that any attempt made by new test constructors to include a built-in component of teaching is a good move toward correction of the previous static approach and a good start toward a more accurate assessment. The problem is that neither the structure of static tests nor the nature of the items in them has been designed originally for teaching. In other words, static tests may be very good for the purposes for which they were designed. Attempts to include teaching items is a small step in the right direction, but why should one be satisfied with a small step when a total "full-blooming" DA approach is already available?

(3.) *Deficient cognitive functions.* One of the key components of DA is to discover what specific deficient cognitive functions are responsible for failure in performance and how modifiable they are as a result of mediation. A detailed description of cognitive functions is given in the following section.

The examiner's role is to intervene in order to modify deficient cognitive functions and observe changes in the child's performance following the intervention. It should be noted that with young children it is suggested to use a positive definition of the cognitive function (i.e., systematic exploratory behavior) rather than a negative one (i.e., deficient systematic exploratory behavior). Cognitive functions of young children are still in a process of development and are difficult to define as deficient.

(4.) *Nonintellective factors.* Assessment of the nonintellective factors is considered as important in DA as the "pure" cognitive factors in determining the child's learning and academic success (Tzuriel, 1991a; Tzuriel et al., 1988). The remediation of the nonintellective factors during a DA process can be diagnostic about the child's difficulties. The DA approach in this sense is considered as a holistic approach where cognitive, emotional, and behavioral tendencies are observed and modified. For example, some children show resistance to accepting mediation, even when it is clear to them that the examiner does not provide the answer. Speaking metaphorically, there are children who have developed "antibodies" against mediation and, in a way, become "immune" to mediation given to them by an adult. This phenomenon happens frequently with special education children who had been "overmediated" in the past and consequently have developed sensitivity to mediation offered to them. The inaccessibility to mediation can also characterize bright children who interpret the help offered as a failure on their part (a detailed discussion of the nonintellective factors is given in Chapter 5).

(5.) *Maintenance and transfer of learning.* An important aspect of DA is the assessment of the extent to which the newly learned cognitive principle is maintained (in a parallel problem) as well as how it is applied adequately to solve more difficult problems (transfer). The performance on a more difficult or a novel problem might be considered as an indicator for transfer of learning. Since the test items gradually become more difficult, it is possible to observe how principles learned in previous items are applied to new problems that gradually become more difficult.

(6.) *Type of modality.* This goal refers to the assessment of the differential preference of children for one or another type of modality of presentation of a problem. For example, some children function better when a task is presented visually whereas others prefer a verbal or pictorial modality. Some children prefer to start solving a numerical dimension of a problem whereas others prefer a dimension such as color, height, size, or position. Studies with the Children's Seriational Thinking Modifiability test (CSTM; Tzuriel, 1995b) showed that most 5- and 6-year-olds begin to solve seriation problems by concentrating on the *number* dimension. Choosing number as the first priority was evident in spite of the fact that developmentally number is considered as more abstract than other test dimensions (i.e., *size* or *shading*).

(7.) *Effects of different mediation strategies.* The last goal is to assess the differential effects of different mediation strategies on modifying the child's performance. Some children respond more positively when *mediation for meaning* is carried out by means of the emotional tone of the examiner and enthusiasm. Others respond more positively when the examiner emphasizes *mediation for transcendence* (i.e., rules, generalizations, and principles). The different mediations used by the examiner depend on the task dimensions such as simple versus complex, familiar versus novel, type of operation (i.e., analogy, seriation, sequential progression), and language of presentation (i.e., figural, numerical, verbal).

In regard to this goal it is important to note that a decrease in mediation during DA is also considered to be a sign of modifiability. With some children there is need to repeat the mediation given with each problem. However, the intensity of the mediation decreases with each problem. This decrease indicates that the child has made some progress in spite of the fact that functioning is not yet autonomous.

COGNITIVE FUNCTIONS

The cognitive functions are considered a key concept in identifying the specific strengths and difficulties of the child's performance. Originally the concept was defined negatively as deficient cognitive function in order to point to the difficulties and mediation required (Feuerstein et al., 1979). However, when assessing young children the cognitive functions are usually phrased in positive terms. Cognitive function is a "conglomerate" of inherited tendencies, learning habits, and attitudes toward learning. Clinical experience has shown that it is difficult to identify the exact source of the cognitive function and that such knowledge of the source is not critical for intervention purposes.

A list of deficient cognitive functions in the *input, elaboration,* and *output* phases were described in detail by Feuerstein et al. (1979, 1988, 1995). The distinction among input, elaboration, and output is helpful on a methodological level, but eventually there is much overlap among them (Tzuriel & Samuels, 2000). The following list examines the cognitive functions that are more common among young children.

Input Phase

1. *Planned, reflective, and systematic exploratory behavior.* This function is characterized by the child's relatively slow reaction to a stimulus and consideration of all its components in a systematic way. Deficient systematic exploratory behavior in young children can be an expression of an innate temperamental trait, or a behavioral tendency to respond impulsively when confronting tasks that require contradictory demands (i.e., speed and accuracy). The intervention here can be relatively simple: delay of the child's response while providing opportunities for consideration of all aspects of the problem. With some children the intervention should be more intensive such as motor inhibition, verbal analysis of the behavior with the child, and mediation for insight.

2. *Receptive verbal tools.* Receptive verbal tools help the child in the process of information gathering, generalization of data, and its expression. Recognition of concepts and terms enables the child to identify the information related to them and to distinguish between different phenomena. Different concepts enable description of relationships (i.e., opposite to, above–below, similar to, identical, inside–outside) and include events and objects under an organizing conceptual framework. A distinction should be made between a *concept* and a *term.* Very frequently children know the concept but are not familiar with the specific term. For example, a child might know the concepts of "horizontal," "vertical," and "diagonal" but does not know the specific terms for them. The child might use instead such terms as "standing line" or "lying down line." In diagnostic processes examiners should verify whether children's difficulty is a result of lack of the concept, lack of the specific term, or just inefficiency in retrieving and using the correct concept. Teaching of the concepts and terms in DA is not for the purpose of mere verbal enrichment but rather for preparing the child to distinguish among stimuli, perform generalizations, and communicate efficiently and accurately.

3. *Spatial and time orientation.* The spatial and time orientation functions are central in affecting children's thinking processes and daily tasks (i.e., estimation of sizes, reading maps, following directions, understanding instructions for assembling instruments, understanding causal relations, and following a time schedule). Deficiencies in those functions usually derive from difficulties in mental representation and from its conceptualization in terms of direction, order, and proximity. It is possible to recognize developed spatial functions when the child relies on mental representation in orienting him- or herself in space rather than on his or her body, in understanding of the relativity of left and right directions, and in projecting three-dimensional objects into two-dimensional objects. The examiner can easily diagnose these aspects when asking the child to point to the right and left hand of the examiner when facing the child and then when asking the child to point to objects to the left and right of both the child and the examiner.

4. *Needs for precision and accuracy.* Needs for precision and accuracy are related to the individual's ability to gather information in a complete way and express it using precise terms. These needs are not necessarily related to the child's intellectual ability and reflect frequently cultural factors and previous learning opportunities. For example, a child can be very precise in comparing the amount of ice cream he or she receives to that of his or her brother. The child in this case has a need to be precise. However, when it comes to computing a math problem, reading a paragraph, organizing the room or school bag, and sharing experiences with others, the child demonstrates lack of precision and/or apathy to inaccuracies. Intervention here involves creating cognitive conflicts, which focus the child's attention on the importance of being accurate.

5. *Considering two or more sources of information simultaneously.* This function is identified when the child can relate to several aspects of an object or event simultaneously. Deficiency in this function is related to a high level of "egocentricity." Deficient function in simultaneous consideration of a few sources of information affects understanding of relativity concepts and varied types of problems that require integration of several components. For example, some children show difficulty in relating simultaneously to dimensions of color and shape of a block, even after these dimensions were taught. Intervention for considering all dimensions involves both development of metacognitive strategies and repetition of the acquired function.

Elaboration Phase

1. *Selection of relevant cues for solving a problem.* The relevance of a cue or a dimension for solving a problem depends on the clarity of the goal. The clearer the specific goal for the child, the easier is the distinction among the relevant dimensions in the perceptual field. For example, if the solution of a problem

requires mental operation on dimensions of size and height, selection of number and color would make the solution impossible. In the intervention process the examiner can point to the different dimensions involved in the problem and the different alternative solutions. The examiner can also ask the child to define the differences among different solutions and justify why one alternative is better than the others.

2. *Spontaneous comparative behavior*. This function is the basis for creation of relations among objects, people, and events. Spontaneous comparative behavior is usually an internal need, which does not require special effort. This function depends on the existence of directing concepts in the child's conceptual repertoire. When the child does not master certain concepts or does not have the need to use them, he or she will not make efforts to compare an external event to an internal existing concept or compare two stimuli that relate to the same concept. An example of this function is when the child spontaneously compares a piece of a puzzle to the original model or between two words that sound similar but have different meanings.

3. *Need for summative behavior*. This function is related to the child's orientation to quantify information and summarizing the reality. Comparing different amounts of objects or events using addition, subtraction, multiplication, and division can reflect summative behavior. Spontaneous counting of plates on the dining table or the number of pencils in a box are expressions of summative behavior. There are children who do not know exactly how many brothers and sisters they have because they have never related to that question. Each time they are asked, they need to count the number of siblings in their family. Summarizing of reality can also be expressed on a conceptual level when the child attaches a comprehensive generalized concept to a group of objects or a string of events. A deficient summative behavior affects a wide range of learning and memory processes.

4. *Need for pursuing after logical evidence*. The need to pursue after logical evidence and provision of logical justification is related to many thinking processes, especially when the child confronts conflicting phenomena or inadequate explanations. Need for pursuing logical evidence is characterizing children who have opportunities for mediation focused on search after logical and consistent explanations. The most frequent example of a deficient function is observed when a child is asked "Why?" and answers "Because." It should be emphasized that this deficiency is related to the *need* and not the *ability* for logical reasoning. Mediation for enhancement of the need for logical evidence can be done by asking several reasons for an answer or challenging the child by presenting purposefully a mistaken answer. Other intervention techniques are to ask the child for justifications of correct and incorrect answers and role playing where the child is the teacher who has to explain the solution for a problem.

5. *Internalization (transfer of a principle across cognitive domains)*. Internalization of a cognitive strategy or mental operation is expressed when the child

uses generalized signs, symbols, and concepts rather than concrete behavior. A deficient internalization is characterized by use of concrete cues, rather than mental representation, to manipulate stored information. Internalization can help the child in transformation of information, in transcending the concrete "here and now" and delay of immediate satisfaction for the sake of a remote goal. For many children labeled as mentally retarded, lack of internalization is a result of an educational (and philosophical) approach of concretizing of reality. Psychologists and educators who argue for teaching by concretizing believe that these children have difficulties in abstraction and therefore need a concrete approach. The educational approach in DA is to bring the child, as much as possible, to use representational processes rather than relying initially on concretizing of reality.

6. *Hypothetical thinking and strategies for hypothesis testing.* Hypothetical thinking is characterized in the child's readiness to adopt several alternatives in searching for a solution, mental representation of several possible solutions, and delay of immediate gratification until accurate examination of all possibilities. Children who did not have many opportunities for mediation in the past have difficulties in hypothetical thinking and relate to reality in a concrete way. The terms of "if–then" characterize a thinking pattern that requires representational skills, cause-and-effect understanding, and use of existing information to predict future results. Hypothetical thinking and hypothesis testing requires examination of opposite and rival hypotheses, their systematic exploration, and logical selection of one. For example, in the Children's Inferential Thinking Modifiability test (CITM; Tzuriel, 1989b, 1991b) the examiner may identify this function by asking the child to point to a possible consequence of a premise ("if the car goes to the red house where will the dog be?") or describe several alternative solutions ("what are all the possible pictures that can enter this house?").

7. *Planning behavior.* Planning behavior is one of the basic cognitive functions, which influence a whole range of other functions and behaviors, especially the tendency for impulsivity and systematic exploratory behavior. Planning behavior connects between past and future processes, is related to representation of goals, and distinction between goals and means. Planning behavior is developed in families where life conditions are organized and/or predicted. Mediation within the family helps children to internalize predicted reality, to mentally represent principles, and to develop an internal locus of control. Planning behavior can be expressed in a variety of academic (e.g., preparing homework, solving a puzzle, writing a paper, organizing a school project) and social areas (e.g., planning of a trip, organizing a party, business management, family expanses).

8. *Elaboration of cognitive categories.* This function is characterized by the child's tendency to develop the information in order to create a wide conceptual system and "condense" known concepts by connecting them to others (networking of concepts) so that the picture portrayed will not be limited and laconic.

Output Phase

1. *Egocentric communication.* Egocentric communication, which is very frequent with young children, derives from a difficulty to perceive reality from someone else's perspective in communicating information. Egocentric communication is related to deficiency in perception of self as differentiated from the other. It is expressed in giving partial answers, lack of precision, and lack of attempts to convince and clarify a point of view based on the assumption that the other person probably understands the meanings and intentions. Egocentric communication characterizes children who come from families with deficient communication patterns and lack of mediation for detailed and precise explanations. Many children fail in written or oral tests because they do not communicate efficiently the end product of their thoughts and give the impression that actually they do not understand the subject. It is possible in DA to change the egocentric communication by asking provocative questions, bringing the child's answers to the absurd, and modeling of efficient communication.

2. *Blocking behavior.* Blocking behavior is observed when the child does not perform well on a problem after showing mastery on a similar problem. Blocking behavior usually appears after a failure in performance. It seems as if the child "panics" and reacts in a way that might give the impression that all that has been learned is forgotten. Mediation in this case involves encouragement of the child (mediation for feelings of competence), analyzing the response, and bringing into awareness that failures are an integral part of the learning process.

3. *Visual transport.* This cognitive function is related to children's ability to preserve a mental image and transport it from one place to another without losing it or parts of it. Deficient visual transport can be identified in tests where the child has to complete a missing part. The child can anticipate the answer, motorically or verbally, but has difficulties in pointing to the correct answer from several alternatives. The difficulty can be derived from lack of perceptual stability, which causes irrelevant stimuli to distract the child from focusing on the central stimulus. One of the reasons for deficient visual transport is lack of a reference system, which is used as a support system for the transported visual stimulus. The support system enables control against interference of irrelevant stimuli. For example, in the Sequences-II subtest of the Cognitive Modifiability Battery (Tzuriel, 1995a, 2000d) the child has to grasp the systematic way in which blocks change position across three "plates" (wooden boards with open windows) and figure out the position of a block in the last empty "plate." This subtest was found to be efficient in assessing visual transport and modifying this cognitive function.

4. *Projection of virtual relationships.* Projection of virtual relationships is defined as the ability to transfer a principle or a rule learned in one context or situation to another unfamiliar context. In some cases, where it is clear that the

child learned a principle, a change in the way a problem is presented, or in the modality of presentation causes "forgetfulness" of the principle. This difficulty is related to internalization of the learned principle in the elaboration phase. It is possible to observe this cognitive function in DA when the child, after learning how to solve analogies in one area, can solve analogy problems that are different on one or more dimensions.

FOUR SHIFTS FROM STANDARDIZED-CONVENTIONAL TESTING TO DA

According to Feuerstein et al. (1979) there are four changes that differentiate DA from standardized-conventional testing. These changes relate to the nature of the tasks, the process of testing, the test situation and especially the examiner–examinee relationships, and the interpretation of findings.

1. *Shift in the nature of the tasks.* The tasks in DA have been constructed for teaching and assessment of cognitive changes rather than for measuring the individual's status relative to his or her peers. In the standardized static approach, the selection of items for inclusion in the test is based on their psychometric properties of differentiating among individuals and their goodness of fit to the normal curve. Selection of items in DA is based on the nature of the item in terms of possibilities to teach important cognitive strategies, and enhance cognitive functions. The items are graduated so that learning of one item prepares the child to perform a more advanced item.

2. *Shift from end product to process orientation.* The shift from end product to process orientation is reflected in the focus given to the changes in the child's performance and to the specific deficient cognitive and nonintellective factors that affect the child's functioning. The emphasis given in DA is not so much on the typical level of performance but on the nature of behavior and the process and the intervention required in bringing about a certain level of performance. The questions asked in DA are "how" and "why" rather than "what" and "how much." Some children learn fast but tend to forget or not transfer their learning. Others may learn slowly but whatever is learned is maintained and even transferred to other cognitive areas. The specific ways in which the child learns and the specific cognitive functions and mediation required to facilitate the child's performance are the process components that are of interest.

3. *Shift in the context of the assessment situation.* One of the most important shifts is the interactive nature between the child and the examiner. In DA, the whole context of the testing situation changes from a standard formal approach to an interactive–dynamic one. The examiner intervenes to modify the child's performance and changes his or her mediation with the child's

improvement. Feedback is given during the testing process using the MLE criteria. The interactive process is characterized by the following behaviors: (1) regulation of the child's behavior through inhibition and control of impulsivity and by sequencing and organizing the task dimensions; (2) improvement of deficient cognitive functions by the MLE criteria; (3) enrichment of the child's cognitive operations (i.e., comparative behavior, analogies, seriation); (4) enrichment of task-related contents (e.g., labeling of relationships such as "opposite," "up–down," "vertical–horizontal–diagonal," "equal to," "left–top"); (5) creation of reflective and insightful thought processes (metacognitive processes).

One of the implications of the interactive nature of DA relates to the *teacher–examiner relationships*. The DA findings, which are based on learning processes, permit an efficient communication between the examiner and the teacher. Both the teacher and the examiner base their observations on parameters of learning and change. The common background of teaching and learning processes creates a communication bridge between teachers and examiners. This bridge is missing in many situations in which the examiner and the teacher come from different conceptual worlds and find themselves entrenched in their positions, concepts, and attitudes without understanding the language of one another. This communication gap risks making the assessment process infertile and eventually not helpful to the assessed child's welfare (Tzuriel & Haywood, 1992).

4. *Shift in interpretation of results.* The interpretation of results is based mainly on qualitative aspects of the child's performance, on analysis of the child's deficient cognitive functions, and on the mediational efforts required to modify them. The child's peak performance is taken as indicative of the child's ability rather than an average of all responses. Sometimes one bright answer indicates that the child has the potential to reach a high level of thinking. The examiner should explain, however, what the possible factors are that block the individual from performing as well in other items.

Tzuriel (1992a) summarized the most articulated characteristics of Feuerstein's DA approach as follows:

- The assessment is focused mainly on learning processes.
- The specific deficient cognitive functions serve as "keys" for understanding the learning difficulties.
- The degree and type of modifiability of deficient cognitive functions during assessment provides strong indications for future change.
- The degree and type of mediation required for cognitive change as well as the changes that take place during assessment in the mediational efforts provide indications for cognitive modifiability.
- The role of the examiner–teacher in relation to both the examinee and the helping agents is of crucial importance.

- The role of nonintellective factors as determinants of the individual's performance as well as their modifiability is important and integrated within the cognitive factors.
- The inclusion of behavioral and nonintellective factors within DA provides the assessment with a holistic view of the individual.

A TRIADIC MODEL OF EXAMINER, TASK, AND CHILD

One way to look at DA is by taking into account the transaction among three basic components: the mediator, the child, and the task. Deutsch (1998) has constructed a tripartite learning partnership model, which characterizes the interaction among the Task, Mediator, and Child in the DA (or any learning situation). This model is presented in Figure 4.1.

As can be seen in Figure 4.1 the mediator–child interaction requires the mediator to analyze the cognitive functions and respond accordingly. The mediator can analyze the child's behavior and functions with the child him or herself in order to bring to awareness these behaviors and cognitive functions. The child, on the other hand, might require mediation from the mediator based on his or her experience with the mediator. I would like to point out here that some children

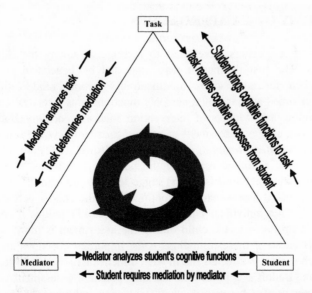

Figure 4.1. Tripartite model of task, mediator, and student. (By permission of Ruth Deutsch, London.)

reveal resistance to mediation in regard to a specific deficient cognitive function or a specific cognitive strategy whereas others demonstrate a high level of change exactly in the same deficient function or strategy. For example, with some children an impulsive tendency to respond is easily modified by using a simple motor strategy ("put your hands under the table until I give you a sign to point to the answer"). With other children a verbal approach ("when you touch it before looking carefully at all components you can make a mistake") is more successful than a motor strategy. Some children refuse to anticipate verbally an answer before performance (cognitive strategy) or apply a novel term to process information whereas others adopt new strategies and verbal terms quite easily.

The relation between the mediator and the task is characterized by analyzing the task characteristics (i.e., level of abstraction required, levels of complexity and novelty) in order to determine the type and amount of mediation required for teaching the task and to understand the child's difficulties. The mediator must consider simultaneously the child's functions and the task characteristics and adapt the level of mediation to those factors.

The third side of the triangular model is the child–task relation. The child brings his or her own cognitive functions to the specific task, and is a factor that should be taken into account in the mediation process. On the other hand, different tasks require different cognitive functions.

TAXONOMY OF DA APPROACHES

Several researchers have tried to distinguish among the different DA approaches. The first distinction was suggested by Feuerstein et al. (1987) between *functional* and *structural* modification. Functional modification refers to intervention aimed at changing a person's functioning as it relates to interaction with a specific task. Models of intervention such as *coaching* (Budoff, 1967, 1987) or those used in assessment of *zone of proximal development* (Vygotsky, 1978) and *graduated prompting* (Campione & Brown, 1987) are referred to as functional, since a limited aspect of the person's functioning is targeted for change. Missiuna and Samuels (1988) suggested that although the clues and aids given in functional assessment are contingent on the child's performance, the intervention is not individually modified for the child's unique needs. In other words, the help given to the child during the assessment is more-or-less standardized. Because of these limitations some important questions are left unresolved, such as who is affected and in what dimension one is best affected by the intervention. Budoff's approach to learning potential assessment is criticized from this perspective because of classifying those who benefit from teaching ("gainers") and those who do not show improvement ("nongainers"). It is only a short step from this classification approach to the search for some stable, fixed, and pervasive intellectual characteristic.

The concept of structural cognitive modifiability (Feuerstein et al., 1979), as opposed to functional cognitive modifiability, is aimed at producing and seeking changes of a structural nature. Structural changes are pervasive and determine cognitive functioning in a broad array of mental activities.

Campione (1989), who suggested three dimensions along which DA approaches are differentiated, has produced another taxonomy: focus, interaction, and target.

Focus refers to the methods of measuring change potential and reflects the distinction between qualitative and quantitative assessment. At one end of the continuum we can find the test–teach–retest procedure (e.g., Budoff, 1987). Children are tested as in a static test, then given an intervention phase and finally retested. The amount of improvement is taken as an indication of learning potential. At the other end of the continuum observations are made on the underlying processes involved in learning such as specific strategies used, deficient cognitive functions, and the quality of the thinking operations.

Interaction refers to the type of examiner–examinee interaction. The assessment may be structured and standardized or flexible and of a clinical nature. Campione and Brown (1987), for example, use a standardized interview and count the number of prompts given to the children, and compare it with the cognitive performance and transfer of learning. By contrast, Feuerstein et al. (1979) suggested a completely clinical approach in which the examiner adapts his or her mediation to the child's responses. Tzuriel (1997a, 2000c, 2000d) suggested the possibility of using either a *clinical/educational* or a *measurement/ research* version of DA (see distinction in Chapter 5). The use of each version is determined by the objectives of the assessment, and the educational system requirements.

The last dimension, *target*, refers to the type of assessed processes or skills, whether they are in domain-specific areas, or generalized across domains. Thus, within the DA movement two traditions coexist, one using traditional psychometric method and the other a clinical approach. Both traditions have their origins in the ZPD concept, although each is interpreted in a different way. The first group (Budoff, 1987; Campione et al., 1985; Guthke, 1992) bases their approach on standardized scripted prompts that provide quantitative measures of the child's learning ability. The second group (Feuerstein et al., 1979; Tzuriel, 1997a, 2000d) bases their approach on *mediated learning* strategies and clinical observations of the child's responses. It should be noted that my approach integrates both the clinical and psychometric approaches by using either the clinical/educational or the measurement/research approach (see Chapter 5 for description).

Haywood (1997) categorized the DA approaches according to the *degree*, *quality*, *purpose*, and *intensity* of the intervention. Based on these dimensions he distinguished among three levels of DA interventions: (1) restructuring of the test situation (e.g., Budoff's "training tests," Carlson and Wiedl's "optimizing test administration," Haywood's "enriched input"), (2) learning within the test (e.g., Guthke's learning tests), and (3) metacognitive intervention such as teaching concepts and principles that can be generalized (e.g., Feuerstein's mediated learning, Paour's induction of logic structures). For a detailed description of each approach the reader is referred to Haywood's (1997) paper.

A recent elaborated description of DA approaches was suggested by Grigorenko and Sternberg (1998), who suggested comparing various approaches along the following aspects:

- *Method of testing* (e.g., coaching, hinting, teach-to the limit, mediated learning)
- *Target population* (e.g., mentally retarded, learning disabled ethnic minorities)
- *Format of testing* (e.g., test–mediate–test, multiple conditions)
- *Nature of testing* (e.g., outside the school context, abstract reasoning, specific domains, psychometrically oriented)
- *Outcome measures* (e.g., structural cognitive changes, improved test performance, extent of benefit from help)
- *Focus of test* (e.g., child-driven, task-driven)
- *Predictive power of the approach.*

Based on these parameters, Grigorenko and Sternberg (1998) used a four-point scale to evaluate the empirical data of four clusters of approaches, those suggested by Haywood (1997) and a fourth cluster characterized by training a single cognitive function. The last approach included Swanson's (1995) working memory battery, Spector's (1992) test of phonemic awareness, and Pena, Quinn, and Iglesias's (1992) test of narrative performance. The four clusters were evaluated by four criteria: (1) comparative informativeness, (2) power of prediction, (3) degree of efficiency, and (4) robustness of results. Readers are referred to Grigorenko and Sternberg's (1998) paper for a detailed discussion of the different approaches to DA as well as their evaluation.

The DA of young children approach developed by Tzuriel (1997a, 1998, 2000c) in the last two decades is based on the mediated learning approach with some modifications. The approach was tested both clinically and empirically. In the following chapters the basic characteristics of this approach of testing young children (Chapter 5) and the DA instruments for young children (Chapter 6) are described, followed by chapters presenting three types of DA research: educational (Chapter 7), developmental (Chapter 8), and cognitive intervention (Chapter 9).

CONDITIONS FOR USE OF DA

DA is perceived in this book as a complement to standardized testing, not a substitute for it. It is also conceived as a broad approach, not a particular test. Given the myriad of performance problems one encounters, it is often useful to shift from one kind of test to another. The question frequently raised by educators and psychologists, however, is when to use DA? Clinical experience has shown that it is useful to use DA in the following conditions:

- When standardized tests yield low scores
- When standardized tests hover around margins of adequate cognitive functioning
- When there are discrepancies between the child's aptitude and performance
- When the child comes from a low socioeconomic or culturally different background, or is linguistically different
- When the child shows some emotional disturbance, personality disorder, or learning disability

5

Dynamic Assessment of Young Children

Principles, Approaches, and Procedures

Tzuriel's (1992a, 1997a, 1998, 1999a, 2000a, c, d) approach with young children is based on both, Vygotsky's sociocultural approach and Feuerstein's MLE theory. The assessment approach is characterized by innovations of test materials, assessment procedures adapted for the developmental stages of young children, and a recording and scoring system. This approach is summarized in the following 10 aspects identified in Table 5.1.

ADAPTATION OF TEST MATERIALS TO CHILD'S DEVELOPMENTAL LEVEL

The first aspect is characterized by the use of three-dimensional test materials that contain gamelike features rather than the two-dimensional features of the paper-and-pencil instruments used in other systems of static assessment and DA (i.e., the LPAD). The gamelike materials were found to be potent in attracting and maintaining the child's attention and motivating him or her toward exploratory task-intrinsic behavior. The examiner allows the child to manipulate the test's components, change the answer parts, and rearrange them until he or she reaches convenience level and is satisfied with the answer. Experience shows that despite the gamelike nature of the instruments, the "naive" and simple look of the problems, and the concrete operations stage of the child, the problems presented require a high level of abstraction and thinking.

Table 5.1. Unique Characteristics of DA of Young Children

Adaptation to developmental requirements
- Test materials are geared to concrete operations
- Attractive, manipulative, gamelike aspects of materials
- Procedures of testing take account of short-attention-span features of child function

"Bridging" of concrete operations to abstract level of functioning

Communication aspects
- Tuning-in to young child's needs
- Adapting examiner's tone of voice and gestures to child's state
- Use of optimal verbal abstraction

Use of clinical/educational and measurement/research versions of testing

Baseline preliminary phase as an integrative component of DA

Use and significance of two scoring methods in measurement/research version
- "None-or-all"
- Partial credit

Use of transfer problems as a component of testing and use of a mediation phase with transfer problems

Comparison of modifiability indices across items' difficulty levels and task dimensions

Assessment of nonintellective factors and their modifiability as integrative component of DA
- Accessibility to mediation
- Need for mastery–curiosity, aspiration, task–intrinsic motivation
- Frustration tolerance
- Fear of failure and defensiveness
- Confidence in correct response
- Locus of control
- Vitality and alertness

Creativity in construction of problems by examiner and child

"BRIDGING" OF CONCRETE OPERATIONS TO ABSTRACT LEVEL OF FUNCTIONING

Presentation of the problems should be carefully graduated with regard to complexity and/or abstraction levels. The reason for graduation of problems is that the mediation given on one item should prepare the child to solve the following item. The concrete natures of the materials and of test procedures serve as a basis for bridging of the learned principle(s) to understanding of abstract rules and generalizations. Clinical experience and research findings (Tzuriel, 1992a, 1997a, 1998) have shown that children can reach an abstract level of functioning with the adult's help; much higher than what is expected without the adult's guidance. One should not expect this high level of functioning to be maintained and/or crystallized. However, it reflects the child's cognitive modifiability, and points to future mediational efforts that are required in order to actualize and crystallize the evolving functions within the DA procedure.

COMMUNICATION ASPECTS IN DA OF YOUNG CHILDREN

A significant aspect of assessment of young children is the adjustment of the examiner's communication style to the child's developmental level and specific needs. Since young children cannot express orally their thoughts and feelings, the examiner should "tune in" to the child's needs, implicit or explicit. For example, the examiner's tones of voice, facial expressions, and body gestures are calibrated to the child's psychological state. They can be soft when the child is in stress, and authoritative, demanding, and "activating" when the child can handle demanding tasks, or when he or she is trying to manipulate the situation. The examiner's level of verbal abstraction should also move flexibly along the concrete—abstraction dimension, depending on the child's accessibility to mediation (Tzuriel, 1991a) and readiness to internalize new operations and concepts offered within the DA situation.

CLINICAL/EDUCATIONAL AND MEASUREMENT/ RESEARCH VERSIONS OF DA

It is suggested that DA will be used in either the *clinical/educational* or the *measurement/research* version. The clinical/educational version is conducted by assessment of qualitative aspects of the child's performance. The examiner, for example, assesses the quality of the child's performance, the amount and nature of mediation needed in different phases of the test, the level of task difficulty in relation to the child's answer, behavioral tendencies that affect the child's cognitive responses, and nonintellective factors that affect performance. The examiner might analyze with the child the sources for a mistake, repeat a dimension or rule that was overlooked, teach a general rule, focus the child on articulated aspects of the problem, and give more opportunities to solve similar problems. In the clinical/educational version the examiner presents the child an initial item to be solved independently. If the child shows some difficulty, mediation adapted to the child's level is given. As a rule, the mediation level should not exceed the difficulty level of the child. After presenting one or more parallel item(s) aimed at assessing the child's learning (maintenance) and transfer, the examiner might present a more difficult problem. Once the child shows an adequate mastery level of one level it is possible to move to a higher level. Sometimes, however, it is possible to present a problem that is remote of the present mastery level in order to test the child's coping behavior and adaptation of learned strategies to problems of a much higher level of difficulty. As will be explained later, the examiner is encouraged to create his or her own problems, in addition to those provided in the test. These problems should be based, however, on the same principles of the item in which the child showed difficulties. The amount and type of mediation are recorded, and compared to the performance level before and after teaching. An example of a recording sheet for the clinical/educational version of the Children's Analogical Thinking Modifiability test (CATM) is presented in Figure 5.1.

In the measurement/research version of administration, Pre-Teaching and Post-Teaching phases are given without mediation and the child's responses are

Name of Child: _____   Date of Birth: _____   Date of Testing: _____

Level I of Difficulty

	Item 1	Item 1	Item 1
Correct			
Mediation			
DCF			
Behavior			
	Item 2	Item 2	Item 2
Correct			
Mediation			
DCF			
Behavior			

Level II of Difficulty

	Item 3	Item 3	Item 3
Correct			
Mediation			
DCF			
Behavior			

DCF= Deficient Cognitive Functions

Figure 5.1. Example of a recording and scoring sheet from the CATM Test (Clinical/Educational Version).

scored. A short-term mediation, which is given between the tests, is usually intensive but is not "tailored" to the child's specific needs. In the measurement/ research version the scoring methods are applied and a total score is computed by summing all scores from the items. A gain score can also be computed by deducting the score of the Pre-Teaching test (A) from the score of the Post-Teaching test (B). Careful examination of gain scores should be applied since gains of children with different initial levels of performance cannot be compared. Separate scores for the easy versus difficult items or for various test dimensions can also be computed for detailed analyses. The decision about the version to be used depends on the assessment goals (i.e., need to provide objective scores). Examples of recording and scoring sheets from the CSTM, CMB (Analogies subtest) and Seria-Think Instrument are presented in Figures 5.2, 5.3, and 5.4, respectively.

BASELINE PRELIMINARY PHASE AS AN INTEGRATIVE COMPONENT OF DA

A preliminary baseline phase is given in any version of administration so as to both (1) prepare and familiarize the child with the task dimensions and problem solving rules and (2) observe the child's initial cognitive performance. Initial observation can help to determine whether and what skills should be mastered before moving to other phases. The examiner might decide to start with the test's items or to work on prerequired cognitive functions before solving the test items. This phase can be of crucial importance for some individuals because it reveals basic perceptual processes, behavioral tendencies, and cognitive difficulties. For example, the baseline phase can reveal specific difficulties in classification, simultaneous consideration of two or more sources of information, mental representation, attention deficits, impulsive tendencies, deficient verbal tools especially, and emotional blocking.

SCORING METHODS FOR THE MEASUREMENT/RESEARCH VERSION

For most of the tests developed by Tzuriel (Tzuriel, 1989a, 1995a, 2000d; Tzuriel & Klein, 1987, 1990) two scoring methods were constructed: "none-or-all" and a "partial credit" method. According to the "none-or-all" method a score of 1 is given to each correctly solved problem. Full answers, which include all dimensions (e.g., color, shape, and size), are given a score of 1; no score is given for missing one or more dimensions. According to the "partial credit" method a score of 1 is given to each correct dimension. Both scoring methods should be

Child's Name _____   Date of Birth _____
Father's Occupation _____   Date of Test _____
Mother's Occupation _____   Age (in months) _____

ITEM	DIMENSION	PRE TEST			POST TEST				TRANSFER	
		ORDER	CHOICE	SCORE	ORDER	CHOICE	SCORE		ORDER	SCORE
Bee	number							Cube		
Elephant	size									
Bear	darkness							House		
Bird	number / darkness									
Horse	number / size							Stairs		
Turtle	darkness / size							Scale		
Fish	number / darkness / size							Horse		
Leaf	number / darkness / size							Painter		
TOTAL										

Figure 5.2. Example of a recording and scoring sheet from the CSTM Test.

Child's Name ________ Date of Birth ________ Date of Testing ________
Grade ________ School ________ Age ________

PRETEACHING			TEACHING	POSTTEACHING		
Item	Method 1	Method 2	Comments	Item	Method 1	Method 2
AN1-A G4	___	C N H P1 ___		AN1-B Y1	___	C N H P1 ___
AN2-A B1 B1	___	C N H P1 ___		AN2-B Y4 Y4	___	C N H P1 ___
AN3-A Y4	___	C N H P1 ___		AN3-B R4	___	C N H P1 ___
AN4-A G1	___	C N H P1 ___		AN4-B Y4	___	C N H P1 ___
AN5-A G1 G1	___	C N H P1 ___		AN5-B B4 B4	___	C N H P1 ___
AN6-A Y2	___	C N H P1 ___		AN6-B B4	___	C N H P1 ___
AN7-A Y4	___	C N H P1 ___		AN7-B Y1	___	C N H P1 ___

Figure 5.3. Example of a recording and scoring sheet from the CMB Analogies Subtest.

Name _____ Grade _____ Sex: 1. Male 2. Female

Date of Birth _____ School _____ Age _____

		Pre 			Post 	
Item 1	Score	Insert	Measure	Score	Insert	Measure
		③ ① ①	③ ① ①		③ ① ①	③ ① ①
Item 2	Score	Insert	Measure	Score	Insert	Measure
		⑦ ③ ①	⑦ ③ ①		⑦ ③ ①	⑦ ③ ①
Item 3	Score	Insert	Measure	Score	Insert	Measure
		① ⑤ ①	① ⑤ ①		① ⑤ ①	① ⑤ ①
Item 4	Score	Insert	Measure	Score	Insert	Measure
		⑨ ⑦ ①	⑨ ⑦ ①		⑨ ⑦ ①	⑨ ⑦ ①
Item 5	Score	Insert	Measure	Score	Insert	Measure
		⑤ ⑨ ①	⑤ ⑨ ①		⑤ ⑨ ①	⑤ ⑨ ①
Item 6	Score	Insert	Measure	Score	Insert	Measure
		③⑦①⑨⑤	③⑦①⑨⑤		③⑦①⑨⑤	③⑦①⑨⑤
TOTAL						

Figure 5.4. Example of a recording and scoring sheet from the Seria-Think Instrument.

used as each provides different types of information. For example, comparison of modifiability rates of both methods may show lack of improvement on the "none-or-all" but significant improvement on the "partial credit" method. This difference indicates a difficulty in integrative capacity; the examinee improves his or her performance at least on several dimensions but cannot integrate all of them to perform a "full blooming" answer. The "partial credit" method allows analysis of performance on each of the task dimensions (e.g., color, height, number, size, shape, and position) as well as analysis of their differential modifiability.

TRANSFER PROBLEMS

A major indication for the child's cognitive modifiability is the level of transfer of learning the child demonstrates following a learning process. In several DA measures developed by Tzuriel (i.e., CITM, Tzuriel, 1989a, 1992b), a Transfer phase was developed to assess the extent to which the individual internalized the problem-solving principles. The transfer problems are different from the original problems in terms of the level of complexity and the level of abstraction. The principles for solving the problems are constant across the different sections of the test. Furthermore, in one of the recent tests (CMB, Tzuriel, 1995a, 2000d) a *mediation* component was also included within the Transfer phase. Thus, pre- to post mediation improvement can be compared in Testing versus Transfer sections. In a research context where the test problems reach a ceiling level for the children's age it is possible to add the transfer problems to the pool of items.

COMPARISON OF MODIFIABILITY INDICES ACROSS DIFFICULTY LEVEL AND TASK DIMENSIONS

An intriguing question raised in relation to the effects of mediation is to what extent mediation has a differential effect on levels of task-difficulty and test dimensions. It was found, for example, that the higher was the difficulty level the higher was the improvement following a teaching phase (Tzuriel, 1989a). Level of difficulty can interact with type of children, mediation strategies, and specific task domain. Consideration of task dimensions (i.e., color, shape, number, and position) is crucial for understanding of type and amount of modifiability within a developmental framework. Clinical experience and research findings (Tzuriel, 2000d) showed that position or location of blocks on the CMB reflects a spatial orientation skill that is much more difficult for children than color, height, or number.

ASSESSMENT OF NONINTELLECTIVE FACTORS
AND THEIR MODIFIABILITY

The importance of nonintellective factors in DA, as determinants of the child's performance, has been discussed earlier (Tzuriel, 1991a; Tzuriel et al., 1988). For some authors, cognitive functioning and motivational–affective factors are conceived as inseparable, representing two sides of the same coin (Haywood, 1992b; Scarr, 1981). Extensive clinical–educational experience, with DA processes, teaching thinking skills, and using cognitive psychotherapeutic procedures, has suggested the following nonintellective factors as being inherently related in MLE and cognitive modifiability processes.

Lack of *accessibility to mediation* is manifested by actively rejecting the mediator's attempts to teach or by passively withdrawing from the situation. Very often the reason for lack of accessibility to mediation is related to previous negative experiences with a mediator (i.e., parent or teacher) or exessive mediation given to overcome a learning problem. The child who is over mediated tends to develop "antibodies" against mediation and reacts negatively whenever he or she feels that the interaction with the adult is oriented in a mediational direction.

Need for mastery is one of the most important factors determining test results, learning processes, and school achievement. Operationally, it may be expressed by the child's persistence on a task, attempts to work independently, without the examiner's help, pleasure in finding a solution and experiencing progress, and in willingness to continue to work on other tasks that are not related to the previous task. The child's need for mastery cannot be totally separated from the mediator's approach. A sensitive mediator who "feels" the child's lack of interest can energize the child, focus her attention, confront her with challenges, and direct her toward task-intrinsic motivation.

A *frustration tolerance* in learning and/or problem-solving situation is related to the individual's ability to delay the immediate gratification of finding a quick solution to a problem and a willingness to work persistently, even when no clue for a solution is in sight. The child's frustration tolerance may be expressed by giving up easily after experiencing difficulty, or showing signs of anger when asked to solve another task or to explain and elaborate on an answer. The role of the examiner is to control and "soften" the child's frustration by ensuring high rates of success, by preparing the child for difficult items, and by using various therapeutic procedures.

Locus of control refers to individuals' perception of themselves as responsible for the outcome of their behavior and for control over life events. The child's sporadic responses, persistent guessing behavior, passive approach toward problem solution, reliance on task-extrinsic rewards, an expressed surprise about a successful answer, and blaming of others following failure manifest indications of external locus of control in teaching situations.

One of the most debilitating factors in learning and performance is *fear of failure and defensiveness*. Fear of failure and defensiveness are especially aroused in tasks that remind the child of previous failures or that seem to be too complicated to deal with.

Confidence in a correct response refers to the child's believing the answer given is correct even when challenged or asked to explain his or her answer. Uncertainty and lack of confidence might reflect a lack of crystallization of the learned content but very often it is related to emotional–attitudinal variables which have little to do with the child's cognition. One way of mediating to a child to be aware of his or her confidence level is by asking the child "are you sure about this solution?" even when the answer is correct, and analyzing with the child the meaning of the hesitating response.

Vitality and alertness refer to the level of activity, energy, vividness, attentiveness, and interest the child shows in the interaction with the mediator. It is judged subjectively and requires a certain amount of experience with different types of children. While vitality and alertness can be observed during any learning session, the ease with which this factor can be modified is best ascertained during DA. Some children who begin the assessment with an apathetic, lifeless approach and a lack of attention and interest start to show clear signs of engagement, vividness, emotional openness, and cooperation. This is manifested by an increased willingness to invest effort, an increased responsiveness to humorous remarks, more relaxed body language, and great mental alertness.

CREATIVITY IN CONSTRUCTION OF PROBLEMS BY EXAMINER AND EXAMINEE

A frequent problem DA examiners face, especially with very slow learners, is the absence of parallel items to assess level of maintenance of performance. Based on the author's experience it is suggested that the examiner would design his or her own problems based on the test's principles. Thus, the examiner's role is perceived, in an innovative way, not only as reproductively dispensing and teaching the test items but also creating his or her own items. Furthermore, the child can be asked after a certain degree of performance, to create problems based on mediation of problem solving rules. Thus, if all parallel items at some difficulty level have been used to mediate the problem, new items can be created.

Learning processes, especially with young children, require very frequently coping with complex data and exploring systematically several dimensions, in order to solve a problem. The tasks become even more difficult when the child's span of attention decreases, working memory is overloaded with information, or when the child reaches a "saturation" level. Clinical experience in a DA situation showed that it is helpful to use two practical cognitive strategies in order to expand children's span of attention, engagement, efficiency, and motivation. I prefer to label these cognitive strategies as *one-by-one* and *one-more* strategies.

The one-by-one strategy refers to gathering information, analyzing, and solving one dimension of a problem at a time. The child can move to the next dimension only after reaching a solution of the first dimension. In this kind of activity the child is helped to avoid another dimension while working on one. Children with a tendency for impulsivity and overinclusiveness are especially helped by this strategy. For example, in solving analogies from the CMB (Tzuriel, 1995a, 2000c) the child has to consider four dimensions: color, number, height, and position. In addition, in some problems, where they can be solved only by a transformation rule (as opposed to categorization), the child must compare changes of blocks placed on a plate, which occur from right to left as well as changes from top to bottom. Many children have a strong tendency to start to analyze the *color* dimension but before reaching a conclusion they are distracted by another dimension (i.e., height, location, or number) and start to work on it. Before they finish with the first dimension they "jump" to a second dimension, then back to the first and then move to a third one. The final result is that they actually do not solve any of the dimensions. This type of cognitive deficiency is also reflected in schoolwork, or in other problem solving situations. For example, in solving Math problems the child has to pay attention to several pieces of data and gather information systematically by finishing up with one component and then moving to another. The one-by-one strategy helps the child concentrate on one dimension at a time before integrating them for the correct complete solution.

The one-more strategy is a cognitive–motivational strategy, which might be applied when the child's span of attention is short or when the child reaches a relatively high level of saturation, after working on a set of problems. In some learning tasks the end result is not immediately achieved and the child is required to gather information sequentially and to delay immediate gratification. In a DA situation, the examiner might want to observe whether the child is able to recruit energy and invest mental efforts to do some more problems. The child's ability to invest mental efforts in a DA situation is indicative of the child's willingness to tolerate frustration until solving a problem or completing a task or a project. The use of the one-more strategy is carried out in the following way. After the examiner (teacher) observes that the child is "tired" he or she encourages the child to work on one-more problem ("You have done so good till now, is it ok if we try to do one more"?). Usually children respond positively, as they know that the examiner (teacher) will provide the necessary help, if needed. After solving the problem the child is asked whether he or she would agree to solve one more problem. With some children (mostly older ones) this strategy is presented in a somewhat humorous way, as both the child and the examiner know that the trick is transparent. The examiner of course has to be sensitive not to overstretch this strategy and respect the child's genuine decision not to continue with more problems. Clinical experience with young 5- to 6-year olds showed that they can double or even triple their efforts and that their attention span is significantly extended when the one-more strategy is used.

6

Dynamic Assessment Instruments for Young Children

The objective of this chapter is to provide a brief description of each of the DA tests developed by Tzuriel for young children. The presentation of tests follows the *measurement/research* version, which specifies each test's phases and procedures. There have been several attempts to develop DA measures for young children by different authors (Bryant, 1982; Burns, 1991; Gamlin, 1989; Hessels, 1997; Kahn & King, 1997; Lidz, 1991; Mearig, 1987; Resing, 1997; Waters & Stringer, 1997) most of which are based on Feuerstein's and Vygotsky's theories. Because of space limitation, the following tests developed by my colleagues and I at Bar-Ilan University will be examined:

- *The Children's Analogical Thinking Modifiability Test (CATM)*
- *The Children's Inferential Thinking Modifiability Test (CITM)*
- *The Frame Test of Cognitive Modifiability (FTCM)*
- *The Children's Seriational Thinking Modifiability Test (CSTM)*
- *The Complex Figure Test*
- *The Cognitive Modifiability Battery (CMB): Assessment and Intervention*
- *The Seria-Think Instrument*
- *The Children's Conceptual and Perceptual Analogies Modifiability Test (CCPAM)*

THE CHILDREN'S ANALOGICAL THINKING
MODIFIABILITY TEST

The purposes of the CATM are to test children's learning strategies, accessibility to mediation, employment of high-order concepts and operations, and use of a variety of cognitive functions to solve problems. The major required operation is the operation of analogy, which has been considered by many authors as a powerful tool for a wide range of cognitive processes and as a principal operation for problem solving activities (Gentner & Markman, 1997; Goswami, 1991; Holyoak & Thagard, 1995, 1997).

Description of the CATM. The CATM (Tzuriel & Klein, 1985, 1987, 1990) is composed of 18 colored (red, blue, yellow) blocks and three sets of analogical problems for Pre-Teaching, Teaching, and Post-Teaching phases. Each set contains 14 analogical problems increasing in level of difficulty. The blocks are different in dimensions of color by size by shape ($3 \times 2 \times 3$).

A Preliminary baseline phase is given before presenting the analogical problems. In this phase the child is asked to name the colors, sizes and shapes of the blocks and build up a matrix using classification strategy. Next the child is asked to label the main dimensions of the matrix using the high-order concepts of shape, color, and size and to "move" flexibly in labeling them between rows that represent the same color and columns that represent the same shape.

In a following activity the child is asked to hand the examiner blocks based on description of the three dimensions. This is done to observe whether the child can relate simultaneously to three dimensions of information.

Following the completion of the matrix (see Figure 6.1) there is an optional phase in which the examiner can play a game with the child. The examiner closes his or her eyes and the child is asked to take away and hide one block. The child has to tell the examiner to open his or her eyes and tell what block is missing. The child can replace the block in the matrix after the examiner has identified all three dimensions of the block. The examiner purposely, makes "mistakes" in describing one of the dimensions and the child has to identify the mistake and express it in terms of high-order concepts. This activity requires sorting out the correct dimensions from the incorrect dimension without looking at the hidden block. Some children however need to peek at the block to detect the "mistake." Roles can be reversed with the child closing his or her eyes and the examiner taking away the block. The child is encouraged to mentally represent the dimensions of the block without checking it visually, to repeat simultaneously all sources of information (dimensions), and use high-order concepts rather than concrete labels.

The last step of the Preliminary phase consists of an analogical problem that is presented to the child in the form of A:B::C:?.

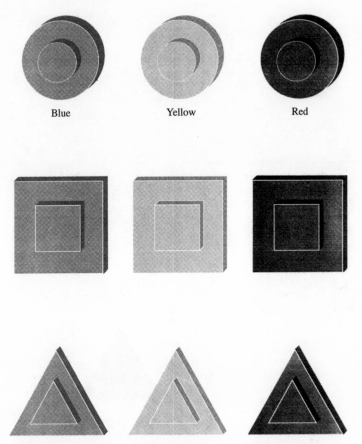

Blue   Yellow   Red

Figure 6.1.   The CATM matrix based on dimensions of color, shape, and size.

In each problem the examiner places three blocks and asks the child to compare the first two blocks (A:B) and find which block should be placed to match the third one (C:D). The child is asked to explain his or her solution regardless of whether it was correct or incorrect. Mediational strategies such as conflict arousal, focusing, and labeling are used to lead the child toward a correct solution.

The CATM problems are constructed in four levels of task difficulty (see Figure 6.2). In the first level only one dimension changes, in the second level two dimensions change, and in the third level three dimensions change. In order to solve the problems the child has to identify the relevant dimensions, infer the relation between the first two components and apply it in the second pair of components. For example, in Level III the child should conceive that while the color

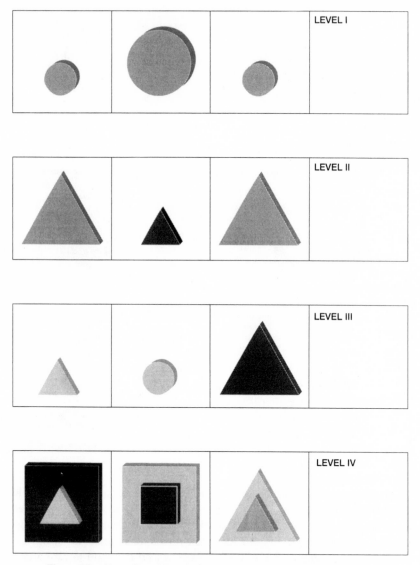

Figure 6.2. Example problems in four difficulty levels from the CATM test.

and size are similar, the shape changes (yellow triangle changes into yellow circle
but both are small). This rule should be applied to the second pair (blue triangle
changing to blue circle but both are big).

In Level IV difficulty each section of the problem is composed of
two blocks one on top of the other. In some of the problems of this level
(see Figure 6.2) the child has to understand the concept of "opposite." The child

has first to grasp the opposite relationship (of colors) between the first pair and apply it to the second pair. In addition the child has to apply the relationship of shape and size and finally choose the right blocks for the solution. The task requires a high level of systematic exploratory behavior, simultaneous consideration of several sources of information, need for accuracy, and control of impulsivity.

The Pre-Teaching phase following the Preliminary phase serves as a baseline for the assessment of a child's analogical thinking modifiability. This phase is compared to the performance in the Post-Teaching phase. Each of the 14 items included in each of the phases is presented in the ascribed order. No intervention is given at the Pre- and Post-Teaching phases and the child's full response is recorded on the answer sheet. For some children who have problems of short attention span and difficulties of concentration, the other two phases of Teaching and Post-Teaching test can be given on another day. The objectives of the Teaching phase are to teach the child how to (1) search for relevant dimensions required for the analogical solution, (2) understand transformational rules and analogical principles, (3) search systematically for correct blocks, and (4) improve efficiency of performance. For each teaching item the child has to choose the correct block initially with no intervention.

The mediation strategies vary from nonverbal focusing, labeling, and "rhythmic intonation" of contents (i.e., "RED-circle : BLUE-circle") to direct teaching of classes and transformational rules. For most problems there are two main ways of teaching the analogy. The first approach is analytic; each dimension is analyzed separately so that the child has to determine the color of the missing block, then to move on and find the required shape, and finally its size. The integration of all dimensions of the missing block is carried out after the child has correctly identified all of them. With some young children it was found as useful to emphasize relations between blocks in a personified way such as "The red circle is a *friend* of the red square here [tester points to first two blocks] so who should be a friend of this red circle [Tester points to the third block.]?" The second intervention approach involves teaching of transformation rules as described in the following example: "Here the red one becomes blue [tester points to the first two blocks] so what would happen to the red one here [Tester points to the third block and to the fourth empty place]?"

A specific technique found to be helpful with young children is to articulate the information in a special "rhythmic intonation." The tester pronounces loudly one dimension and softly the second one (i.e., yellow-CIRCLE). A little pause is introduced between pairs of blocks. The "rhythmic intonation" can be used efficiently on problems involving one or two dimensions but becomes complicated when all three dimensions are involved. When all blocks share a common dimension (i.e., all blocks are red, or circle, or big) the "rhythmic intonation" should relate to the other two dimensions. Both quantitative and qualitative aspects are taken into account. The amount of improvement serves as an indication of the child's modifiability rather than as evidence for a lasting and stable achievement.

Cronbach-alpha reliability coefficients for the Pre- and Post-Teaching phases were computed using the measurement/research version. The coefficients are .85 and .89, respectively (Tzuriel & Klein, 1985). The validity of the CATM as well as its effectiveness with different groups of children, have been established both clinically and empirically (Missiuna & Samuels, 1989; Samuels, Killip, MacKenzie, & Fagan, 1992; Tzuriel, 1992a, 1997a; Tzuriel & Caspi, 1992; Tzuriel & Ernst, 1990; Tzuriel & Hatzir, 1999; Tzuriel, Kaniel, Zeliger, Friedman, & Haywood, 1998; Tzuriel & Kaufman, 1999; Tzuriel & Klein, 1985, 1987; Tzuriel & Weitz, 1998; Tzuriel et al., 1999). A recent review of the CATM was reported by Samuels (1998a).

THE CHILDREN'S INFERENTIAL THINKING MODIFIABILITY TEST

The CITM, designed by Tzuriel (1989b, 1991a) is based on the principles of the Organizer test from the LPAD (Feuerstein et al., 1995). The objectives of the CITM are to assess the young children's ability to solve problems that require inferential thinking as well as their ability to modify their performance following a process of mediation.

The CITM is composed of four sets of problems for Pre-Teaching, Teaching, Post-Teaching, and Transfer phases. The child is presented with a set of 24 familiar pictures (i.e., clothes, animals, and furniture) and he or she is asked to name them. Naming pictures is aimed at establishing familiarity with the objects. Next the child is presented with two example problems, and instructed in the rules for solving them and in the procedures for gathering information. The problems are composed of a set of figural "sentences". Each "sentence" presents information about the possible location of objects in houses with different colored roofs. In terms of Feuerstein and colleagues' (1979) list of deficient cognitive functions, the task requires systematic exploratory behavior, control of impulsivity, spontaneous comparative behavior, planning, inferential-hypothetical ("iffy") thinking, and simultaneous consideration of many sources of information. The operations required for solving the task are related to *negation*-negative inference ("the chair is not in the red house and not in the blue house"), and inductive reasoning. An example of a problem from the CITM (L7) is presented in Figure 6.3.

In item L7, three houses are presented at the top of the page with black, white and red roofs. The child is instructed to place cards with pictures into the appropriate houses at the top of the page. To solve the problem the child is given three rows, at the bottom of the page, with each row containing part of the information. The rules are that in each row the objects in the left should enter the

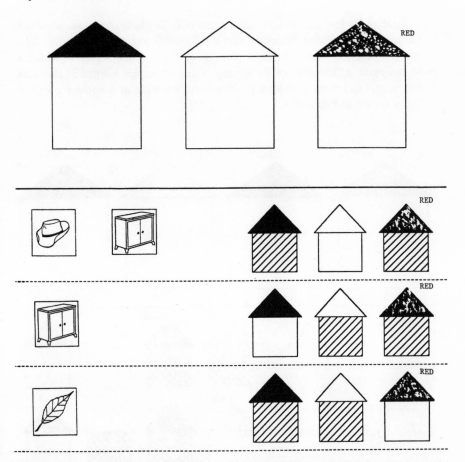

Figure 6.3. Example problem (L7) from the CITM test. (Copied by permission from *Educational Psychology Review*, *12*, 385–435.)

houses with patchworks to the right. In the first row, the Hat or the Cabinet should go into the houses with lines (black and red); it is not known at this stage which object will be in which house. In the second row, the Cabinet should go into either of the houses with lines (white or red); but one does not know which object goes into which house. In the third row, the Leaf should enter one of the houses (black or white).

The task requires systematic exploratory behavior, control of impulsivity, spontaneous comparative behavior, planning, inferential-hypothetical ("iffy") thinking, and simultaneous consideration of several sources of information. The operations required for solving the task are related to negation-negative inference ("the chair is not in the red house and not the blue house"), and inductive reasoning.

Each of the Pre-Teaching, Teaching, and Post-Teaching phases is composed of 12 items of increasing difficulty, and the Transfer phase is composed of 10 items. The objective of the Transfer phase is to examine the degree to which a child can make a "transfer" of the strategies and principles learned in previous problems and use them with new problems. An example of a transfer problem (TR6) is shown in Figure 6.4.

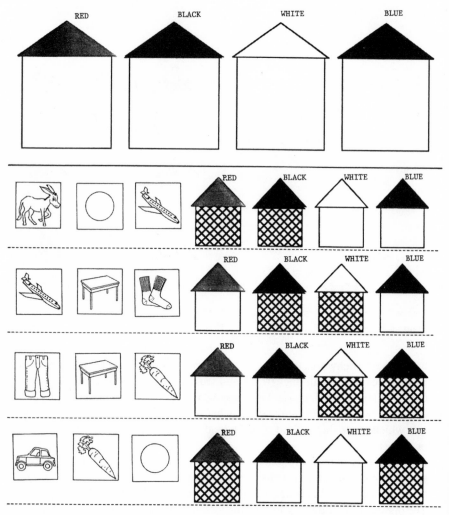

Objects on left cannot enter the meshed houses

Figure 6.4. Example problem (TR6) from the CITM test—Transfer phase.

As seen in item TR6, four houses are presented at the top of the page with red, black, white, and blue roofs. The task is to place cards with the correct pictures into the appropriate houses at the top of the page. To solve the problem the child is given four rows, at the bottom of the page, with each row containing parts of the solution. The rules are that in each row the objects in the left *should not* enter the meshed houses to the right. In the first row, the Donkey, Circle, and Airplane *should not* enter the meshed houses (black and red); it is not known at this stage which object will be in which house. In the second row, the Airplane, Table, and Socks *should not* go into either of the meshed houses (white or black); but again one does not know which object goes into which house. In the third row, the Pants, Table, and Carrot *should not* enter the white or blue houses. In the fourth row the Car, Carrot, and Circle *should not* enter the red and blue houses. The task requires systematic exploratory behavior, control of impulsivity, spontaneous comparative behavior, planning, inferential-hypothetical ("iffy") thinking, and simultaneous consideration of several sources of information. The operations required for solving the task are related to negation-negative inference ("the chair is not in the red house and not in the blue house"), and inductive reasoning.

The Transfer problems cover several dimensions, such as consideration of a different aspect of the data, coping with complex presentation of information, using "negative" information, and eliminating irrelevant clues. In several problems two or more dimensions of transfer are involved making these problems more difficult.

The total score in each of the phases is 37. A Free-Recall phase, given after the Transfer phase, is aimed at examining the child's free-recall ability as an indication of incidental learning. The child is asked to memorize all of the objects (pictures) that he or she saw. The last phase of the CITM—Classification—is aimed at examining whether or not the child can classify the 24 objects into categories. The categories are animals, clothes, furniture, shapes, transportation means, and plants. The child is first asked to classify all objects into groups according to some principle, and give an explanation for his or her answer. If the child fails to make the classification or makes incomplete classification, mediation is given. The examiner chooses one of the categories and explains the common characteristic of all objects and then asks the child to re-sort out again the objects according to similar characteristics. Cronbach-alpha reliability coefficients of the Pre-Teaching, Post-Teaching, and Transfer phases are .82, .82, and .90, respectively (Tzuriel, 1991b). The CITM validity was established in several developmental and educational studies (Tzuriel, 1989b; Tzuriel & Eran, 1990; Tzuriel & Kaufman, 1999; Tzuriel & Weiss, 1998). A recent review of the CATM was reported by Samuels (1998b).

THE FRAME TEST OF COGNITIVE MODIFIABILITY

The FTCM (Tzuriel & Klein, 1986) is composed of four frames, beads (40) in four colors (red, green, yellow and blue) and a set of problem cards for Pre-Teaching, Teaching, and Post-Teaching phases; each set is composed of 12 problems. The objectives of the FTCM are to assess the child's cognitive modifiability, and deficient cognitive functions in areas of numerical progressions and spatial orientation. The procedure of administration is that the examiner presents four frames to the child and asks him/her to count the frames as well as the numbers of corners in each frame. In identification of corners both dimensions should be used simultaneously, the vertical (top–bottom) and the horizontal (left–right). A fifth frame is not used at this phase; but used later for demonstration in the Teaching phase. In the Preliminary phase, specific focus is given to recognition of the different types of corners, and observing the pattern of change from corner to corner across the frames. The child is asked to name the colors of beads and to demonstrate that he or she can count to four. The child's concept of number is examined by using a Piagetian approach asking the child to (1) give the examiner a certain number of beads, (2) count backwards, (3) match numbers by placing beads on the table, and (4) compare two rows with the same number of beads but spaced differently. Rules for problem solving are taught by using three example cards. After the examiner places the beads in the first three frames (left to right for the child), the child is asked to find the bead(s) of the fourth frame. Examples from the FTCM test are presented in Figure 6.5.

Reasons for correct answers are then discussed using the main dimensions of color, number, and location (corner). Qualitative aspects of the child's behavior and performance observed in this phase are related to spatial orientation, counting strategies, the number concept, conservation of quantity, simple numerical progression, level of cooperation, accessibility to mediation, impulsiveness, anxiety, self-confidence, and efficiency of performance.

The objectives of the Pre-Teaching phase are to assess the child's initial level of problem solving and the extent to which the Preliminary phase was sufficient in solving the FTCM type of problems. The intervention allowed in this phase is minimal and limited to general focusing ("did you look at all frames?") and regulation of behavior ("be careful, don't hurry," "look carefully on each corner"). The examiner should be careful not to comment on the specific solution offered by the child after solving the problem and thus cueing him or her for the examiner's remarks. Comments and focusing can be provided before the child gives the solution.

In the Teaching phase full mediation is given by helping the child to work systematically, efficiently, and independently, use rules for solving the problems, restrain impulsivity, and focus attention on different dimensions of the stimuli. Problems are analyzed systematically to gather the accurate information and to

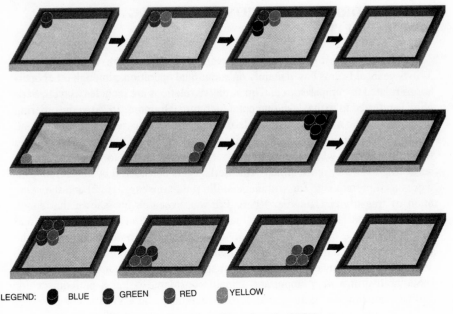

Figure 6.5. Example problems from the FTCM test.

place the correct beads in the correct corner of the fourth frame. Teaching of rules is carried out usually by analyzing each dimension across the frames. To facilitate learning, the examiner places the fifth frame parallel to each of the frames and replicates the beads placed on them sequentially. This procedure helps the child find out which corner is still empty, and combine the information of all three frames into one frame. The use of the fifth frame helps the child detect not only the remaining corner but also the progressive sequence of "movement" of beads from one frame to another, the numbers in each corner, and the order of the colored beads. In other words, the examiner helps the child to synthesize the information presented in separate frames. During this phase, the child's responses are not scored, but his or her behavior and the specific cognitive difficulties are recorded and interpreted qualitatively.

The objective of the Post-Teaching phase is to assess the child's improvement in solving the problems as well as the difficulties that are still to be remedied after the intervention. Mediation in Pre- and Post-Teaching phases is limited to focusing and regulation of behavior, but not to rule teaching.

Cronbach-alpha reliability coefficients for the Pre- and Post-Teaching phases are .85 and .90, respectively (Tzuriel & Klein, 1986). The FTCM developmental features and validity aspects were reported in several studies (i.e., Tzuriel & Baruch, 1995; Tzuriel & Klein, 1986).

THE CHILDREN'S SERIATIONAL THINKING MODIFIABILITY TEST

The CSTM test is a dynamic–interactive (Tzuriel, 1995b) test designed for 3- to 5-year- olds. It is based mainly on seriational operation, although other operations related to comparisons and quantitative relations are included as well. Seriation is referred to in the developmental literature (Brainard, 1979) as the ordering of objects along a single or multiple dimensions such as length, color, weight, and size. In a single seriation the child is asked to order the objects according to one dimension whereas in multiple seriation the task is to order the objects according to two or more dimensions. Seriation is considered by several investigators as a prerequisite for arithmetic skills (i.e., Ginsburg, 1977) and the operation of transitivity (Kingma, 1983). Previous research has shown that single length seriation is acquired earlier than multiple seriation (Kingma, 1983) and that performance on a developmental scale of seriation predicted ($r = .80$) the performance on a number line comprehension task (Kingma & Ruevekamp, 1984). The importance of the CSTM is that it allows the assessment of cognitive modifiability in a very important domain considered being a prerequisite for further mathematical skills and transitive relations. The CSTM is composed of unique problems that require not only an arrangement of stimuli on a certain continuum but also the controlling for one or more dimensions that are imbued within the same set of stimuli. In several of the items, for example, the examinee is required first to order the set according to one dimension (i.e., size) while trying to avoid interference of other dimensions within the given set. Then the examinee is asked to rearrange the stimuli on another continuum. Each of the CSTM items is composed of five cards depicting one or more continua within the same set of cards.

In the Preliminary phase the child is presented with three sets of cards, representing seriation of darkness, size, and number, respectively. Each set contains only three cards presented in a mixed order and the child has to order them according to the dimension presented and label the dimension correctly. If the child does not know the label it is provided, and repetition of the task is carried out. It is then explained to the child that the purpose of the following items is to order the cards according to some order that he or she will find.

The problems in the Pre- and Post-Teaching phases are identical. In the first three problems the series are composed of one dimension each (number, size, and darkness). The child has to find and order the cards according to the relevant dimension. Three more series are composed, each with two dimensions (i.e., size and number); however, the child has to work on the first dimension and then shift to the second one "filtering out" the first dimension. The last two series are each composed of three dimensions and the child is required to work at each one

Figure 6.6. Example problem ("horses") from the CSTM test—two solutions.

separately controlling for the nonrelevant dimensions. An example from the testing phase (the "horses" problem) is presented in Figure 6.6.

In the "horses" problem, the examinee is required first to order a set of horses drawn on five cards according to one dimension (number or size). Following the first seriation the examinee is asked to rearrange the stimuli on the second dimension. This mental activity requires cognitive flexibility, as the child should make a shift in reordering the same set of stimuli and use another conceptual dimension. While ordering the horses along one dimension—number—the examinee has to avoid interference of another dimension—size—which is included within the given set (see Figure 6.6).

The Teaching phase includes three items; each is composed of a set with three dimensions. The first set is of five cylinders varying along dimensions of height, width, and darkness (dark blue to light blue). The second and third items (Square, Car) each include three dimensions (darkness, size, and number). For research and clinical purposes it is possible to use only one of the Teaching items, a combination of two, or all the three items and recording the degree of mediation. A two-dimensional schema of the cylinders is presented in Figure 6.7.

The major approach of teaching the seriation is by analyzing each of the dimensions separately. The examiner concentrates on one of the dimensions and avoids the others. Only after ordering the set according to one dimension should the examiner mix the set and ask the child to re-order it using another order. When moving from one dimension to another within the same set it is possible to observe the child's flexibility of moving from one dimension to another without confusing the dimensions.

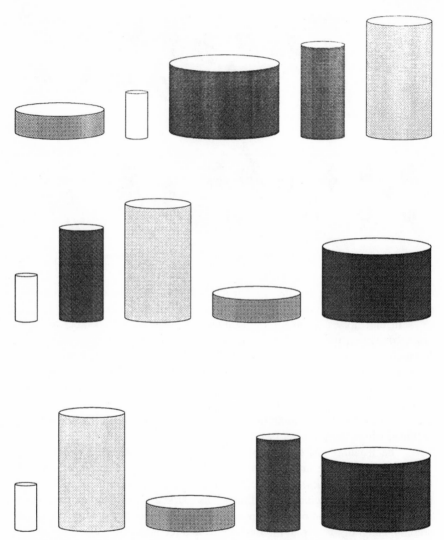

Figure 6.7.   The Cylinders problem from the CSTM test. (Copied by permission from *Educational Psychology Review, 12*, 385–435.)

Another major mediational strategy is to ask the child, after successfully completing ordering the set in a certain dimension, to order another set along the dimension of the completed set, using the same dimension for both sets. In this activity the child has to control nonrelevant dimensions of both sets and focus only on the common one. We found it useful to use both approaches of teaching in order to bring the child to internalize the operation of seriation. A specific technique found to be helpful in teaching the dimension of width of the cylinders is to put them vertically one on top of another, from the widest to the narrowest. However, the child has to see immediately that the same set can be ordered identically when the cylinders are placed horizontally. In this way the child's flexibility for ordering the same dimension in different shapes is facilitated.

Cronbach-alpha reliability coefficients for the Pre-Teaching, Post-Teaching, and Transfer phases based on a sample of kindergarten children ($n = 129$) were .87, .85, and .70, respectively (Tzuriel, 1995b). Validation of the CSTM has been shown in two studies carried out with different groups of disadvantaged and advantaged kindergartners (Tzuriel, 1995b) and with special education kindergartners who participated in a cognitive education program (Tzuriel & Eiboshitz, 1999).

The CSTM was developed as a multimedia program and used in two studies. In the first one the effects of computer-assisted DA were compared with a regular DA procedure (Tzuriel & Shamir, in press). In the second study the computerized program was used as an intervention tool in which third graders children mediated seriational principles to their peers in first grade. In the second study the effects of a program for peer-mediation on mediation strategies and children's cognitive modifiability were investigated (Shamir & Tzuriel, 1999). The program for peer-mediation is presented in Chapter 9.

THE COMPLEX FIGURE TEST

The Complex Figure test was originally developed by Rey (1956) but was elaborated as a DA measure by Feuerstein et al. (1979) and adapted for young children by Tzuriel and Eiboshitz (1992, 1999). The Complex Figure, which is part of the LPAD (Feuerstein et al., 1979), is used extensively in clinical and educational settings.

Two versions (A and B) of the Complex Figure test were developed for young children; version B is more difficult than version A. The two versions allow assessment of transfer of learning from the easy version to the difficult version. Another possibility is to use the two versions for evaluation of cognitive education programs before and after their implementation. Figure 6.8 shows the two versions.

The Complex Figure test is composed of five phases:

In the first phase (Copy-I), the child is asked to copy the figure on a rectangular blank page. This phase might take between 2 and 5 minutes. No help is given in this phase except encouragement to perform the task in case the child is inhibited from starting the task.

In the second phase, the child is required to draw the figure from memory (Memory-I). The child does not know in advance of that requirement and no help

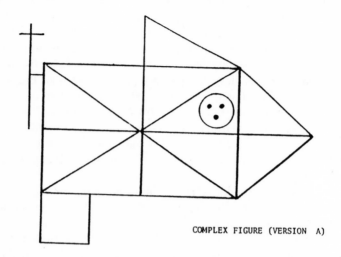

COMPLEX FIGURE (VERSION A)

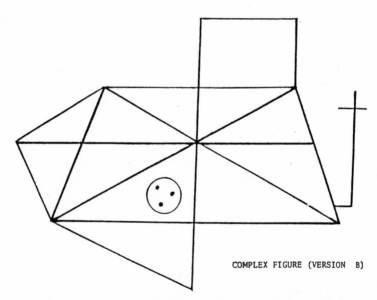

COMPLEX FIGURE (VERSION B)

Figure 6.8. Two versions (A and B) of the Complex Figure Test for young children. (Copied by permission from *Educational Psychology Review*, *12*, 385–435.)

is given except encouragement to start performance when the child shows signs of inhibition.

The third phase is a Teaching (mediation) phase in which the child is taught efficient strategies of drawing. The strategies include gathering the information systematically, planning the construction of the figure (i.e., drawing first the major lines and then secondary lines, going in clockwise order), and paying attention to precision, proportions, and the quality of lines.

The fourth phase is a second copy phase (Copy-II) similar to the first phase (Copy-I).

The fifth phase is a second memory phase (Memory-II) similar to the second phase (Memory-I).

Comparison of copy and memory phases before and after teaching provides information about the cognitive modifiability of the child's performance in terms of accuracy, precision, and organization of the figure.

The Complex Figure has 11 components, each one given 1 point for accuracy and 1 for location, for a possible total score of 22. A third, qualitative, score, ranging from 1 (low) to 7 (high), is given for organization. The reliability of the test was studied on a sample of 15 kindergartners and first graders by two independent raters who were previously trained to rate the Complex Figure and had extensive experience in rating (Tzuriel, 1999a). For the sake of clarity the Accuracy and Location scores were summed up, as both scores revealed a similar pattern for the majority of children. The interrater reliability coefficients computed by Pearson correlation for Accuracy + Location scores were as follows: Copy-I .99, Memory-I .98, Copy-II .98, Memory II .97. The parallel reliability coefficients for Organization scores were Copy-I .90, Memory-I .95, Copy-II .48, Memory II .78.

The Complex Figure test has been validated previously with different groups of preschool children with learning disabilities and with academically high-risk disadvantaged children (Tzuriel & Eiboshitz, 1992, 1999) as well as with 5- to 8-year olds who were born as very low birth weight (Tzuriel & Weitz, 1998). It was found effective in predicting treatment effects of the Bright Start program aimed at developing deficient cognitive functions and learning skills of preschool children with learning difficulties (Tzuriel et al., 1999).

THE COGNITIVE MODIFIABILITY BATTERY: ASSESSMENT AND INTERVENTION

The CMB (Tzuriel, 1995a, 2000d) was designed for both assessment and intervention processes. The tasks were constructed originally to cover kindergartners to fourth graders but they also can be used with older children who have learning difficulties. The CMB is composed of five subtests, each tapping different areas of cognitive functioning. The subtests are Seriation (S), Repro-duction of Patterns (RP), Analogies (AN), Sequences (SQ), and Memory (ME). For each subtest there is a set of problems, designed for Pre-Teaching, Teaching, and Post-Teaching phases. For two of the five subtests (Analogies and Sequences) there is also a Transfer phase which includes problems that are remote from the original ones. Unlike previous tests, the Transfer problems also have Pre-Teach-ing, Teaching, and Post-Teaching phases. This allows comparison of modifiabil-ity on test versus transfer problems. The CMB is constructed of 4 plates, 64 colored blocks, 36 wooden squares to cover "Windows" on the plates, recording and answer sheets for the five subtests, and a squared cardboard with the "Windows" picture that is used in the Memory subtests and an instruction manual. Each of the plates contains nine squared "Windows" arranged in a 3 by 3 pattern. The squared "Windows" can be covered by the small wooden covers to create different patterns of open "Windows" required for the different CMB tasks. The number of "Windows" used varies in different subtests. Examples of prob-lems from the CMB subtests of S, RP, AN, SQ-I, and SQ-II are presented in Figures 6.9–6.13.

The administration of the first two subtests, S and RP, has two goals: (1) to assess the child's functioning on relatively simple tasks of seriation and reproduction of patterns and (2) to prepare the child for the more difficult sub-tests of Analogies and Sequences (I and II) that follow these subtests.

Seriation (S). The goals of the SR subtest are to evaluate the child's initial comprehension and mastery of the seriation operation as well as his or her cog-nitive modifiability following mediation. The tasks require ordering the colored blocks according to one or more rules presented to the child in a sequential order. The rules include progression of height (i.e., high to low), sequence of colors (i.e., red–green–blue–yellow), and progression of numbers. The first tasks are based on one rule followed by tasks based on a combination of two or more rules. An example of a seriation task (item S3) is given in Figure 6.9.

In the Preliminary phase the goals are to familiarize the child with the task dimension (height and color) and basic rules of alternating them systematically. The teaching processes include several strategies of seriation (e.g., working from extremes to the middle, working gradually by choosing the next lower, or higher), focusing the child on mistakes and self-reflection, teaching task-specific rules and strategies, and mediating self regulation of responses (metacognitive aspects). In general, mediation always begins with simple focusing and prompting to detailed teaching of rules, principles, and generalizations.

Reproduction of Patterns (RP). The RP subtest is based on the simple visual-motor task requiring copying three-dimensional patterns. The copying requires distinction of the dimensions of color, height, number, and location. The tasks begin with very simple patterns increasing in level of difficulty to very complex patterns, requiring fine distinctions on all dimensions.

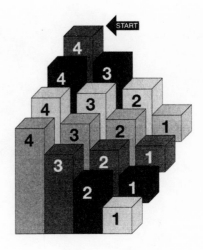

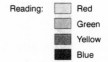

Figure 6.9. Example problem from the CMB Seriation Subtest.

The RP subtest is composed of 27 problems divided into three parallel sets; each contains nine problems for the Pre-Teaching, Teaching, and Post-Teaching phases. In each problem the child is presented with a pattern of blocks on a plate and asked to reproduce it exactly on another plate. An example from the RP subtest is presented in Figure 6.10.

In the Preliminary phase the child is helped to identify the number of "Windows" on the plate, understand their 3 by 3 pattern, name their relative position (e.g., top-left, middle-right, bottom-middle), and be familiar with the inner location of blocks within the "Window". The labeling of the position of the "Windows" enhances the child's spatial orientation—an important requirement for the following Sequences (Levels I and II) subtests. The items are constructed with increasing level of difficulty.

The mediations given in the RP subtest are composed of focusing attention on spatial orientation, labeling of stimuli, location of correct "Windows," and development of a need for precision, especially in regard to the correct location and height of blocks. Mediation of correct performance is also used, i.e., focusing on comparative behavior, spatial orientation, and summing the number of blocks, and verbalizing the task. On this subtest, all of the "Windows" on the plate are open and the child has to recognize the exact location of colored blocks.

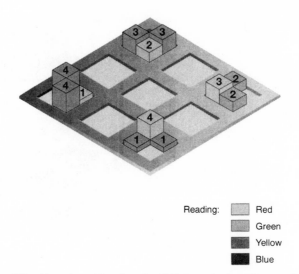

Reading: Red
          Green
          Yellow
          Blue

Figure 6.10. Example problem from the CMB Reproduction of Patterns Subtest.

Analogies (AN). The subtest contains two sections: Testing and Transfer. Each section has three parallel problems for each item. The Testing section is composed of 14 items (14 × 3 = 42 problems), while the Transfer section is composed of 9 (9 × 3 = 27 problems). Unlike conventional tests, the Transfer tasks here have a double role: (1) to assess the level of internalization of the analogy principles with tasks increasing in level of abstraction and novelty and (2) to assess the level of modifiability on the Transfer tasks themselves. The subtest is presented with four "Windows" open (see Figure 6.11). The examiner places the blocks in three "Windows" and asks the child to complete the analogy in the last open "Window". The empty "Window" is always to the "bottom right" of the child. An example of the subtest (a Transfer problem) is given in Figure 6.11.

In all analogies the child has to compare the blocks in the top two "Windows" (or the two left "Windows", understand the rules that govern the changes from left to right (or top to bottom), and apply them to the bottom (or right) two "Windows." In some problems the child has to consider changes both from left to right and from top to bottom. The analogies are based on four dimensions: color, height, number, and location. The combination of some or all of these dimensions creates three levels of task difficulty.

The Transfer problems are different with regard to the number of dimensions involved and the abstraction level required. Each of the Transfer items is composed of three problems that can be used both for measuring the level of Transfer from the Post-Teaching phase and for the continuation of the mediation

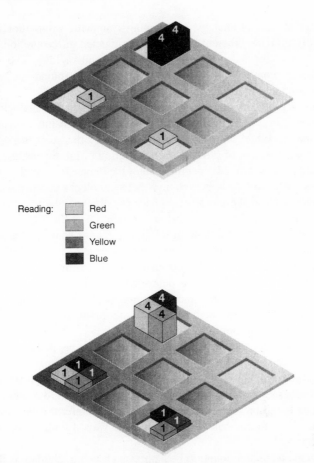

Figure 6.11. Example problems from the CMB Analogies Subtest (Testing Phase and Transfer Phase).

process with more difficult problems. In the clinical/educational version, the examiner continues administering the Transfer items and mediates, when necessary, immediately after each item. In the measurement/research version mediation is given only in the Teaching phase.

In the Preliminary phase the child is familiarized with the task dimensions and the basic rules of solving the CMB analogical problems. The Pre-Teaching phase then serves as a baseline for the modifiability of the child's analogical thinking. While the examiner places the blocks on the plate, the child observes the process of problem construction.

The Teaching phase includes mediation strategies such as (1) searching for relevant dimensions—especially the spatial component, (2) understanding transformational rules of analogy, (3) learning systematic exploration of dimensions, and (4) applying efficient performance, reflected in recognition of a need for accuracy, and the balance between accuracy and rapidity. The mediation strategies include nonverbal focusing, labeling, "rhythmic intonation," and teaching classification and transformational rules directly.

For most problems there are two ways of teaching the analogy: *analytic* and *transformational*. In the analytic approach each dimension is analyzed separately so that the child has to determine separately the color, the height, the number, and the location of blocks. The integration of all dimensions is carried out after the child has correctly identified all of the dimensions. With some young children it is useful to emphasize relations between blocks in a personified way, i.e., "The red block at the top left is a *friend* of the red block at the top right [examiner points to the two top blocks], so who should be the *friend* of this green block [examiner points to the bottom-left block]?". For some problems there is no need to go over all dimensions, especially in problems where all blocks have the same color or height. The transformational intervention approach involves teaching of transformational rules as described in the following example: "Here the yellow one *becomes* green [examiner points to the top two blocks] so what would happen to the yellow one here?" [examiner points to the third bottom-left block and the empty bottom-right "Window]?"

It is useful to mediate with both approaches at the beginning of the Teaching phase, and then judge, according to the child's response, which of the two is preferred by the child. Some children prefer the transformational strategy because they do not remember, when working on the second or third dimension, what they have just found on the first one. Other children prefer the personified style in which they have to find *friends*, or the analytic way of finding one dimension after the other.

A specific technique found to be helpful with young children is the articulation of information in a *rhythmic intonation*. The examiner pronounces loudly one block (e.g., yellow-right) and softly the second one (e.g., yellow-left). The rhythmic intonation can be used efficiently on problems involving one or two dimensions but becomes complicated when three or more dimensions are involved. When all blocks share a common dimension (e.g., all blocks are red, or high, or have the same number) the rhythmic intonation should relate to the other dimensions. In many cases the child selects a block that is partially correct (i.e., only one or two dimensions are taken into consideration). In this case the tester leads the child to pay attention to the dimension(s) that are incorrect. Sometimes a simple nonverbal focusing can change the child's response. A simple question such as "What is the height of these blocks?" or "How many are there?" may suffice to trigger a correct solution. The Teaching phase is longer than any of the other phases and may take between half an hour and an hour. A break of 5 minutes may be given to the child between and/or within the test phases. For complex problems, especially Transfer problems, the use of a "one-by-one" analytical approach is suggested where each dimension is analyzed separately and the combination of all solved dimensions is integrated into the solution.

The subtest is scored by two scoring methods: "all-or-none" (Method 1) and "partial credit" (Method 2). According to the first method, each correctly solved *problem* is given a score of 1, while according to the "partial credit" method a score of 1 is given to each correctly solved *dimension* (i.e., color, height, number, and location). A total score is computed by summing all scores from all items, and a gain score is computed by deducting Pre-Teaching (A) from Post-Teaching (B) scores. The maximal scores of the Testing section for Methods 1 and 2 are 14 and 56, respectively. The maximal scores of the Transfer section for Methods 1 and 2 are 9 and 36, respectively. Separate scores for the different levels of difficulty may also be attained.

Sequences Level I (SQ-I). The SQ-I subtest is composed of two sections: Testing and Transfer. The problems are presented on one plate with all "Windows," except the middle one, open. The middle one is covered. A progressive pattern beginning at the upper-left "Window" is presented sequentially in the first six peripheral "Windows" (see Figure 6.12).

The Testing section is composed of 10 items, each containing three parallel problems. The Transfer section is composed of 6 items; each of these also contains three parallel problems. The examiner presents the problem to the child by placing blocks in six "Windows" (1–6) starting from the "top left" and the child has to place blocks in the last two open "Windows" (7 and 8), completing the sequence. The SQ problems are based on systematic changes of two or more dimensions (e.g., color and height, color and number).

Sequences Level II (SQ-II). In SQ-II the problems are presented on the first three plates and the child has to complete the blocks in the last (fourth) plate. In some problems the blocks change their location from one plate to another as well as their inner position within the "Window". The change of location across plates is systematic and can be visualized as a "movement" of blocks governed by hidden rules that should be discovered. In Figure 6.13, a problem, which involves "movement" of blocks, is presented.

In most of the SQ-II problems the child needs to use a visual transport strategy in order to carry the pattern perceptually from one plate to another. The easy problems include only two changing dimensions whereas in more difficult problems three or more dimensions are involved. The child has, in general, to take into consideration the dimensions of color, number, position within the "Window", and position of "Windows" across plates. Each item is composed of three parallel problems for the Pre-Teaching, Teaching, and Post-Teaching phases. The Testing and Transfer sections are composed of six and nine items, respectively.

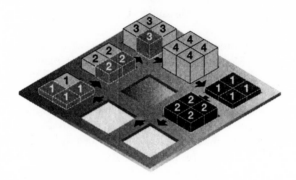

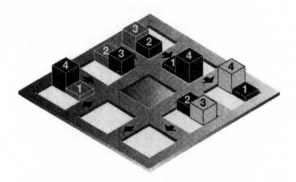

Figure 6.12. Example problems from the CMB Sequences Level-I Subtest (Testing Phase and Transfer Phase).

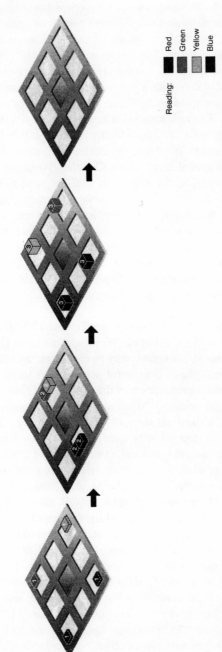

Figure 6.13. Example problem from the CMB Sequences Level-II Subtest (Transfer Phase). (Copied by permission from *Educational Psychology Review, 12,* 385–435.)

Memory (ME). The Memory subtest is composed of nine positional learning tasks. Each task is constructed of a different pattern of open "Windows" represented on four plates, stacked one on top of the other. In some ways the ME subtest is similar to the Plateoux Test (Feuerstein et al., 1979; Rey, 1950). The difference is that in the Plateoux the instrument is set to present one problem only. The CMB contains the possibility of creating many patterns of problems by using different combinations of open "Windows" starting from very simple patterns to complex ones. The task involves a series of trials where the child must learn the position of the open "Windows". After each trial, the child has to point to the location of the open "Windows" on cardboard, placed on the top of the plates with a two-dimensional representation of the "Windows." Scoring starts after the first trial and involves the number of trials required to reach a learning criterion (three) and the number of correct answers for each trial.

The ME subtest is composed of two phases: Learning and Rotation. In the Learning phase, the child is asked to point, for each plate, to the position of the open "Window(s)." The plates are presented in a series of trials until a criterion of three consecutive correct solutions is reached. The ME is given for 10 trials or until the child memorizes correctly all of the "Windows." The examiner may decide, based on the child's age and cognitive level, which of the items to choose.

In the Rotation phase the examiner turns the plates 90° and then 180° and asks the child to point to where the open "Windows" are now. There is no learning or repetition of rotations. This phase may be considered an indication of internalization of the learning phase. Successful performance usually indicates that the child created a mental representation of the positions of the open "Windows."

The position of the selected "Window(s)" for each plate in each trial is recorded. For each trial a maximal score of 4 may be achieved, 1 point for each plate. The ME subtest is stopped after three consecutive successes or after 20 trials. The child's errors are analyzed and a learning curve can be depicted.

Cronbach-alpha reliability coefficients were computed on a sample of kindergartners and first graders ($n = 222$) who were administered the CMB as well as other static and DA measures (Tzuriel, 2000d). The reliability coefficients based on the "partial credit" scoring method for Pre- and Post-Teaching phases, respectively, were as follows: Seriation, .62 and .64; Reproduction of Patterns, .91 and .94; Analogies, .84 and .77; Sequences-I, .88 and .90; Sequences-II, .69 and .67. Except for Sequences-II, the reliability coefficients were higher for the "partial credit" method of scoring than for the "all-or-none" method.

An exploratory factor analysis using the principal component method with an oblique rotation revealed three factors. Factor 1, containing the highest explained variance (35.23%), was composed mainly of Sequences-I, Sequences-II, and Analogies variables. Factor 2 was composed of Reproduction of Patterns (18.45%) variables and Factor 3 was composed of Seriation (16.46%) variables.

A Weighted Smallest Space Analysis (WSSA) performed on the CMB data revealed a three-dimensional solution with *coefficients of alienation* of .07 and .07 for Methods 1 and 2, respectively. The WSSA showed four clusters of factors, each cluster containing the Pre- and Post-Teaching scores of the same subtests. The clusters were as follows: (1) Seriation. (2) Reproduction of Patterns, (3) Sequences Level-II, and (4) Analogies and Sequences Level-I, which constitute one cluster. These clusters, besides confirming the factorial pattern found above, suggest two major independent dimensions along which the CMB subtests can be arranged. The first dimension relates to *abstraction level* of the task and the second dimension relates to the *task-specific strategy* component. Looking at the first dimension, Reproduction of Patterns and Seriation require a relatively low level of abstraction and are separated from the other subtests. Sequences Level-II, on the other hand, was found to be the most elaborated and sophisticated task requiring the highest level of abstraction from all of the other subtests. On the second dimension, task-specific strategy, Reproduction of Patterns requires simple copying of a model and, therefore, was low on this dimension. Seriation, on the other hand, depends to a large degree on task-specific strategies of arrang-ing the seriational tasks. The other three subtests—Analogies, Sequences Level-I, and Sequences Level-II—were found somewhere in the middle along the task-specific-strategies dimension.

The WSSA findings implied that the cognitive domain of each subtest, as represented by its Pre- and Post-Teaching scores, was more interrelated than across cognitive domain. Seriation and Analogies are relatively closer cognitive domains, as both require abstract logical processes and are relatively free of the spatial orientation component that characterizes the other subtests.

The CMB was used as an intervention instrument by several researchers and was found as useful in facilitating cognitive change (i.e., Elliott & Lauchlan, 1997; Lauchlan, 1999). A detailed description of the CMB as an intervention measure is given in Chapter 9.

THE SERIA-THINK INSTRUMENT

The Seria-Think Instrument (Tzuriel, 2000a) is a novel DA instrument aimed at assessing and teaching children a variety of arithmetic skills based on the operation of seriation, in combination with mastery of math skills of addition and subtraction. The rationale behind this is that measures of modifiability are more closely related to teaching processes, by which the child is taught how to process information, than are standard measures of intelligence. The mediational

strategies used within the DA procedure are conceptually congruent with learning processes in other life contexts, and therefore, give better indications about
future changes of cognitive structures.

The Seria-Think Instrument was designed for first to third graders, based
on the DA principles for young children (Tzuriel, 1997a, 1998, 2000a, c), but it
can be used with older children who have different kinds of difficulties in the
arithmetic domain. The problems of the instrument require several cognitive functions; the most important of them are planning behavior, systematic exploratory
behavior, simultaneous consideration of a few sources of information, and control
of trial and error behavior.

The Seria-Think Instrument (see Figure 6.14) is composed of a wooden
Block ($10 \times 6 \times 12$ cm) with three rows of holes, a set of cylinders (with heights

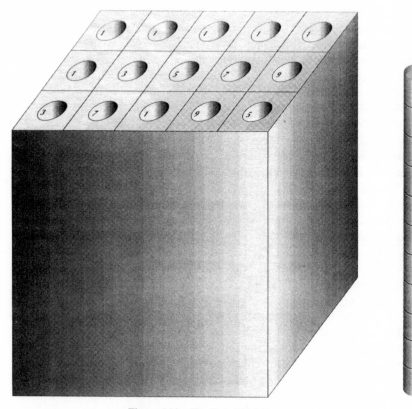

Figure 6.14.   The Seria-Think Instrument.

of 3, 5, 7, 9, 11, 13, and 15 cm), and a measuring rod divided equally into 11 units (1 cm each).

The wooden block (placed horizontally) has three rows of holes, five holes in each row. The holes in the first row are all have the same depth (1 cm). The depth of the holes in the second row varies gradually from left to right (1, 3, 5, 7, and 9 cm). The depth of the holes in the third row is similar to the second row except that the order is mixed (3, 5, 1, 9, and 7 cm). In addition there is a measuring cylinder.

The tasks in the Seria-Think involve insertion of the cylinders inside the holes so as to get lines of cylinders with (1) equal height, (2) an increasing height, and (3) a decreasing height. Most of the problems are presented when the wooden block is turned vertically, thus creating five rows; each contains three holes in it. In each row the child is asked to insert cylinders so as to obtain a row having cylinders of equal height, a row having increasing height, or a row having decreasing height.

The child is instructed to be careful as much as possible to insert a cylinder in a hole only once. In order to avoid trial and error behavior the child is encouraged to use the measuring rod as many times as he or she wishes and plan the solution. In order to solve the problems the child has to calculate the depth of the holes and the height of the cylinders. For example, in order to get a height of 2 cm with three holes of 5, 1, and 9 cm, the child has to insert cylinders of 7, 3, and 11 cm.

The Seria-Think can be used as a dynamic test or as an intervention instrument; for either there is a Preliminary baseline phase. The goals of this phase are (1) to prepare the child and familiarize him or her with the task dimensions and problem-solving rules and (2) to observe the child's performance and determine whether there are some skills to be mastered before moving to the test's problems. The examiner can choose to begin with the test's items or to discontinue the test and work with the child on required functions before presenting the test items. With some children this phase is most revealing in terms of basic perceptual, behavioral, and cognitive difficulties. This phase is composed of two steps: (1) familiarity with the task dimensions and (2) practice of two example problems. In the first step the child is presented with the wooden block and explained the set of holes in it. The child is encouraged to insert the measuring cylinder and measure the depth of each hole, compare them, and comprehend the pattern of their depth. It is important to emphasize here that there is no way of knowing the depths of some of the holes without first measuring them with the measuring cylinder. In the next step the child is given two examples. In Example 1, the child is asked to seriate the set of red cylinders in the first row (horizontal). Since all holes in this row have the same depth (1 cm), the child should start with the smallest cylinder and seriate them without taking into account the depth. In Example 2, the child is asked to insert the cylinders in the second (horizontal) row so that the final height will be equal. Since the depth of the holes changes progressively

(1, 3, 5, 7, and 9 cm), the child has to insert cylinders that are progressively longer (3, 5, 7, 9, and 11 cm).

There are six problems in each of the test's phases. In the first five items the wooden block is placed vertically (to create five rows of three holes in each) and the child is asked to seriate the cylinders in each row in an increasing order (Pre-Teaching), equal height (Teaching), or decreasing order (Post-Teaching). In the sixth problem, which is more difficult, the block is placed horizontally and the child is asked to seriate the cylinders in the third row (where five holes are arranged in a mixed order). The number of times the child inserts cylinders in each hole, and the number of times the child uses the measuring rod are recorded for each item.

The focus of mediation in the Teaching phase is on planning behavior (i.e., preparing the solution outside the holes before inserting the cylinders), restraint of impulsiveness in data gathering, need for precision (measuring the depth of the hole), comparison of the depth of the hole to the required height, and computation of length (by subtraction) of the cylinder minus the depth of the hole. The mediator tries to install in the child feelings of competence by giving feedback about successes and use of efficient strategies even if the solution is not correct.

The child's responses are recorded according to three criteria: correctness of solution, efficiency as indicated by the number of insertions (few insertions for a correct answer indicate higher efficiency level), and number of measurements required to solve the problem. A derived score of number of insertions by number of measurements is also available. Each of the first five items can have a maximal score of 3 (1 for each correct height) and the sixth item a maximal score of 5. The total score for each of the Pre- and Post-Teaching phases is 20 ($5 \times 3 + 5 = 20$). The combination of number of insertion and number of measuring times can reveal qualitative aspects about the child's patterns of dealing with the problems. For example, a child who measures less and makes many unnecessary insertions can be perceived as impulsive as compared with a child who is using more measurements and makes fewer insertions who can be considered as having planning behavior and reflective approach.

Cronbach-alpha reliabilities were computed (Tzuriel, 2000a) based on a sample of second graders ($n = 48$) who were administered the Seria-Think. The coefficients of the Pre- and Post-Teaching scores for Number of Measurements were .37 and .66, respectively. The coefficients for Number of Insertions were .78 and .85, respectively.

The findings also showed that an experimental group of children who were mediated on the Seria-Think Instrument decreased significantly their number of insertions and concurrently increased their number of measurements from Pre- to Post-Teaching. A control group of children who received a practice manipulative phase showed almost the same pattern of response before and after the treatment.

THE CHILDREN'S CONCEPTUAL AND PERCEPTUAL ANALOGIES MODIFIABILITY (CCPAM) TEST

The CCPAM (Tzuriel & Galinka, 2000) is a DA test of young children composed of two subtests of analogical problems, *conceptual* and *perceptual*. The conceptual subtest is comprised of 40 items, 20 for the Pre-Teaching and 20 for the Post-Teaching phases of the test. The perceptual subtest is comprised of 32 items, 16 for the Pre-Teaching and 16 for the Post-Teaching phases of the test. For each subtest there are two more analogies used for instruction before administration of the test. Each problem is formatted in a 2 × 2 matrix (A:B::C:D) and presented in a pictorial colored modality at the top of the page. At the bottom of the page there are four alternative answers, only one being the correct answer. The child is required to think about the relationship between the first pair of pictures in the problem, apply it to the second pair, and choose the right answer from the four given alternatives. Examples of items from the conceptual and perceptual subtests are presented in Figures 6.15 and 6.16.

Each problem in the Pre-Teaching phase has a parallel problem in the Post-Teaching phase in terms of the relation expressed in the analogy. For example, the analogy Bird:Nest::Dog:Doghouse in the Pre-Teaching phase parallels the analogy Bee:Beehive::Parrot:Cage in the Post-Teaching phase. Both analogies represent the same relationship, i.e., the first lives in the second.

Conceptual Analogies Subtest. The conceptual analogies are composed of three types according to the relationship expressed in the analogy: *functional* relation (i.e., A lives in B), *part–whole* relation, and *categorical* relation. The four alternative answers are divided into four categories based on the Goswami and Brown (1989) suggestion: semantic association to the C term of the analogy, different semantic category, categorical relation, part–whole relation. For example, in Figure 6.15, which taps functional analogy, the correct answer is Sandwich. The other alternatives are *House* (a different semantic relation), Man (categorical relation), and Head of a Girl (part–whole relation). In functional analogies the correct answer is a functional association related to the C term whereas in part–whole analogies the answer is part of the C term. Systematic construction of the noncorrect answers allows analysis of mistakes before and after the teaching phase.

Perceptual Analogies. The tasks here are based on adaptation of Goswami (1991), but instead of using geometrical shapes the analogies in the perceptual subtest are based on familiar objects (see Figure 6.16). In each analogy the

Figure 6.15.   Example of a conceptual problem from the CCPAM test.

relation between terms in the analogy was of three types: (1) *difference* (change of color, position, number, or type of object), (2) *existence* (an objects appears or disappears), and (3) *opposite* (i.e., object is above the chair changes to object under the chair). For example, in Figure 6.16 terms A and B of the analogy are similar in the color of the Box but differ in the position of the Cat. Terms A and C are similar in the position of the Cat but differ in the color of the Box. In order to solve the analogy the child has to pay attention to both task components (position and color), and use both of them to find the correct solution. Each problem contains three alternative diversions: a picture identical to term B, a picture identical to term C, and a random picture, which relates to an irrelevant part of the objects presented in the problem (i.e., the Cat is in front of a pink Box).

Each correctly solved analogy gets a score of 1. The maximal scores for each of the conceptual and perceptual subtests is 16. Separate scores can be

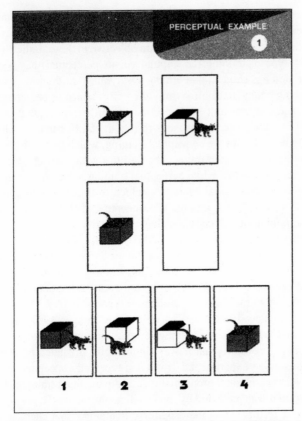

Figure 6.16.   Example of a perceptual problem from the CCPAM test.

computed for the type of mistakes in both subtests and patterns of mistakes can be compared before and after the training. Cronbach-alpha reliability coefficients were attained in three samples of kindergartners between the ages of 4 and 6 (Tzuriel, 2000b; Tzuriel & Galinka, 2000). The first sample ($n = 48$) was composed of 4-year olds, and the second ($n = 70$) and third ($n = 229$) samples were composed of 5- year olds. The Cronbach-alpha reliability coefficients for the Pre-Teaching Conceptual Analogies subtest ranged between .64 and .74 and for the Post-Teaching between .70 and .85. The reliability coefficients of the Pre-Teaching Perceptual Analogies subtest ranged between .83 and .87 and for the Post-Teaching between .90 and .91.

The validity of the CCPAM was examined in two separate studies in which children received either a conceptual training of solving analogies or a perceptual training (Tzuriel & Galinka, 2001). Both types of training were compared with a control condition where children were trained only to understand the relation between the first pair of the analogy (A:B) but without application of the relation to the second pair (C:D). The main objective in these studies was to investigate which type of training (conceptual versus perceptual) has better transfer effects. The findings showed that among very young children (4 years old), perceptual training helped to improve only the performance of perceptual analogies and that conceptual training had no effect on either conceptual or perceptual analogies. The authors explained these results by the fact that the children were too young to benefit from the conceptual training, which by nature requires more abstraction than perceptual training. The findings with older children (five years old), however, showed that while perceptual training helped to improve only perceptual analogies, conceptual analogies helped to improve both conceptual and perceptual analogies. Thus, training of conceptual analogies had better transfer effects than training of perceptual analogies with five-year olds.

In other studies (Flor-Maduel, 2001; Tzuriel, 2001b, Zilber, 2001) the CCPAM Pre- and Post-Teaching scores were used to predict expressive language processing, emergent literacy, auditory associations, and readiness for math, among kindergartners. Tzuriel (2001b) investigated the prediction expressive language processing, as measured by the Hebrew version (MA'ASE, Rom & Morag, 1999) of the Language Processing Test (Richard & Hanner, 1987), by the CCPAM Pre- and Post-Teaching scores. Stepwise regression analysis of expressive language processing revealed that it was significantly predicted by Post-Teaching analogy scores in an experimental group that received conceptual training (R^2 = .34) and in an experimental group that received perceptual training (R^2 = .40). In a control group it was predicted by the Pre-Teaching score (R^2 = .23). The explanation of these results is that the "cognitive mapping," that characterize analogical thinking is required also in expressive language processing. It should be noted that in both experimental groups the predictive variable was the CCPAM Post-Teaching score, whereas in the control group the predictive variable was the Pre-Teaching score.

Flor-Maduel (2001) found that Pearson correlations of Emergent Literacy with Pre- and Post-Teaching scores of conceptual analogies were .37 (p = ns) and .55 (p < .0001), respectively. The correlations of Emergent Literacy with Pre- and Post-Teaching score of perceptual analogies were .00 (p = ns) and .39 (p = ns), respectively. As reported in previous studies, the Post-Teaching scores are more powerful in predicting the criterion variables than Pre-Teaching scores. Also, the predictive power of conceptual analogies was found to be higher than that of perceptual analogies.

Zilber (2001) investigated the prediction of readiness for math by the CCPAM with a sample of kindergartners. Her findings showed that Pearson correlations of Readiness for Math with Pre- and Post-Teaching score of Conceptual Analogies were .20 (p = ns) and .79 (p < .0001), respectively. The correlations of Readiness for Math with Pre- and Post-Teaching score of Perceptual Analogies were .31 ($p =$ ns) and .61 ($p < .0001$), respectively. She explained these findings in regard to analysis of the common cognitive processes that characterize math and analogical thinking, as well as previous findings, which indicate higher prediction by DA post- than by pre-teaching scores.

7

Educational Aspects of Dynamic Assessment

The aim of this chapter is to present the utility of the DA approach in regard to educational issues such as predictability and group differentiation. Most of the presentation is based on studies with different groups of young children. The DA studies derive mainly from the theoretical approaches of Vygotsky and Feuerstein and on instruments developed by me and colleagues. In all studies data were gathered using the measurement/research version of administration. The review of educational studies is followed by a case study of a child with specific learning difficulty.

The major issues investigated in this chapter are related to the utility of DA with children from different SES and cultural backgrounds and children with specific learning difficulties, language difficulties, and mental handicap. Other sections refer to the effectiveness of different mediational strategies and prediction of school performance by DA measures as compared with conventional measures. In a separate section I review studies on the relation between cognitive style of impulsivity-reflectivity and problem solving in DA tasks. Finally, a case study is presented that portrays the complexities of DA with children having specific learning difficulties.

THE UTILITY OF DA WITH CHILDREN OF DIFFERENT SES LEVELS

One of the main questions regarding DA is to what degree learning processes within the test situation improve the performance of children from diverse cultural backgrounds and various SES groups. It was expected that children who had not been exposed to adequate MLE in the past, because of internal or external reasons, would benefit more from the mediation given in the DA procedure than would children who had relatively rich learning experiences. It should be emphasized that very frequently the distinction between socioeconomic level and cultural difference is not possible. This distinction is done mainly for methodological reasons. Nevertheless, in the following section, I present research in which children differed mainly on the basis of *SES level* or *cultural difference*. Previous findings with adolescents (e.g., Tzuriel & Alfassi, 1994; Tzuriel & Feuerstein, 1992) showed that children coming from low SES backgrounds achieved higher level of performance within a DA situation than that manifested in a standard psychometric test. In the following section the focus is on DA with young children.

Previous research has shown generally that standardized intelligence scores underestimate the cognitive ability of children coming from low SES backgrounds (e.g., Hamers, Hessels, & Van Luit, 1996; Hessels, 1997; Lidz & Thomas, 1987; Resing, 1997; Tzuriel, 1989b). In one of the first studies on kindergartners, Tzuriel and Klein (1985, 1987) explored the utility of the CATM with four groups: students identified as being advantaged, disadvantaged, as having needs for special education, or as MR. The kindergartners were 5 to 6 years old, whereas the last group was composed of older MR children with a mental age equal to the kindergarten level. The findings showed that the highest gains from Pre- to Post-teaching phases occured, among disadvantaged and advantaged children as compared with children with special needs for education and MR children who showed small gains. The MR group, however, showed significant improvement when a "partial credit" scoring method was applied. In this method credit is given for each correctly solved dimension (color, size, shape). This last finding indicates that the MR group has difficulty in integration of all sources of information and therefore showed modifiability only according to the "partial credit" method. Another important finding indicated that performance on the CATM was higher than performance on the RCPM (Raven, 1956). This finding was more articulated when the analogical items of the RCPM were compared with the analogical problems of the CATM. The advantaged and disadvantaged children scored 69 and 64% on the CATM, respectively, versus 39 and 44% on the RCPM, respectively.

The effects of DA procedures with young children from different SES levels were investigated further in several other studies (i.e., Lidz & Thomas, 1987; Tzuriel, 1989b). Lidz and Thomas (1987) administered the Preschool Learning Assessment Device (PLAD) to an experimental group composed of 3- to 5-year-old Head Start preschool children, mostly black and Hispanic. The experimental children were compared with control children who had experience with the same materials but *without mediation*. The PLAD is based on Feuerstein's MLE approach and Luria's (1976) neuropsychological theory as elaborated by the Naglieri and Das (1988) PASS model (Planning, Arousal, Simultaneous,

Successive). The testing procedure is basically a test—intervention—retest model using readiness tasks for 3- to 5-year-old preschool children. The testing procedure is anchored to the Triangles subtest of the Kaufman Assessment Battery for Children (K-ABC; Kaufman & Kaufman, 1983). The tasks include human figure drawing, building steps with cubes, and copying parquetry designs. The authors reported that the mediated children showed higher gains than the control children who showed no change. Significant strong correlations were also reported between the magnitude of gains and a social competency measure.

An important question raised by Tzuriel (1989b) was whether the effects of mediation in a DA procedure, found with children from disadvantaged families, are more articulated in difficult as compared with easy tasks. This question was studied with a group of disadvantaged ($n = 54$) and advantaged ($n = 124$) children in kindergarten and first grade. The children were administered both a DA test—the CITM—and a static measure (the RCPM). The objectives of the CITM are to assess young children's ability to solve problems that require inferential thinking as well as their ability to modify their performance following a process of mediation (see Chapter 5 for test description).

The findings of Tzuriel's (1989b) study showed a significant Group by Time (2×2) interaction that indicates higher improvements from Pre- to Postteaching scores for the disadvantaged than for the advantaged children. This interaction was also modified by the level of *task complexity*. The triadic interaction (see Figure 7.1) indicates that the degree of improvement of the disadvantaged children over the advantaged children was higher in the medium- and high-complexity-level problems than in the low-complexity-level problems.

These results verify what is known clinically, that mediation is most effective and therefore most needed in complex and/or abstract tasks. We should recognize the fact that the higher gains of the disadvantaged children over the advantaged children might also be caused by a ceiling effect, but the magnitude of gains clearly indicates that mediation is more effective with children who have a lower initial performance level.

One of the questions raised frequently with all children is which of the test findings is more reflective of children's ability: the pre- or postteaching performance? The differences in some tests might be very large. For example, results on the CITM test (Tzuriel, 1991b) with 5- to 6-year-old kindergartners ($n = 223$) revealed significant differences on each of the 12 items. In some of the items the improvement was about 50%. On item 7 from the CITM, 15.1% solved correctly all three houses in the preteaching phase as compared with 64.4% in the postteaching phase. It should be noted that the CITM task is relatively complex and abstract, in Piagetian terms, yet can be taught to kindergartners. Furthermore, a high level of transfer of learning was found on transfer items that are different from the original ones. The transfer problems are different on several dimensions such as negative information ("the bird is not in the red house"), inconsistent

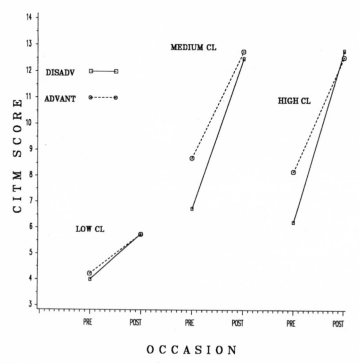

Figure 7.1. The CITM pre- and postteaching scores as a function of complexity level (CL) and social level (advantaged, disadvantaged). (Reproduced by permission from *The International Journal of Dynamic Assessment and Instruction, 1*, 73.)

location of colored roofs across rows, additional nonrelated objects, and reversal solution of the problem. My argument, which is based on theory, clinical experience, and extensive research, is that the postteaching performance reflects much more accurately children's intellectual ability than does the preteaching performance.

The differences between children from low and middle SES groups were examined recently in two studies using the CSTM (Tzuriel, 1995b). The CSTM is a DA measure designed for 3- to 5-year-olds. It is based mainly on operation of *seriation*, although other operations related to comparisons and quantitative relations are included as well. The CSTM allows the assessment of cognitive modifiability in a domain considered as a prerequisite for further mathematical skills. The CSTM is composed of unique problems that require both an arrangement of stimuli on a certain continuum and the controlling for one or more dimensions that are embedded within the same set of stimuli. In several of the items, for example, the examinee is required first to order the set according to one dimension (e.g., size) while trying to avoid interference of other dimensions within the given set (see test description in Chapter 6).

In both studies with kindergartners, large pre- to postteaching gains were found. In the first study, a sample of disadvantaged ($n = 69$) kindergartners showed performance initially lower than that of advantaged children ($n = 62$), but they significantly improved ($p < .001$) their performance from the pre- to post-teaching phase and narrowed the gap with the advantaged group. The pre- to post-teaching gains were especially articulated in problems with a high level of complexity (e.g., containing more dimensions in one set) than in problems with a low level of complexity. These results are very similar to Tzuriel's (1989b) findings with another test (CITM) and another sample. The most difficult dimension was that of *size* followed by *darkness* and *number*. The children scored higher on number, in spite of the fact that, developmentally, number is a more abstract dimension than size or darkness. This result was explained by schooling effects, i.e., kindergarten teachers emphasize mastery of quantitative relations over other dimensions.

In the second study (Tzuriel, 1995b) the CSTM was administered to a sample of kindergartners. The sample was randomly assigned to experimental ($n = 40$) and control groups ($n = 40$). The experimental group received the teaching phase, whereas the control group received no teaching. The results showed very clearly that the experimental group significantly improved its pre- to post-teaching performance as compared with the control group, which showed only slight improvement. The higher gains of the experimental group over the controls were similar across dimensions of size, number, and darkness. Similar to previous findings in other DA measures (i.e., Tzuriel, 1989b), mediation was more effective in complex than in simple problems.

DA OF CHILDREN WITH MENTAL HANDICAPS, DEVELOPMENTAL DELAYS, AND SPECIFIC LEARNING DIFFICULTIES

DA research on children with various learning difficulties has focused on the effects of mediation on children's cognitive performance and on identification of efficient mediation techniques that produce the highest change.

Reinharth (1989) conducted one of the first studies on a sample of developmentally delayed children ($n = 36$) between the ages of 2 years 7 months and 11 years (MA ranged between 20 and 63 months). The PLAD (Lidz, 1991) was administered to experimental and control groups who were matched by age and cognitive level. The experimental children received a mediation phase, whereas the controls were exposed to the materials with no mediation. The findings showed, as expected, higher pre- to posttest improvement in the experimental than in the control group. Of most importance, however, was the finding showing that 2 weeks after test administration the differences between the two groups increased. The experimental children continued to improve their performance, whereas the control group remained at the same level. These findings contradict those of Tzuriel and Klein (1985) on kindergartners identified as needing special education. These children did not show an improvement on the CATM after a mediation phase. Missiuna and Samuels (1989) tried to explain why these children showed no pre- to postteaching improvement by referring to the type of mediation, which was rather short and simple (detailed discussion of their findings is reported below in regard to use of different mediation strategies in DA). The differences between Tzuriel and Klein's study and Reinharth's study raise a crucial question regarding comparison of different DA studies without controlling for the amount and type of mediation administered in each of them. When making such a comparison the level of mediation should be described in detail so that comparison of changes in performance could be attributed to the level of mediation.

The importance of DA with learning disabled children was demonstrated also by Resing (1997) on groups of second graders from classes of slow learners (n = 74, mean IQ = 67.8), learning disabled (n = 80, mean IQ = 83.8), and regular education students (n = 80, mean IQ = 95.3). Following Campione and Brown's (1987) graduated prompt approach, Resing designed a learning potential test based on two inductive reasoning tests: exclusion and verbal analogies (i.e., Pencil:Writing::Mouth:____). In exclusion, the child has to compare a set of geometrical forms and indicate which of them is different. These tests were taken from the Revised Amsterdam Kindergarten Intelligence Test (RAKIT, Bleichrodt, Drenth, Zaal, & Resing, 1984). The inductive reasoning tests were chosen because of their centrality in theories of intelligence, their central role in cognitive development, and the frequency with which a variety of tasks are solved by inductive and analogical reasoning processes. Both the number of hints necessary to reach a specified amount of learning and the amount of transfer on various tasks defined learning potential. A system of graduated prompts was designed starting from metacognitive hints ("What do you have to do?"), cognitive hints ("What is the relation between pencil and writing?"), and training steps, each being composed of several graduated steps. Her findings showed slow learners and learning-disabled children needed two and three times, respectively, as many hints as mainstream education children. Unlike the static test, the learning potential test revealed, as expected, more qualitative information about the child's cognitive functioning (e.g., type of hints needed, type of strategies used) than did the static test performance. Both learning potential scores had significant additional predictive value for school performance. Resing (1997) concluded that the learning potential tests are of most importance when there are doubts about the child's real intelligence level because of cultural background or disadvantaged educational history.

An interesting issue related to the validity of DA versus standard tests is the prediction of various criteria of school attendance and success with mentally handicapped children. Samuels et al., (1992) explored this issue with an experimental group of handicapped preschool children who participated in the Bright Start program (Haywood et al., 1986) for one year. These children were compared with a control group that received a good but noncognitive program. At the end of the program both groups were given dynamic (CATM) and static (RCPM, PPVT-R) tests. While the findings did not reveal any significant treatment effects, in a follow-up assessment stage, 2 years later, the researchers reported an interesting finding on an unobtrusive measure of regular versus special education class attendance. Of all measures taken at the end of the program, 1 year earlier, *only the CATM postteaching score significantly predicted class attendance.* Children attending regular classes had higher CATM postteaching scores than did children who ended up attending special education classes. The authors interpreted this result as supporting the notion that postmediation scores of mentally handicapped children are better predictors of future learning than is initial performance on a static measure.

DA OF DEAF CHILDREN

Intellectual functioning of deaf children using standardized tests has led to conflicting conclusions regarding their mental level as compared with hearing individuals (Keane et al., 1992). Some authors argue that, relative to their hearing counterparts, they are cognitively inferior (Pintner, Eisenson, & Stanton, 1941). Yet others claim that they are intellectually normal but cognitively different (Myklebust, 1960), or that there is no difference between deaf and hearing individuals (Moores, 1978).

The application of the MLE theory and DA procedures seems to be reasonable with deaf children because, through mediation, one can overcome barriers caused by deafness and identify the individual's learning potential. Braden (1985) opposed this view by showing that deaf children perform better than minority children on nonverbal IQ tests. According to Braden, this finding challenges the notion that lack of MLE was the proximal etiology in deficiencies of the deaf. Other researchers argue that MLE presents a reasonable framework for understanding the manifest characteristics of the deaf and that DA provide tools for testing this hypothesis with such a population (Keane et al., 1992).

The only known study on deaf kindergartners is that of Tzuriel and Caspi (1992), in which both DA and conventional measures were used. In this study, deaf kindergartners were matched to hearing children on variables of age, sex, and a developmental visual—motor test. Both groups were tested on the CATM and RCPM tests. On the CATM postteaching test the hearing and deaf children scored 66 and 54% ("all-or-none" scoring method) and 86 and 81% ("partial credit" scoring method), respectively, as compared with 42 and 39% on the RCPM. These findings indicate that both groups have a higher level of learning potential than is indicated by static test scores. Comparison of pre- to postteaching tests revealed that the deaf children performed lower than the hearing children on the preteaching test but showed greater improvement after the teaching phase; no significant group differences were found in the postteaching test.

Other findings of this study showed a differential prediction pattern of the CATM postteaching scores by cognitive and family factors in both deaf and hearing groups (Tzuriel & Haywood, 1992). Using stepwise regression analyses it was found that, in the deaf group, the CATM postteaching score was predicted by mother's occupation, the overall score of the Home Observation for Measurement of the Environment (HOME) inventory (Bradley & Caldwell, 1984), and the CATM preteaching score ($R^2 = .70$). In the hearing group, only one significant ($R^2 = .62$) predictor was found: an analogy subtest of the Snijders-Oomen Nonverbal (SON) test (Snijders & Snijders-Oomen, 1970). For this group the similar psychometric qualities (both tests tap the analogies domain) take precedence over the family factors. Those results indicate that the contribution of family factors—as indicated by the level of cognitive stimulation and emotional warmth given in the family—was more critical in the deaf group in overcoming the mediational barriers and in actualizing the upper level of the ZPD than in the hearing group.

THE RELATION BETWEEN ITEM DIFFICULTY AND PERFORMANCE IMPROVEMENT AFTER MEDIATION

The effects of mediation on different levels of task difficulty were investigated in several studies by correlating item difficulty with pre- to postteaching improvement. These studies were based on the hypothesis that the more difficult the task is, the more the mediation given will be effective in improving the child's performance. Findings from several studies using different tests and samples indicated repeatedly, significant positive correlations between item difficulty and level of change. Findings from various studies are summarized in Table 7.1.

These results of several studies indicate a tendency to benefit more from mediation, given within the test situation, in the higher levels than in the lower levels of item difficulty. It should be noted, however, that some caution is required in interpreting the results. Some of the variance can be attributed to a "ceiling effect"; the easier the item the less room is left for improvement. In spite of

Table 7.1. Summary of Correlations of Item Difficulty with Pre- to Post-Teaching Improvement Scores on DA of Young Children

Study	Test[a]	Grade	Sample	n	r
Tzuriel & Klein (1985)	CATM	K	Advantaged	42	.84**
		K	Disadvantaged	45	.40
		K	Special education	20	.70*
			MR[b]	18	.30
Tzuriel (1989b)	CITM	K	Advantaged	80	.82**
		K	Disadvantaged	92	.92**
Tzuriel (1995b)	CSTM	K	Advantaged	52	.85**
		K	Disadvantaged	92	.87**
Tzuriel (1998)	CATM	K	Heterogeneous	130	.57**
	CITM	K	Heterogeneous	130	.70**
Tzuriel (1998)	CATM	K	Advantaged	26	.87**
	FTCM	K	Disadvantaged	26	.77**
	CATM	1	Advantaged	26	.76**
	FTCM	1	Disadvantaged	26	.91**
Tzuriel & Kaufman (1999)	CATM	1	Ethiopian	29	.45
		1	Israeli-born	23	.95**
	CITM	1	Ethiopian	29	.94**
		1	Israeli-born	23	.93**
Tzuriel (2000d)	CMB				
	RP	K + 1	Heterogeneous	222	.84**
	AN				.91**
	SQ-I				.39
	SQ-II				.47

[a]CATM, Children's Analogical Thinking Modifiability; CITM, Children's Inferential Thinking Modifiability; CSTM, Children's Seriational Thinking Modifiability; FTCM, Frame Test of Cognitive Modifiability; CMB, Cognitive Modifiability Battery; RP, Reproduction of Patterns; AN, Analogies; SQ, Sequences.
[b]Older subjects with mental age equivalent to kindergarten age.
*$p < .01$. **$p < .001$.

this possible effect, some of the variance is attributed to the effectiveness of mediation. However, one might argue that as the item becomes more difficult the more mediation is required to overcome the difficulty.

DA OF CULTURALLY DIFFERENT CHILDREN

The assessment of culturally different children raises several theoretical and practical questions. The answers to these questions can be dramatically different based on the evaluation tools used. A conventional standardized approach might reveal a different picture than a DA approach.

- What is the influence of exposure to cultural conflicts on children's cognitive development?

- Are DA findings of culturally different children better predicting academic achievements than static test results?
- What are the effects of the DA approach on changing educational practices of culturally different groups?
- What are the effects of cognitive intervention programs, based on mediation processes, on narrowing academic gaps between culturally different groups and main stream groups?
- What is the role of mediation within a specific culture as a factor that equips individuals with *cognitive plasticity* (i.e., individual's ability to modify cognitive structures as a response to environmental demands)?
- In what way do culturally different children have basic readiness to transfer acquired mediation strategies given in their culture to another? In other words, how do these children internalize novel *symbolic mental tools* (Vygotsky, 1978) with transition from their culture to another and does it help them to develop resiliency in coping with cultural conflicts?

Culturally different children might show low performance in conventional tests because of negative environmental conditions and lack of learning opportunities. DA, on the other hand, was found to be more accurate in revealing these children's cognitive abilities (Guthke & Al-Zoubi, 1987; Skuy & Shmukler, 1987; Hessels & Hamers, 1993; Kaniel, et al., 1991; Shochet, 1992; Tzuriel & Kaufman, 1999), especially with minority students or culturally different students. The reason is that the interactive-teaching nature of the test allows for undeveloped cognitive capacities to mature (Vygotsky, 1978), and provides the possibility to observe learning processes and to go beyond the children's manifested cognitive performance.

One of the most extensive studies was carried out by Hessels (1997) in the Netherlands on a sample of Moroccan and Turkish ($n = 445$) minority children who were compared with Dutch children ($n = 115$) on the Learning Potential Test for Minorities (LEM). The LEM is based on a short-term learning test model (Guthke & Wingenfeld, 1992) and is composed of five subtests: classification, number series, figurative analogies, word—object association (recognition and naming), and syllable recall; the first three subtests address inductive reasoning. Achievements on these tasks are age related, sensitive to individual differences, and substantially correlated with school achievement. The test's reliability and validity were reported in several studies (Hessels, 1997; Resing & Van Wijk, 1996).

Hessels's (1997) findings indicated a correspondence between children's scoring average or high on a static intelligence test (RAKIT) and their scoring average or high on the LEM. However, children who scored low on the standard test scored low, average, or even high on the LEM. About 10–15% of the minority children and 10% of the Dutch children were labeled as intellectually impaired, whereas their learning potential scores were average or above average. Similar results were reported by Resing and Van Wijk (1996) using another static test (RCPM). Prediction of academic gains in classroom settings showed that the learning potential scores were better predictors of academic achievements than were static scores, and that higher prediction was found among children with high learning potential than among children with average learning potential.

Tzuriel and Kaufman (1999) demonstrated the efficiency of DA with a group of first-grade Ethiopian immigrants to Israel compared with a group of Israeli-born first graders on two DA measures. A major question raised recently with Ethiopian immigrants to Israel is how to assess their learning potential, in view of the fact that their cognitive scores on static tests are low and that standard testing procedures inaccurately reflect this population's cognitive functioning. It should be noted that the Ethiopian immigrants had to overcome a "civilization gap" in order to adapt to Israeli society. This issue transcends the specific context of the Ethiopian immigrants, both theoretically and pragmatically.

The main hypothesis of Tzuriel and Kaufman (1999) was that many of these immigrants would reveal cultural difference but not cultural deprivation (see discussion in Chapter 3), and therefore would show high levels of modifiability within a DA situation. An Ethiopian group ($n = 29$) was compared with a group of Israeli-born children ($n = 23$) on the RCPM and on two young children's DA measures: the CATM and the CITM (Tzuriel, 1989b, 1992b; see description of tests in Chapter 6).

The findings showed initial superiority of the Israeli-born comparison group over the Ethiopian group in all tests. ANOVA of Group (Ethiopian-born versus Israeli-born) by Time (pre- versus postteaching) in each of the DA measures revealed significant interactions for the CATM and the CITM (see Figures 7.2 and 7.3).

The Ethiopian children performed lower than the Israeli-born children in the preteaching phase, but they improved their performance more than the Israeli children and closed the gap in the postteaching phase. The gap between the two groups was narrower even in the transfer phase, which consists of more difficult problems.

The data were analyzed further by ANCOVA with the postteaching as the dependent variable, the Group as an independent variable, and the preteaching score as the covariate. The analyses showed no significant Group differences for any of the DA tests. It should be noted that in spite of the initial superiority of the Israeli-born children in every test, after a short but intensive teaching process, the Ethiopian group significantly narrowed the gap.

These findings are similar to those reported previously on older Ethiopian children (Kaniel et al., 1991) and to findings in other countries showing smaller differences between minority and mainstream groups after a mediation given

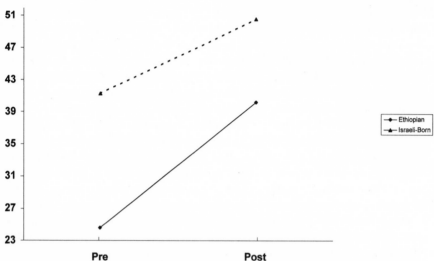

Figure 7.2. CATM (Method 2) pre- and postteaching scores of Israeli-born and Ethiopian children. (Reproduced by permission from *Journal of Cross Cultural Psychology, 30,* 359–380.)

within a DA process (Guthke & Al-Zoubi, 1987; Hessels & Hamers, 1993; Skuy & Shmukler, 1987). The difference between the two groups in a Free-Recall subtest was shown to be very small and insignificant. The lack of inferiority of the Ethiopian children on this task probably reflects Ethiopia's culture of oral learning and rote learning strategies. Correlation analyses showed that the Free-Recall was significantly correlated with the RCPM score only in the Ethiopian group (Fisher's $Z = 2.89$, $p < .01$). This result was explained by the Ethiopian children's tendency to use similar cognitive processes in solving both tasks, as compared with the Israeli-born children's tendency to apply different processes.

One of the most impressive results was found in classification subtest scores of the CITM test. In this subtest the child is asked to classify the pictures he or she has already been exposed to in the inferential problems. After the preteaching phase, the child is given a short teaching phase in which a brief (1–2 minutes) mediation is given about the principles of classification. This is followed by a parallel postteaching phase in which each of the pre- and postteaching phases has a maximal score of 12. The Ethiopian group showed much higher improvement (from .70 to 9.00) relative to the Israeli-born group (10.20 to 12.00). The investigators explained the very low initial performance of the Ethiopian children as being due to the lack of familiarity with classification tasks rather than to lack of ability. These results coincide with cross-cultural research findings indicating that individuals in many non-Western nations classify items into functional rather than

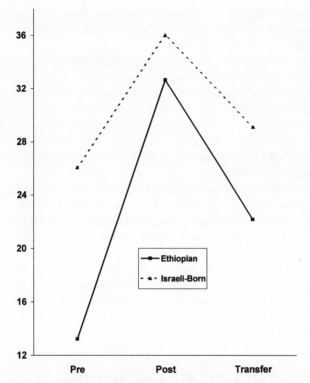

Figure 7.3. CITM preteaching, postteaching, and transfer scores of Israeli-born and Ethiopian children. (Copied by permission from *Journal of Cross Cultural Psychology*, *30*, 359–380.)

taxonomic categories (i.e., Luria, 1976; Scribner, 1984; Sharp, Cole & Lave, 1979). These results coincide with those of Sternberg (1997) who emphasized the role of environmental context on definition and assessment of intelligence. What is learned in terms of both declarative and procedural knowledge may differ radically from one environment to another.

DA OF CHILDREN WITH LANGUAGE DEFICITS

DA has been adapted by several speech-language pathologists to provide a valid means for differentiating children with language differences from children with language disorders and in assessment of reading difficulties (Jeffrey, 1997; Kester, Pena, & Gillam, in press; Lidz & Pena, 1996; Olswang & Bain, 1996; Sharoni & Greenfeld, 1999). Pena and Gillam (2000) showed, for example, that with a group of low SES children (the majority of whom were from culturally and linguistically diverse backgrounds), cognitive strategies rather than intervention materials influenced gains on a labeling task in a DA procedure (for a detailed discussion see the next section).

Sharoni and Greenfeld (1999) developed an integrative model for remedial teaching of reading that combines three approaches: (1) cognitive strategies involved in reading, (2) a mediated learning approach, and (3) cognitive behavior strategies. They applied this model in a seminar for teachers as well as in a clinic for assessment and remedial teaching of reading difficulties. In a single case study they reported the effectiveness of their paradigmatic integrative approach both with college students, who learned teaching processes, and with children diagnosed in the clinic.

Using a clinical approach Jeffrey (1997) and Jeffrey and Tzuriel (1999) demonstrated the efficient use of the CMB (Tzuriel, 1995a, 2000d) to assess and intervene with children showing language difficulties. The CMB tasks were used to identify various difficulties: definition of verbal categories, memory deficits, number concepts, directionality, grammatical markers of comparison (e.g., big*gest*), self-talk strategies, and limiting of options strategies. In all of these areas the CMB tasks were used to "bridge" newly acquired concepts to letter formation, directionality of letters, and word formation. In conclusion, the clinical use of DA in content related domains and the research in this area is relatively scarce, but the novel attempts for applications are promising.

COMPARISON OF DIFFERENT MEDIATIONAL STRATEGIES IN DA

One of the issues raised frequently in DA is the effect of different mediation strategies used on children's performance. Missiuna and Samuels (1989) tried to explain an unexpected finding in Tzuriel and Klein's (1985) study, namely, the low level of modifiability on the CATM found for the special education group. They argued that the mediation given in Tzuriel and Klein's (1985) study was standardized (i.e., given similarly to each child without taking into account the unique difficulties of the specific individual tested). They hypothesized that special education children are especially sensitive to the type of mediation given to them and that mediation that is "tailored" to the children's specific needs is more effective than the mediation given regularly in the teaching phase of the DA procedure. In their replication study, they introduced two adjustments. (1) Learning-disabled kindergartners were randomly assigned to treatment conditions of either "instruction" or "mediation". "Instruction" was similar to the original Teaching phase in that the children received the same nonprescribed mediation. The "mediation" condition, however, was tailored to the unique difficulties demonstrated by the child during assessment (i.e., attention span, labeling, and self-regulation). (2) The CATM was administered twice before the Teaching phase with no mediation in between. This was done in order to rule out the possibility that the children's gain could occur partially because of simple familiarity with test problems and practice. The findings showed no practice effect, as evidenced by the lack of improvement between the two administrations. The main findings, however, showed clearly that the handicapped children significantly improved their scores, whereas the "instruction" group showed no change. Thus, the minor improvement of the "instruction" group replicated Tzuriel and Klein's (1985) results with the special education group, using the regular mediation given. The modifiability of the special education group was demonstrated more impressively with use of the "partial credit" scoring method (e.g., a score is given for each correct dimension of the solution) than with the "all-or-none" method. This result might be explained by the difficulties of the children in simultaneously considering and integrating all three sources of information that are within the task. Also, the "mediation" group required significantly more time to solve the postteaching problems than did the "instruction" group, a result that was explained by better control of impulsivity and awareness of different options for problem solving strategies. Missiuna and Samuels (1989) concluded that mediation within DA should be tailored to children's unique learning difficulties in order to reveal their learning potential.

Burns (1991) supported this position by comparing two DA procedures: the *MLE* and the *graduated prompt* procedures (Brown & Ferrara, 1985) with the static test approach, on a sample of high-risk preschool children. Burns (1991) used a preschool DA measure, which is based on Arthur's (1947) Stencil Design Test. The findings revealed that the children performed higher when given DA than when given static tests. DA using the MLE approach was associated with higher cognitive performance on the test and higher transfer scores (using the Animal House subtest from the WPPSI) than was either the graduated prompt or static testing procedure.

Other attempts to compare different intervention conditions in DA were carried out by Kester, Pena and Gillam (2000) on a sample of low SES preschool children, the majority of whom were from culturally and linguistically diverse backgrounds. The intervention approaches were *direct instruction*, *MLE*, and *hybrid methods* for instructing children about labeling. The primary learning goal of all three interventions was to teach labeling skills. The interventions varied according to the type of procedures and the type of materials that were used. The findings indicated, first, that the labeling performance of children in the three instruction groups improved significantly relative to that of children in a no-treatment control condition. Second, the effect size of the direct intervention gain was approximately half as large as the effect size for the hybrid group, and more than three times smaller than the effect size for the MLE group. The authors explained these results as follows: Children in the direct intervention group learned some new labels for objects but did not learn strategies for single words that could be applied to word learning or to labeling contexts in general. The MLE approach was most effective because it involves understanding of transcendent rules for labeling beyond specific context. The cognitively oriented approaches (MLE and hybrid) were found to be more effective than the procedures that were used in direct instruction, regardless of the materials that were used. These findings are consistent with earlier theory and research (i.e., Missiuna & Samuels, 1989; Rogoff, 1990, Rogoff & Morelli, 1989; Tzuriel, 1998; Vygotsky, 1956, 1978, 1981) about the importance of using mediation within the child's zone of proximal development.

PREDICTION OF SCHOOL ACHIEVEMENT
BY STATIC VERSUS DA MEASURES

Prediction patterns of school achievements by DA measures versus conventional standardized tests might provide important information about the validity of the tests. Conducting comparative prediction research, however, carries a methodological problem, i.e., the academic achievement scores are usually measured in a static way, thus giving priority to static tests. In other words, there is a greater chance of a higher relation between a standardized test and academic achievements scores (both are static tests) than between DA measures and academic achievements. In spite of this difficulty, two studies have been reported with first graders (Tzuriel, 2000d; Tzuriel et al., 1999). In both studies, reading comprehension and math scores in Grade 1 were predicted by different DA measures as compared with conventional static tests.

In the first study (Tzuriel et al., 1999) a group of experimental children who participated in the Bright Start program in kindergarten were followed up in Grade 1 and compared with a control group (see Chapter 9 for detailed description of this study). Both groups received reading comprehension (Ortar & Ben-Schachar, 1972) and math (Minkowich, 1976) tests 1 year after the end of the intervention as well as static (e.g., the RCPM) and dynamic measures (e.g., the CATM and the Complex Figure test). A series of stepwise regression analyses were carried out for each of the criterion variables in the experimental and the control group. It was found that reading comprehension scores were significantly predicted by the RCPM, in both the experimental ($R^2 = .19$) and the control group ($R^2 = .26$). The prediction of math scores, however, showed that the dynamic measures were far more powerful in prediction of the math scores than the static test of the RCPM. In the control group the only score that predicted math was the CATM Post-Teaching test ($R^2 = .54$) and in the experimental group two scores have evolved as significant predictive variables ($R^2 = .26$): the Postteaching CATM ($\beta = .47$) and the RCPM ($\beta = .39$).

In the second study (Tzuriel, 2000d) sample of children in Grade 1 ($n = 35$) were administered a reading comprehension test (Ortar & Ben-Schachar, 1972) and a math test (Kidron, 1989), both tests are standard group tests. The predicting variables were the CMB Pre- and Post-Teaching scores of five subtests (S, RP, AN, SQ-I, and SQ-II). A detailed description of the subtests is given in Chapter 6. All subtests were administered using the measurement/research version. Thus, the Pre-Teaching scores can be considered as static tests. A stepwise regression analysis approach was applied to predict the academic scores by the CMB subtests' scores. Two regression analyses were carried out, one for reading comprehension and one for math as criterion variables. The predicting variables were the Pre- and Post-Teaching CMB scores.

The findings showed that reading comprehension was predicted by *Post-Teaching Seriation* and *Post-Teaching Analogies* scores ($R^2 = .45$) and that Math was predicted by *Post-Teaching Seriation* and *Pre-Teaching Reproduction of Patterns* ($R^2 = .57$). It should be noted that in prediction of reading comprehension the Analogies Post-Teaching score was more powerful ($\beta = .60$) than the Seriation Post-Teaching score ($\beta = .27$). This finding might be explained by the fact that Analogies taps an abstraction domain, which is closer to reading comprehension than Seriation. Seriation characterizes the individual's ability to learn task specific strategies, which is a cognitive function related to the technical skills required in reading which, in turn, affect performance on comprehension of a written text.

The regression analysis showed that math was predicted by Pre-Teaching Reproduction of Patterns and Post-Teaching Seriation scores ($R^2 = .57$). Both scores explained 57% of the variance. In prediction of math, the Pre-Teaching Reproduction of Patterns score was more powerful ($\beta = .69$) than the Post-Teaching Seriation score ($\beta = .43$) score. Detailed task analysis of these domains showed that both tests require *needs for precision and accuracy*, a cognitive function that is required in math performance. In addition, Seriation requires systematic exploratory behavior and learning of task-specific strategies, which characterizes successful math performance.

In conclusion, the findings of both studies indicate that the Postteaching scores are more powerful than static tests in predicting academic achievement scores. It is assumed that were the academic performance to be measured dynamically, their prediction by dynamic tests would be much higher than what has been found to date.

DA AND REFLECTIVITY-IMPULSIVITY DIMENSION

Cognitive styles have been found as strongly affecting learning and performance on a variety of cognitive domains. Clinical experience in DA shows that impulsivity is a deficient cognitive function that affects cognitive processing in a pervasive way across domains and phases of the mental activity (input, elaboration, output). One of the goals in DA is to change children's impulsive style to a reflective mode of responding. The effects of impulsivity on cognitive functioning and change of impulsivity was investigated in three studies.

In the first study, the effect of DA on modifying impulsivity was investigated in a group of second grade children (Tzuriel & Schanck, 1994). All children were given, individually; the Matching Familiar Figures Test (MFFT; Kagan, 1965), followed by the CATM and the CITM adapted for school-age children as group DA tests. Testing procedures included an instructions phase with 3 examples, preteaching, teaching, and postteaching phases. The Teaching phase was composed of 1 hour of group mediation, for each test, which included teaching of strategies for solving the problems, systematic exploration of the dimensions, analytic perception of tasks, simultaneous consideration of several sources of information, hypothesis testing, planning behavior, and understanding the rules governing the problems. The MFFT was administered again 10 days after the intervention; this time delay was set up to control for possible artifacts of the intervention process as well as to ensure stability of changes beyond the immediate intervention effects. A control group was administered the MFFT before and after the intervention, but none of the DA procedures. The initial *number of errors* and *reaction time* on the MFFT were taken as criteria for categorizing the children into four groups: Impulsive, Reflective, Fast/Accurate, and Slow/Inaccurate. One-way analyses of variance carried out on the CITM and CATM preteaching scores revealed significant differences on both tests. The main finding was that the *Reflective* group scored significantly higher than did the other three groups, who scored about the same, including the *Fast/Accurate* group. Two analyses of covariance were carried out, on the postteaching performance of the CATM and CITM tests with Group (experimental-control) and Cognitive Style as independent variables (2 × 4). The covariate was the initial cognitive performance on each test. The findings revealed that the only group that showed high pre- to postteaching improvement was the Fast/Accurate group on the CITM, but not on the CATM scores. The Reflective group, however, continued to be the highest performance group. ANOVA of the MFFT *error* scores revealed a significant interaction of Time × Group, indicating that the experimental participants had changed their cognitive style from pre- to postteaching towards reflectivity, whereas the control participants displayed the same degree of impulsivity. The Impulsivity-Reflectivity scores derived from the MFFT were significantly correlated with the performance scores on the CATM and CITM tests in the pre- and postteaching phases, ranging between .23 and .40.

The results of this study supported the authors' hypothesis that initial cognitive performance is related to the level of impulsivity-reflectivity. Of most importance was the result showing that even the Fast/Accurate subjects achieved lower scores on the CATM and CITM tests (pre- and postteaching) than did the reflective (slow/accurate) subjects. This finding indicates that when abstract thinking skills are involved, a reflective cognitive style is more efficient than any other style including a fast/accurate style. Interpretation of these findings should take into account the nature of tasks that determined the impulsivity-reflectivity dimension. The MFFT task is based on a perceptual process in which the child has to scan several visual stimuli and detect differences between a model figure and several similar alternatives. This type of processing is basically different from the cognitive processing functions required in the CATM and CITM tasks.

The findings showed that although the DA process helped all subgroups to improve their cognitive performance from pre- to postteaching phase, it helped the Fast/Accurate group more than others. These results imply that in teaching processes one should concentrate on the level of accuracy and on inhibition of the tendency to respond quickly. Another interesting result related to the effects of the DA procedure on modifiability of the cognitive style. In spite of the fact that the DA procedure is aimed mainly at modifying the level of cognitive performance, the impulsivity level was also affected.

In a second study (Tzuriel, 1997b) a sample of kindergarten to 3rd grade students (n = 120) were administered the MFFT and were tested individually using the Cognitive Modifiability Battery: Assessment and Intervention (CMB, Tzuriel, 1995a). The CMB tasks were constructed originally to test kindergarten through Grade 3 children, but they can be used also with older children who have learning difficulties. The CMB is composed of 5 subtests: Seriation (S), Reproduction of Patterns (RP), Analogies (AN), Sequences (SQ- Levels II and I), and Memory (ME); each tapping different areas of cognitive functioning. For each subtest there is a set of problems, designed for preteaching, teaching, and postteaching phases. For 2 of the 5 sub-tests (Analogies and Sequences) there is also a transfer phase which includes problems that are remote from the original ones.

The children in each grade level were categorized into four groups (Impulsive, Reflective, Fast/Accurate, and Slow/Inaccurate) in a similar way carried out in the first study. A series of Group × Time (4 × 2) ANOVA's with repeated measures were carried out on each of the 5 subtests (for both "none-or-all" Scoring Method-1, and partial credit Scoring Method-2). The last variable was the within subjects factor. The findings showed significant Group differences in 8 out of 10 analyses, indicating higher performance for the Reflective than for the other subgroups. As was found previously, the Fast/Accurate subgroup was significantly lower than the Reflective (Slow/Accurate) subgroup in all test domains. The higher performance of the Reflective children was on both the pre- and postteaching phases of all subtests. The findings also showed significant Group × Time interactions for Reproduction of Patterns (Method-1), Analogies (Method-1), and Analogies (Method-2). These interactions showed that the Impulsive,

Slow/Inaccurate, and Fast/Accurate groups benefited more than the Reflective group from the teaching phase and also showed higher gains. Correlation analyses showed significant correlations, between all the CMB scores and the number of errors on the MFFT, ranging between .21 and .58.

The objectives of the third study (Tzuriel, 2000a) were to investigate the effects of mediation on change of impulsivity level with young children and prediction of math achievements in seriational-computational tasks by process-oriented measures of impulsivity level. The Seria-Think Instrument measured impulsivity level. The Seria-Think Instrument is a novel DA measure aimed at assessing and teaching children a variety of arithmetic skills based on the operation of seriation, in combination with mastery of math skills of addition and subtraction. The problems of the Seria-Think Instrument require several cognitive functions, the most important of which are regulation of impulsivity, planning behavior, systematic exploratory behavior, simultaneous consideration of few sources of information, needs for accuracy, and control of trial and error behavior. The Seria-Think yields three measures: *performance level* as indicated by the accuracy of the solution, *number of insertions*, which indicates the efficiency level, and the *number of measurements* of the depths, which indicates planning behavior. For a description of the instrument see Chapter 6.

The study was carried out on a sample of Grade 1 children (mean age in months was 92.30) who were assigned randomly into experimental (n = 24) and control (n = 24) groups. All children were administered a pre- and postteaching phases on the Seria-Think. The experimental group received mediation for regulation of behavior with special focus on planning, comparing, and computing (i.e., measuring the depth of holes and length of cylinders, adding, and subtracting), whereas the control group received free-play manipulative experience with no mediation. Following the Seria-Think, both groups received a content related Math test. A MANOVA of *treatment* by *time* (2 × 2) showed a significant interaction, which was explained by both *number of measurements* and *number of insertions*. The interactions are displayed in Figures 7.4 and 7.5.

The findings clearly indicate that, from pre- to postteaching, the experimental children *decreased* significantly their number of insertions and concurrently *increased* their number of measurements. The control group on the other hand showed about the same response pattern before and after the treatment. Of most importance is the result indicating that both process-oriented measures were significant in differentiating between the experimental and control groups; the combination of both characterizes the dimension of reflectivity versus impulsivity.

Other important findings were the prediction pattern of math score by the Seria-Think measures. Stepwise regression analyses showed that math score was predicted in the experimental group by *postteaching number of insertions* ($R^2 = .19$)—the less insertion the child used in the postteaching phase the higher was the math score. In the control group, the math score was predicted by the *postteaching number of measurements* and *postteaching performance* ($R^2 = .54$):

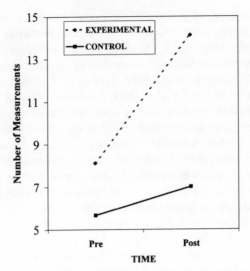

Figure 7.4. Number of measurements in pre- and postteaching phases among the experimental and control groups. (Reproduced by permission from *International School Psychology*, *20*, 173–190.)

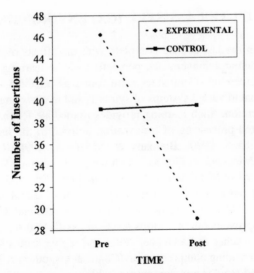

Figure 7.5. Number of insertions in pre- and postteaching phases among the experimental and control groups. (Reproduced by permission from *International School Psychology*, *20*, 173–190.)

the higher the score on both variables the higher was the math score. In both groups the postteaching scores were more accurate in predicting the math scores than were the preteaching scores. The utility of the postteaching score as a more accurate predictor measure than static tests was also demonstrated in other studies (Embretson, 1992; Samuels, et al., 1992; Tzuriel, et al., 1999).

The results of all three studies show consistently that an impulsive inclination is detrimental to cognitive performance, and that even having an accurate mode of processing does not guarantee efficient cognitive functioning if it is *not* accompanied by a slow information-processing tempo. These findings have important implications for the validity of static measures of intelligence, especially the timed tests, which encourage children to work fast. Static tests that rest heavily on timed factors tends to constrain efficiency and ability. Impulsive children frequently manifest a lower level of cognitive performance in spite of their relatively high learning potential and/or abstraction level. Their low performance might be interpreted as *low ability* rather than as *low efficiency*. The findings might have implications for teaching procedures within the school system and for societal values that encourage speed rather than accuracy, and efficiency rather than depth of processing and comprehension.

DA IN A COMPUTER ASSISTED (CA) ENVIRONMENT

Research in the last decade is replete with the effects of computer based learning on academic achievements, perception of the learning processes, and academic self-perception. Computers were found as effective in exposing the learning individual to varied systems of symbols and in attracting and enhancing the learner's attention. Such learning provides immediate feedback, and graduated and organized processing of information tailored to the individual's level (Barba & Merchant, 1990; Biemans & Simmons, 1996; Clariana, 1993; Garrison, 1996; Mevarech, 1993; Kao, Lehman, & Cennamo, 1996; Koszalska, 1999; Miech, Nava, & Mostelletr, 1997; Shamir, 1999; Tzuriel & Shamir, 2001). The use of computer assisted (CA) learning was found useful also with young children (Carlson & White, 1998). Children who received CA intervention demonstrated improvements in various academic skills and memory and visual perception (Goldmacher & Lawrence, 1992) and higher scores in tests of word identification and reading comprehension (Chang & Osguthorpe, 1990) than children who received regular non-computer teaching.

The role of CA learning within a DA procedure which involves mediation, was studied by only few researchers (i.e., Guthke & Backmann, 2000; Jensen, 2000; Tzuriel & Shamir, 2001). Use of mediation in a CA environment raised questions such as: What is the role of the mediator in a CA context? What are the specific attributes of the computer in facilitating of cognitive processes? It becomes more and more evident that the effectiveness of CA learning depends on a match between the goals of teaching, learner's characteristics, the software design, and decisions made by educators.

In a study by Tzuriel and Shamir (2001) the effects of CA learning in a DA context was compared to DA by examiner alone (EO), on pre- to postteaching gains. Based on the *Children's Seriational Thinking Modifiability* (CSTM) test (Tzuriel, 1995b), the CA group was administered a multimedia computerized DA test whereas the EO group was administered the test in the usual way. The specific objectives of the study were to study CA environment as compared to EO, as regards: (1) *initial cognitive performance* on seriational tasks, (2) effectiveness of teaching (mediation), and (3) effect of task dimension (number, size, and darkness) and task complexity level on children's cognitive modifiability.

The sample was composed of kindergarteners (n = 60) who were assigned to either a CA (n = 30) or EO (n = 30) groups. The findings revealed that intervention involving mediation processes in a CA dynamic assessment procedure was more effective in bringing about significant cognitive changes than mediation with only an examiner. A repeated measures ANOVA of Group by Time (2 × 2) revealed a significant interaction ($F(2,216) = 6.51$, $p < .01$) indicating that while both groups improved their performance from Pre- to Post-Teaching, the CA group showed higher gains than the EO group.

Another important findings indicate that the higher pre- to postteaching gain of the CA over the EO group, was more articulated in difficult than in easy tasks. The level of difficulty was studied by two separate criteria: task dimension (darkness was more difficult than number and size), and complexity level which was defined by the number of problems contained in one series of cards (i.e., some series contain one dimension, whereas others contain two or three dimensions). For a description of the CSTM see Chapter 5.

One of the questions Tzuriel and Shamir (2001) asked was whether the measurement process of the cognitive ability in the CA versus EO condition has, by itself, an effect on performance. The findings clearly showed that just measurement has no effect on performance. Comparison of both groups on the Pre-Teaching scores showed no significant differences. The group differences, however, were more articulated when the comparison was carried out between two subgroups (n = 12 in each) who were administered the test's phases as Total CA (i.e., all phases administered with computer assistance) or Total EO (i.e., all phases administered by examiner). The Total CA subgroup doubled its score from Pre-Teaching ($M = 20.25$, $SD = 6.87$) to Post-Teaching ($M = 40.10$, $SD = 3.14$) phase as compared with the Total EO subgroup who improved their score less dramatically from Pre-Teaching ($M = 22.17$, $SD = 8.57$) to Post-Teaching ($M = 31.25$, $SD = 9.19$). The gain achieved by the Total EO subgroup was similar to the gain achieved by the EO group, whereas the gain of the Total CA group was much more articulated than the gain achieved by the CA group. The investigators explained these results in the fact that the measurement technique by itself is not strong enough to have an effect on performance. Only after implementing a learning phase—in which the mediator taught the child how to solve the tasks, using the multimedia modality—did the CA condition have a stronger effect. These findings strengthen the hypothesis that the CA effects should be attributed mainly to the *quality* of the CA learning condition.

CASE STUDY: A CHILD WITH SPECIFIC LEARNING DIFFICULTIES

Adam was 8 years old when referred for psycho-educational assessment to our clinic at Bar-Ilan University. His parents and the Child Development Center of Sheba Hospital in Israel referred him after diagnosing speech difficulties, attention deficits, and behavior problems. The main problems reported were in motor aspects of speech, language expression, especially in acquisition of reading and writing, disorders of attention and concentration, distractibility, and behavior problems in the class. Adam was first diagnosed with DA and later with a battery of graph-motor tests and language tests, which included listening, speech, reading, writing, and memory. The battery of tests included the Raven's Colored Matrices, Auditory Association from the ITPA, Picture Arrangement test, Sentence Construction, Listening Comprehension, and Attention Span.

Dynamic Assessment

Adam was administered two DA measures: the CMB and the Complex Figure test (Rey, 1956; Feuerstein et al., 1979). On the CMB Adam showed basic difficulties of understanding simple instructions, systematic exploratory behavior, simultaneous consideration of more than two sources of information, spatial orientation, verbal anticipation of a solution, and verbal expression and elaboration of solved problems. Throughout the test it was clear that these kinds of difficulties affected the whole spectrum of his performance in school. However, unlike previous reports Adam showed high levels of concentration and intrinsic motivation to accept challenges, and above all a high level of cognitive modifiability. This last aspect was of special importance as it showed that in spite of his basic difficulties, there were many signs that he could modify them, learn abstract principles, and perform on a much higher level than what could be expected based on the reported difficulties.

For example, on the Seriation subtest, Adam learned with relatively little mediation (two explanations), how to seriate the blocks using the specific systematic strategy that was taught. During the learning process he became more reflective in solving the problems, showed more independence and initiative. He uses more a verbalizations to direct his performance, though he still had difficulties in considering simultaneously more than two source of information.

In the Reproduction of Patterns subtest, Adam had an initial difficulty in the area of spatial orientation as reflected in his failure to identify right versus left and top versus bottom. Most of his mistakes were of position. With light mediation (focusing) he improved his performance and could do the most difficult items with no mistakes. In the Analogies subtest (Testing and Transfer) he showed a basic ability to solve problems requiring relatively high abstraction level. This aspect was important to rule out difficulties deriving from central processing deficiencies. His main problems were in mastering the spatial orientation component, in verbally anticipating the answer before proceeding into the solution, and in verbally justifying his response. In the Testing section he reached his highest level of performance with light mediation targeted at considering all dimensions using a "one by one" strategy (Tzuriel, 1999b). The Transfer problems required more mediation, especially regarding the position component.

The last test from the CMB was Sequences I. Here Adam required more mediation than on any other subtest. His main difficulties were considering simultaneously all sources of information, especially the dimensions of height and position. As in the previous subtest he did not verbalize his performance, elaborate a response or provide justification for an answer—correct or incorrect. In spite of the difficulty level of this subtest, Adam showed task-intrinsic motivation, high level of attention, and willingness to accept challenging problems.

The second DA test administered was the Complex Figure. This test is composed of five phases: (1) the child is asked to copy the figure (Copy-I) and then (2) to draw it from memory (Memory-I). (3) The child is taught how to gather the information systematically, to plan the construction (i.e., drawing first the major lines and then secondary lines, going in clockwise order), and to pay attention to precision, proportions, and the quality of lines. (4) The child is asked again to copy the figure (Copy-II) and then (5) to draw it from memory (Memory-II). Comparison of the copy and memory phases before and after teaching provides information about the cognitive modifiability of the child.

Adam showed an initially adequate performance in both copying and memorizing the figure, with some minor difficulties in accuracy. His performance reached a maximum after a short mediation phase. Throughout testing Adam showed adequate task intrinsic motivation, accessibility to mediation, adequate concentration level, and willingness to invest mentally in solving complex problems. For example, when asked if he prefers easy tasks or difficult ones, he preferred difficult tasks and smiled when he managed to reach a solution to a problem independently. When the examiner was occasionally interrupted by a phone call, Adam continued to work on the problem without showing signs of being disrupted by the temporary lack of attention.

The reported attention deficits and behavior problems in the classroom seem to be a function of disinterest in class subjects, repeated failures in verbal domains, and lack of challenges. These behaviors are related probably to the nature of the verbal academic tasks given in the classroom and lack of a mediational approach, and difficulties in expressing and displaying of his performance.

Static Testing

In the domain of *listening skills*, Adam showed difficulties related to pronunciation (i.e., *th* instead of *sh*), distinction between similar vowels, synthesis of letters into words, analyzing words into letters, lexical and phonological awareness. His memory abilities for a string of words and numbers and for following instructions with four components were adequate.

In the *writing domain*, Adam did not know how to write independently all the letters in alphabetical order; he had difficulties even in writing his name, and made mistakes in almost all words dictated to him. His writing difficulties were strongly related to these difficulties in listening skills. Adam's reading skills were deficient, as evidenced by his lack of accuracy, lack of distinction between similar vowels, and lack of knowledge of several basic vowels. He made many mistakes in combination of letters and tried to cope with difficult words by guessing. Attempts to intervene and to teach him to read correctly included focusing on details, inhibition of guessing approach, and generalized rules of reading, all given in a graduated way and combined with interpretation of his success and attempts for mastery. Following these cognitive strategies, Adam showed a quick grasp of the principles, improved his reading, and showed clear signs of satisfaction from achievements.

The combined results of dynamic and static tests indicate that Adam has a specific learning difficulty focused in the area of language. More specifically Adam's difficulties were in coding linguistic information and expression of an elaborated linguistic product. The same response pattern was revealed in both static testing and the DA measures. The DA process, however, provided clearer indications for Adam's modifiability as well as implications for the intervention processes required in the future. It was clear that in spite of the severity of his language difficulties there was a significant improvement after a short intensive mediation. We could identify several deficient cognitive functions that contributed to his inadequate functioning above and beyond the domain specific language difficulties. There were indications that his language and attention deficits could be modified by mediation. The mediation included graduation of task level of difficulty, provision of linguistic tools to gather information, learning how to explore information systematically, control of impulsivity, use of rules and strategies to deal with complex information (i.e., task analysis of dimensions), developing feelings of competence and self-confidence, and enhancing insight processes. These cognitive functions once modified by mediation brought about a meaningful change in Adam's functioning. As a result the following recommendations are offered to enhance Adam's future learning:

- Use of the CMB tasks to develop general cognitive strategies of systematic data gathering, development of spatial orientation skills, verbal anticipation and justification of a solution, and linguistic expression of performance.
- Intervention in content oriented domains such as reading and writing but with heavy emphasis on "bridging" cognitive principles learned in the CMB intervention to subject matters. For example, when Adam has to identify *both* the string of letters and their correct order it was related to *simultaneous consideration of two sources of information* learned in the CMB. Control the pace of reading and stop when tackling a new word was related to *regulation and control of impulsivity* level. Paying attention to differences between similar letters (perceptual) and vowels (auditory) was related to *needs for accuracy and precision*. Elaboration of ideas read in a paragraph and justification of an answer was related to the demands on the CMB for verbal anticipation of a solution, elaboration of verbal answers, and justification of correct and mistaken responses.

Special recommendations were given to enhance Adam's feelings of competence by graduating the tasks in terms of difficulty level thus allowing many successes, by interpreting the reasons for successes and failures, by encouraging successful performance, and by highlighting the changes Adam made in the learning process.

8

Use of DA from Developmental–Cognitive Perspectives

RATIONALE FOR USE OF DA IN DEVELOPMENTAL–COGNITIVE STUDIES

The use of DA in developmental–cognitive research is based on the assumption that *cognitive modifiability* as an explanatory concept of other developmental variables or as an outcome criterion of other factors is more informative than static cognitive measures. Cognitive modifiability indicators were found to be informative both in prediction of changes in various cognitive domains and as predicted outcomes of other educational and developmental factors (Embretson, 1992; Guthke et al., 1997; Lidz, 1991; Tzuriel, 1998, 1999b).

Most studies in this area were carried out in the laboratory at Bar Ilan University with different samples of parents and children. In these studies we investigated the effects of parent–child MLE interactions as a proximal factor of cognitive modifiability. Cognitive modifiability was measured in these studies by means of DA using different instruments. In some studies the focus was on the relative contribution of distal and proximal factors in predicting cognitive modifiability (Tzuriel & Eran, 1990; Tzuriel & Ernst, 1990; Tzuriel & Hatzir, 1999; Tzuriel & Weiss, 1998a). In other studies the focus was on prediction of cognitive modifiability in different situations such as free play versus structured (Tzuriel, 1996; Tzuriel & Weiss, 1998a). In five studies we investigated the prediction of cognitive modifiability by parent–child MLE interactions as a function of children or parent's characteristics. These characteristics included child's low birth weight (Tzuriel & Weitz, 1998), child's personality orientation (Tzuriel &

Weiss, 1998a), gender of child and parent (Tzuriel & Eran, 1990; Tzuriel & Hatzir, 1999), mother's acceptance/rejection of the child (Tzuriel & Weiss, 1998a), and ethnic origin (Tzuriel, Yehudai, & Kaniel, 1994). In all studies we used the Observation of Mediation Instrument (OMI) developed by Klein (1988) for infants and toddlers. The OMI, however, was adapted for kindergarten and school age children (Tzuriel, 1996, 1999b) as well as for different teaching situations (e.g., teaching in small groups, peer mediation) than the original parent–child interactions. The OMI is described below in the methodological section.

A growing body of evidence indicates that specific activities of parents can predict their children's cognitive development, that they are concurrently related to children's mental functioning, and that both child and parent influence the child's mental development (Bee et al., 1982; Belsky, Goode, & Most, 1980; Berk & Spuhl, 1995; Bornstein, 1985, 1988, 1989a, 1989b; Bornstein & Lamb, 1992; Bornstein & Tamis-LeMonda, 1989, 1990, 1997; Bradley & Caldwell, 1984; Carew, 1980; Clarke-Stewart, 1973, 1993; Collins, 1984; Gottfried, 1984; Klein, 1988, 1996; Olson, Bates, & Bayles, 1984; Ramey, Farran, & Campbell, 1979; Sigel, 1982; Tzuriel, 1996, 1999b; Wachs, 1992; Wachs & Gruen, 1992; Wachs & Plomin, 1991). The relation between parent–child interaction and the children's cognitive performance has been studied from different perspectives using different concepts and theoretical frameworks.

The following section examines recent studies on the relationship between parent–child interactions and children's cognitive functioning based on various *cognitive–developmental models*. In these studies only static cognitive measures were used with no attention to indications of learning and cognitive modifiability indicators. Following this section is the main discussion regarding the relationship between parent–child MLE strategies and children's cognitive development and cognitive modifiability. This discussion is based on current research carried out in the last decade (Tzuriel, 1999a). It focuses on Klein's (e.g., 1988) studies with infants, and Tzuriel's (e.g., 1999b) studies with kindergarten and school-age children. I also discuss some methodological issues concerning the measurement of MLE processes in parent–child interactions and of cognitive modifiability using the DA approach.

STUDIES DERIVED FROM GENERAL COGNITIVE DEVELOPMENTAL MODELS

Recent developmental research has shown a relationship between several dimensions of parent–child interactions and a variety of cognitive developmental outcomes. It was shown, for example, that positive *social caretaking* during feeding of 4- to 12-month-olds predicted significantly the children's language performance at 3 years of age and IQ at 4 years of age (Bee et al., 1982). Price, Hess, and Dickson (1981) reported that mothers' *encouragement of verbalization* fostered development of preschool children's verbal–educational abilities. It was correlated significantly more strongly with children's knowledge of letters and numbers than with general indices of Verbal and Performance IQ. Elias, Ubriaco, and Gray (1985) reported that parental strategies of questioning and suggestions helped children to translate their thinking process into operations and search for varied solutions, whereas directives (i.e., telling children what to do) depressed their problem-solving skills and conveyed low self-confidence in their abilities.

Another strategy studied in parent–child interaction is *distancing*, used by parents to develop children's representational thinking. Distancing strategies relate to placing cognitive demands on children by describing relations and raising alternatives and consequences that are not perceptually seen. Parents use distancing strategies to facilitate hypothesis testing, and to evoke mentally represented plans, and task responsibility (Sigel, 1982).

The pattern of mother–child teaching strategies was demonstrated recently with a group of mothers and their learning disabled (LD) children who were compared with a group of mothers and their normally achieving children (Lyytinen, Rasku-Puttonen, Poikkeus, Laakso, & Ahonen, 1994). The mothers were videotaped during a teaching task, which resembled a homework assignment. It was found that the mothers of the LD children used fewer high-level strategies, gave less teaching time, and exhibited more dominance and less emotionality and cooperation than mothers of normally achieving children exhibited. Within the LD group it was also found that a combination of mothers' motivation, emotionality, and proportion of high-level cognitive demands was best at predicting children's success in learning. These results confirm the authors' hypothesis that despite underlying neuropsychological and genetic factors which may be affecting LD learning performance, the mothers' distancing strategies and motivational–emotional factors are still crucial determinants of learning performance.

Another concept used to explain mother–child interactions was *scaffolding*. This concept was used originally by Wood (1989; Wood, Bruner, & Ross, 1976) to describe the informal teaching roles that caregivers adopt in order to facilitate children's cognitive development. Scaffolding has been used as a metaphor for a process by which caregivers assist children to carry out a task beyond the children's capability. The caregivers regulate task components that are initially beyond the children's capacity, permitting them to concentrate on and complete only those elements that are within the children's range of competence. Using the scaffolding concept, Carew (1980) found that sensitive parents tailor their scaffolding behavior to match the infant's cognitive developmental level.

A variety of additional relevant concepts have been suggested to elucidate the relation of parents' behavior to children's cognitive development. Collins

(1984) identified parent *demandingness* as an essential determinant of the quality of the family environment. Rogoff (1990; Rogoff & Chavajay, 1995) has referred to the concept of *apprenticeship* in relation to a sociocultural framework, and Bornstein (1989a) has investigated parental *responsiveness* as a determinant of children's cognitive competence.

In regard to the parental responsiveness, Bornstein (1989a) distinguished between two types of parental responsiveness: *social* and *didactic*. Social inter-action involves physical and verbal parental strategies aimed at expressing feel-ings, and engaging children in exchanges, which are primarily interpersonal. Didactic interactions are characterized by focusing children's attention on objects and events in the environment by introducing, mediating, and interpreting the external world. Didactic interactions involve the parents' strategies for stimulat-ing and arousing their child to attend to external stimuli. "Such interactions include caretakers' strategies in stimulating and arousing their offspring to the world outside the pair, in encouraging attention to properties, objects, or events in the environment, in introducing, mediating, and interpreting the external world, and in provoking or providing opportunities to observe, imitate, speak, and learn" (Bornstein, 1989a, pp. 199–200). The orthogonality of these two modes of inter-action as well as their internal consistency was validated in several studies (e.g., Vibbert & Bornstein, 1989).

The relation between didactic interactions and development of mental skills was demonstrated by several authors (e.g., Carew, 1980). Various studies have shown that positive social interactions predict mental growth in the child (e.g., Olson et al., 1984; Ramey et al., 1979) and that mother–infant didactic interac-tion was significantly associated with infants exploratory competence (Belsky et al., 1980).

In a series of longitudinal studies, Bornstein and his colleagues (i.e., Bornstein, 1985, 1988; Bornstein & Tamis-Lemonda, 1989, 1990) demonstrated that mothers' *responsiveness* to their infants predicted the children's cognitive performance. Bornstein (1985) reported that mother's home-based didactic inter-actions and infant's habituation during infancy, predicted language production and intelligence test scores during childhood. Bornstein and Tamis-LeMonda (1989) have replicated these findings by showing a significant prediction of rep-resentational competence of 13-month-old toddlers according to the mothers' responsiveness to their 5-month-olds. Using a structural equation modeling approach, they demonstrated that the children's representational competence was predicted by the mothers' responsiveness even after partialling out other factors such as the infants' habituation at 5 months and the mothers' noncontingent stim-ulation at 5 and 13 months.

Several studies have focused on cross-cultural comparisons. For example, in a study on Japanese infants, it was found that mothers' responsiveness to their 4- to 5-month-olds significantly predicted their scores at $1\frac{1}{2}$ years on the Peabody

Picture Vocabulary Test (PPVT, Dunn & Dunn, 1981) and on the Cattel Infant Test (Bornstein, 1989b). Bornstein and his colleagues have also reported that specific indices of child's language development were positively related to the degree to which an adult directs the child's attention to specific aspects of the environment (Tamis-LeMonda & Bornstein, 1991; Vibbert & Bornstein, 1989). American and Japanese mothers, for example, who more often encouraged their infants to focus on properties of the environmental stimuli had toddlers and older children who performed better on standardized tests of intelligence and verbal abilities (Bornstein, Miyake, & Tamis-LeMonda, 1986; Tamis-LeMonda & Bornstein, 1991). The specificity of the parent–child interactional pattern and its relationship to the child's cognitive development have also been validated cross-culturally (Bornstein, Azuma, Tamis-LeMonda, & Oginio, 1990; Wachs, Bishry, Sobhy, McCabe, Yunis, & Galal, 1992).

Several studies have established the fact that mother–child object-oriented communication during play predicted preschool IQ scores (Farran & Ramey, 1980; Olson et al., 1984; Wachs & Gruen, 1982). Shure (1987) showed that preschoolers' problem-solving skills in interpersonal areas were negatively related to maternal avoidance of communication, providing solutions, and belittling of the children's efforts. The problem solving skills were positively related to maternal efforts to guide their children, to consider alternative solutions to problems.

In several studies the effects of parent–child interactions focused on children's *metacognitive processes* rather than on intellectual skills. For example, Moss and Strayer (1990) reported that the level of metacognitive competence of gifted and nongifted children during problem solving with their mothers was related to (1) the quality of parental instruction, (2) to the extent to which the child was able to benefit from adult assistance, and (3) a relational context that allows flexible and reciprocal negotiation of roles. They also reported that the emergence of autonomous metacognitive strategies in the problem solving of gifted children was preceded by mothers' direction of their children toward metacognitive processes. However, the way in which the children demonstrated ability for self-regulation during learning served as an important clue for the mothers about how quickly to progress within the children's ZPD.

ADVANTAGES OF THE MLE MODEL

The focus of discussion in this chapter is on the effects of parent–child MLE interactions (especially mothers' interactions) as determinants of children's cognitive development and cognitive modifiability. In my opinion there are three major advantages of the concept of MLE over concepts deriving from other models:

- The MLE concept is explicitly based on philosophical assumptions about the nature of cognitive modifiability and relates to a system of beliefs about the active role of the change agents in their relationship with the developing individual.
- MLE criteria provide us with both comprehensive theoretical principles and specific operational behaviors for parent–child interactions across different domains, ages, and characteristics of children.
- Because the MLE criteria are comprehensive they allow us to include, under the same theoretical umbrella, developmental aspects of parent–child interactions, diagnostic processes, educational intervention programs, and sociocultural aspects of transfer of learning processes and value systems. These common theoretical threads and the universal features across domains allow continuity in observing parental behavior over years and much flexibility in deriving practical guidelines for applying the mediational principles.

METHODOLOGICAL ASPECTS OF THE MLE MODEL

Measurement of MLE Processes

The research reported here is based on the OMI (Klein, 1988, 1996; Klein & Aloni, 1993; Klein, Weider, & Greenspan, 1987). Parent–child interactions are videotaped and then analyzed by trained observers. The MLE criteria were operationalized in terms of the specific behaviors that they represent. Klein (1988) preferred to assess the quality of mother–child interaction by a *macroanalytic* rather than by a *microanalytic* approach. The macroanalytic approach is characterized by observation of a whole event rather than a specific detailed behavior extracted from the situation. For example, when a parent *focused* the child's attention on some aspects of a stimulus (handing a toy to a child), it was coded as a behavior reflecting *focusing* (Intentionality and Reciprocity) only if it was reciprocated by the child's response. Whenever the parent made an attempt to generalize a rule, suggest a concept, or a principle that goes beyond the concrete situation, it was coded as *expanding* (Mediation of Transcendence), regardless of the specific content being conveyed. *The basis of the observation system was an interaction "event" which might contain one or more MLE criteria.* Klein (1988) argued that previous attempts to measure mother–child interactions (e.g., Clarke-Stuart, 1973, 1991; Yarrow, Rubenstein, & Pedersen, 1975) "do not offer clear understanding of which behaviors occurring during parent–child interaction represent necessary and sufficient conditions for learning experience" (p. 56).

The advantages of the MLE molar observational approach are its allowance of the identification of meaningful patterns of continuity in parents' behavior across a developmental dimension. A similar idea was mentioned by Sroufe (1995) who argued that understanding of continuity in child development is not characterized by mere additions of behavioral components but rather on transformations and epigenesis. The qualitative characteristics of the MLE observation approach allow comparison of similarities in behavioral patterns across time. This approach coincides with other patterns such as emphasis on holism and the need to look at the meaning of behaviors within a psychological context rather than as isolated behaviors (Santostefano, 1978; Sroufe & Waters, 1977).

One of the basic assumptions behind the OMI is that observation of MLE processes in a seminatural experimental context reflects the spontaneous MLE processes at home. This assumption was supported in several studies of Klein and colleagues (i.e., Klein, 1988, 1996; Klein & Aloni, 1993; Klein, Weider, & Greenspan, 1987). It should be noted that administering the OMI requires an intensive training of 25 to 35 hours and is always accompnied by videotaping the parent–child or child–child interaction. There are some disadvantages of using the OMI such as overlapping of some of the MLE criteria, in spite of efforts to operationalize the coding system and create mutually exclusive categories.

While Klein's studies with infants focused on situations such as bathing, feeding, and playing, in Tzuriel's studies with kindergarten and school-age children, the MLE interactions were sampled in two distinct situations: *free play* and *structured*. These contexts were hypothesized to represent typical and major parent–child interactions (Tzuriel, 1996). Similar distinction between these two contexts was made earlier by Vygotsky (1978; van Geert, 1994; Valsiner, 1984, 1987; Wertsch, 1984). Vygotsky distinguished between two sources of ZPD: *play* and *instruction*. In play, children create their own ZPD and corresponding level of potential development. On the other hand, in the context of instruction, a competent goal-oriented adult extends the boundaries of the child's ZPD by mediating cognitive functions, operations, or some content to the child. In terms of the MLE theory the adult is intentionally employing transcendent rules to develop the child's cognitive structures.

In Tzuriel's studies (e.g., Tzuriel, 1999b) dyads of parents and children (mostly mothers) were videotaped during *free play* and/or *structured* situations and analyzed later by the OMI. Each mother and her child were videotaped in a seminatural context of an adjunct room of the kindergarten, or in the child's home; both places were familiar to the children and their mothers. A video camera was placed in one corner of the room and focused on a prearranged area of a table and two chairs where the mother and child were invited to sit. The mother and child were told that the study is about "how mothers and children play and learn together." The same person who remained in the background without interfering in was responsible for videotaping for each study in all cases.

In the free play condition, which took 15 minutes, sets of games and play materials were placed on the table: (1) magnetic board with letters, (2) children's picture books and games, (3) Tricky Fingers game (sequencing colored beads according to a model), (4) the Monkey Face game (fitting cards with monkey faces according to color and direction), (5) puzzles of 20 pieces each, (6) the Figure Construction game (constructing a figure from blocks according to models on cards), (7) Numbers Dominoes, and (8) a plate with cookies. The only instruction direction in this free play situation was to the mother: "you can do whatever you want with your child in the next 15 minutes, try to do what you are used to doing at home."

The structured situation, which also took 15 minutes, followed immediately after the free play situation. In this condition, the mother–child dyad was given two problem-solving tasks which the mother had to teach her child. The first task was composed of analogical problems similar to those used in the CATM (Tzuriel & Klein, 1985, 1990), or the CITM (Tzuriel, 1989b, 1992b). The second task was composed of two problems from the Picture Arrangement subscale of the WPPSI. It should be emphasized that while the tasks were explained to the mothers no directions were given as to how to teach the child. During explanation the child was playing in another corner of the room and was not exposed to the task explanation. When the mother understood the tasks she was instructed to work with the child on solving them.

Materials used with kindergartners differed from those used in studies with infants and were adapted for the kindergarten age. Two observers were trained to analyze the videotapes. This training took about 25–35 hours and included other analyses of mother–child interactions that were not included in the sample.

Reliability of the OMI with Infants and Toddlers

Interrater reliability of the MLE total score and of each category was reported in previous studies on mothers of a low-SES population and infants from 4 to 36 months in the United States (Klein, Weider, & Greenspan, 1987) and of Israeli mothers and infants from 6 to 24 months (Klein, 1988). The reliability coefficients ranged between .42 and .93 in the various studies. Intercorrelations between mothers' MLE behaviors over time (when children were 6, 12, 24, and 36 months) averaged .53. The reliability of the OMI was investigated with a group of Israeli mothers and their 3- and 4-year olds; all categories exceeded .87 (Klein & Aloni, 1993).

Reliability of the OMI with Kindergarten and School-Age Children

The reliability coefficients of five studies by Tzuriel and colleagues with kindergartners to second graders are shown in Table 8.1. In one of the studies (Tzuriel et al., 1998) the reliability coefficients are based on observations of teachers interacting with small group of children in the kindergarten. This study

Table 8.1. Reliability Coefficient of MLE Criteria and MLE-Total Scores

MLE criteria	Tzuriel & Ernst (1990)	Tzuriel & Weiss (1998a)	Tzuriel, Kaniel, Zeliger, Friedman, & Haywood (1998)	Tzuriel & Weitz (1998)	Tzuriel & Gerafy (1998)	Shamir & Tzuriel (1999)
Intentionality and Reciprocity	.54	.42	.75**	.95***	.90***	.97***
Meaning	.85**	.73*	.78**	.86**	.85***	.92**
Transcendence	.80**	.83**	.98***	.86**	.53	.97**
Feelings of Competence	.87**	.94***	.80**	.86**	.58	.98**
Regulation of Behavior	.55	.85**	.81**	.95***	.83	.98***
MLE-Total	.93***	.93***	.94***	.85**	.72	.97**

will be discussed later (Chapter 9) in regard to the effects of the Bright Start program on use of mediation by teachers. In another study (Shamir & Tzuriel, 1999) the reliability coefficients are based on observation of peer mediation where third graders mediated to their peers in first grade, using a multimedia program.

The reliability coefficients for young children are very similar to those reported by Klein (1988) for infants. Taking into account the relatively small samples (n = 10) upon which reliability was based in each study, we felt them to be satisfactory.

MEASUREMENT OF COGNITIVE MODIFIABILITY WITH DA INSTRUMENTS

As mentioned above (see Chapter 3), an integrative component of the MLE approach is related to the conceptualization of the developing individual as an open system that is modified by mediating agents (Feuerstein et al., 1979). The conceptualization behind using change criteria as predicted outcome of parent–child interaction is that measures of modifiability are more closely related to mediational processes by which the child is taught how to process information, than they are to static measures of intelligence. The mediational strategies used within the DA procedure naturally matched learning processes in other life contexts more than do conventional static methods and therefore give better indications about future changes of cognitive structures.

Accumulating evidence from educational research provides indications that a score reflecting individual differences in "modifiability" adds substantially to the predictive power of learning in an unrelated program (Embretson, 1992; Guthke & Stein, 1996). The "modifiability" score predicted better than static tests future academic success of young children (Tzuriel, 2000c; Tzuriel et al., 1998), or assignment to special education programs (Samuels et al., 1992). DA measures were found to be efficient in testing theoretical issues such as the effects of MLE processes on learning abilities, the role of specific contexts and of parental and child variables in modifying these effects. The use of both DA and static psychometric measures allows comparison of the relationship of MLE criteria with both types of measures. In all of the studies carried out by Tzuriel and his colleagues, attempts were made to measure the children's *cognitive modifiability* using a DA approach.

One of the problems raised frequently in studying the relation of DA measures to other variables concerns the nature of change scores. Since the starting point of individuals is typically different, equal pre- to postmediation change cannot be considered to be equal. It is much more difficult for individuals to change in the higher range of performance than in the lower range. One of the possible solutions is to analyze DA data by a hierarchical regression analysis. The hierarchical regression analysis seems to be most adequate since the prediction of a child's Post-Teaching (high ZPD level) score by MLE criteria is estimated in a second step after it has been explained by the Pre-Teaching (low ZPD level) score. In other words, the *residual variance* of the Post-Teaching score predicted by the mother–child MLE interactions, after being "washed out" from the initial cognitive performance, reflects the "pure" variance that can be explained by mediation effects within the DA testing situation. This analysis might provide an important indication of the effects of mothers' mediational strategies to the children's cognitive modifiability.

Another procedure developed in several studies is the use of Post-Teaching residual scores (Tzuriel et al., 1999). The residual Post-Teaching scores are based on a regression analysis of the Post- by the Pre-Teaching score of the same parallel test. This procedure was developed to resolve some psychometric difficulties with measurement of gain and interpretation of change scores in different initial ability groups (Bereiter, 1963; Cronbach & Furby, 1970; Embretson, 1992). The residual Post-Teaching score can be considered as an indication of cognitive modifiability since it reflects the child's Post-Teaching performance after controlling for the initial Pre-Teaching performance.

A comprehensive venue for data analysis used in few studies is structural equation modeling (SEM) analysis. The use of SEM for the validation of MLE theory seems to be a promising approach since we can design complex models and infer causal relations among variables without having to use experimental designs. Also the nature of the variables involved in testing the theory are not always given to experimental manipulations, and the accumulated effects that several variables have on outcome variables are not easily given to manipulation simultaneously. The holistic approach used in SEM contributes to understanding of the conceptual whole more than the sum of fragmentary separate analyses.

MLE RESEARCH WITH INFANTS AND TODDLERS

One of the major issues regarding MLE theory is the hypothesized effect of MLE interactions on development of learning skills. Klein and colleagues carried out most studies with infants (e.g., Klein et al., 1987). They found that for a group of infants the amount of mediation that parents gave with their infants was more strongly related to the children's cognitive development than were commonly used measures of early cognitive performance. Klein and colleagues' findings reveal, in general, that 10 minutes of observation of MLE interactions when the children were 12 months old could predict the children's cognitive performance at 48 months of age. Furthermore, different MLE criteria have emerged as dominant predictors at different ages.

The quality of mother–child interactions was also found to be a strong predictor of the cognitive ability of very low birth weight (VLBW) subjects. Klein, Raziel, Brish, and Birnbaum (1987) reported significant prediction for several cognitive measures, whereas no significant correlations were found between birth weight and the same cognitive measures. In two subsequent studies the VLBW children and their parents were assigned to an experimental or a control group. Parents in the experimental group participated in an MLE intervention program for 7 months. Parents were taught how to mediate to their children in different settings. In the first study carried out 1 year after the intervention (Klein, 1991), the quality of MLE in parent–child interactions of the experimental parents was higher than that of the control parents. No significant effects were found, however, for quality of MLE on the children's cognitive scores. In the second study (Klein, 1991) the parent–child MLE interactions and the children's cognitive performance were studied again 3 years after the intervention. Parents in the experimental condition showed higher rates of mediation on all five MLE criteria than did those in the comparison group. Follow-up after 1 to 3 years revealed that mediated Feelings of Competence was the only MLE criterion on which significantly higher scores were obtained after 3 years than after 1 year. Higher scores on cognitive measures were found 3 years later in the experimental than in the control group, although this difference was significant on only one measure, the PPVT (Dunn & Dunn, 1981).

In another intervention study, Klein and Aloni (1993) investigated the immediate and sustained effects of maternal mediating behavior on young children's mediation and cognitive performance. The intervention was carried out in the mothers' homes by mediators who visited the homes for 1 hour weekly, over a period of 7 months. The intervention included explanation of the MLE criteria, videotaping and playback of mothers' interactions with their children followed by focusing on the mediational strategies, and demonstration of mediational principles. The findings indicated that the mothers' MLE behavior could be modified, and that once modified it was sustained over several years. What is more important to our discussion is the finding of a relationship between MLE and improvements in the children's cognitive performance. The experimental group scored higher than the control group on the PPVT, Auditory Reception, and Auditory Association measures. There was also an effect on the children's mediating behavior, especially on the criteria of Meaning and Feelings of Competence.

MLE RESEARCH WITH KINDERGARTEN AND SCHOOL-AGE CHILDREN

The studies carried out with kindergarten (5–6 years old) and school-age children (Grades 1 and 2) were aimed at validating the MLE theory regarding the relationship between mother–child MLE interactions and children's cognitive modifiability as measured by DA procedures. Another objective was to identify *specific* MLE criteria that best predict cognitive modifiability. An attempt has been made to relate specific MLE criteria with cognitive change in specific cognitive domains, specific contexts of interactions between parents and children, and specific child and parent characteristics. Based on the specificity conception of parents–children interactions (Wachs, 1992) I believe that the differential prediction of the child's performance in different cognitive domains by different MLE criteria further elaborates and validates the MLE theory.

In some studies the focus was on the relative contribution of distal and proximal factors as predictors of cognitive modifiability (Tzuriel & Ernst, 1990; Tzuriel & Hatzir, 1999; Tzuriel & Weiss, 1998a). In other studies the focus was on comparison of prediction patterns as a function of situation (free play versus structured; Tzuriel, 1996), or of children's variables (e.g., birth weight, age, gender, ethnic origin; Tzuriel & Eran, 1990; Tzuriel & Hatzir, 1999; Tzuriel & Weitz, 1998; Tzuriel, Yehudai, & Kaniel, 1994). In all studies the same observation technique of the OMI was used with some adaptations for age as required, and a DA approach using Tzuriel's measures (see Chapter 6).

The major findings reported below are briefly summarized in Table 8.2, and discussed later in detail. The findings relate to five main topics:

- Prediction of children's cognitive modifiability by mother–child MLE strategies
- Relative prediction of cognitive modifiability by distal and proximal factors
- The relation between distal factors and mother–child MLE strategies
- Prediction of cognitive modifiability in high risk groups
- Prediction of children's cognitive modifiability by MLE interactions in free play versus structured situations.

Table 8.2. Summary of Studies on Prediction of Children's Cognitive Modifiability by Mother—Child MLE Interactions

Study	Sample characteristics			Distal factors	Tests	Analysis method	Major findings
	Grade	Social Background	n				
Tzuriel & Eran (1990)	K 2	Kibbutz	47		CITM CPM	Stepwise regression	• Preteaching score was predicted by CPM • Postteaching score was predicted by CPM and MLE-Total • Gain score was predicted only by MLE-Total • Transcendence was higher with older than with younger siblings
Tzuriel & Ernst (1990)	K	Low SES Medium SES High SES	16 16 16	1. SES 2. Mothers' IQ	CATM CPM	SEM	• Postteaching score was predicted by Transcendence • Preteaching score was predicted by mediation for Meaning • No distal factor predicted Postteaching score • Distal factors predicted MLE criteria
Tzuriel (1996)	K	Low SES Medium SES High SES	48		CATM	Stepwise regression	• Postteaching score was predicted by MLE-Total in *Structured* situation • Postteaching score was predicted by Mediation for Competence in Structured situation
Tzuriel & Weiss (1998a)	2	Middle SES	54	1. Mothers' acceptance rejection 2. Child's personality	CITM	SEM hierarchical regression	• Postteaching score was predicted by mediations for Transcendence and Self-Regulation • No distal factor predicted Postteaching score • Distal factors predicted MLE criteria • No factor predicted Preteaching score • Postteaching score was predicted by MLE-Total in Structured situation
Tzuriel, Kaniel & Yehudai (1994)	K	Ethiopian Immigrants	20	Cultural difference	CITM CPM	ANOVA Stepwise Regression	• Children of high-mediating mothers improved their CPM scores from Pre- to Postteaching phase more than children of medium- and low-mediating mothers • MLE-Total did not predict Preteaching or Postteaching of CITM scores

Table 8.2. *Continued*

Study	Sample characteristics			Distal factors	Tests	Analysis method	Major findings
	Grade	Social Background	n				
Tzuriel & Weitz (1998)	K-3	Very low Birth weight	26	Birth weight	CATM Complex Figure	Hierarchical Regression	• CATM Postteaching score was predicted by mother's mediation for Transcendence
		Normal birth Weight	26		VMI Draw-a-Person		• CATM Postteaching score was predicted by children's mediation for Transcendence
							• Mediation for Intentionality and Reciprocity predicted *positively* the CATM Postteaching score among NBW children but *negatively* among VLBW children
							• Complex Figure Postteaching score was predicted by mediation for Transcendence
Tzuriel & Hatzir (1999)	K	Low SES	20	Time parents spend with children	CATM Complex Figure	Hierarchical Regression Stepwise regression	• Postteaching. Scores were predicted by parents mediation for Intentionality & Reciprocity and Transcendence
		Medium SES	20		CPM Vocabulary		• Time parents send with children did not predict cognitive modifiability
		High SES	20	SES level	(WISC-R)		• Mothers mediated more than fathers on Meaning and Feelings of Competence
							• Prediction of cognitive modifiability by mothers' MLE is higher with low than with high-functioning children
							• Prediction of cognitive modifiability by fathers' MLE is higher with low than with high SES children set only this role

Note: Modified with permission from *Genetic, Social, and General Psychology Monographs, 125,* 109–156 (the findings of Tzuriel & Hatzir, 1999, have been added to the original table).
CITM, Children's Inferential Thinking Modifiability; CATM, Children's Analogical Thinking Modifiability; CPM, Colored Progressive Matrices; VMI, Visual Motor Integration.

Prediction of Children's Cognitive Modifiability by Mother–Child MLE Strategies

One of the major findings replicated in almost all studies was that children's Post-Teaching scores on DA measures were better predicted by MLE mother–child interactions than static test scores or Pre-Teaching scores of DA measures (which actually are static measures). In our first study (Tzuriel & Eran, 1990) a sample of kibbutz mother–child dyads ($n = 47$) were observed in a free play situation for 20 minutes. The young children (22 boys and 25 girls, age range = 4:7 to 7:8 years) were then administrated the RCPM (Raven, 1956) and the (CITM) test. In order to study the prediction of cognitive performance by mother–child MLE interactions we used a stepwise regression analysis procedure. Three stepwise regression analyses were carried out, in each analysis the RCPM and MLE-Total scores were assigned as predictors of either the CITM Pre-Teaching, CITM-Post-Teaching, and CITM-Gain score. The findings revealed that the CITM Pre-Teaching (static) was predicted only by the RCPM ($R = .40$; $p < .004$), the CITM Post-Teaching was predicted by both MLE-Total and RCPM ($R = .69$; $p < .002$), and the CITM Gain was predicted only by the MLE-Total score ($R = .43$; $p < .001$).

In order to study the pattern of prediction across the three analyses, one should analyze the nature of the predicted variables. The CITM Pre-Teaching score was predicted only by the RCPM scores (first analysis), as both tests are actually conventional-static tests. This result verifies what is commonly known among psychometricians, that the common variance of two cognitive tests is higher than the common variance of a cognitive test with an observed behavior (i.e., MLE mother–child interactions).

The CITM Post-Teaching score (second analysis) seems to be composed of two components: the previously acquired inferential skills as manifested in children's CITM Pre-Teaching performance and what has been learned as a result of mediation given by the examiner within the teaching phase. It is plausible to assume that the first component (Post-Teaching score) is attributed to the RCPM score, and the second component (Post-Teaching score) to the mother–child MLE score. When the Gain score (third analysis) was taken as the criterion predicted variable, only the mother–child MLE score emerged as a significant predictive variable. The progression of the predictability pattern across the three regression analyses is quite intriguing as it shows that *the higher the criterion score saturated with teaching effects, within the testing DA procedure, the higher was the variance contributed by MLE mother–child interaction.*

An interesting finding in this study was related to the comparison of older to younger siblings. Ten children of the whole sample had one brother or sister within the sample, thus creating 10 pairs of siblings. Paired t-tests carried out for each MLE category revealed that mothers used more mediation for

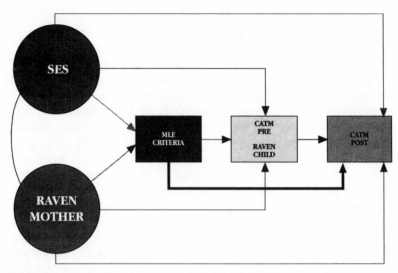

Figure 8.1. A schematic SEM analysis of the effects of distal and proximal factors on cognitive modifiability (Tzuriel & Ernst, 1990). (Reproduced by permission from *International Journal of Mediated Learning and Cognitive Education, 1*, 119–135.)

Transcendence (i.e., teaching of rules and principles) in interactions with older than with younger siblings (t (9) = 2.44, $p < .02$). It seems that mothers intuitively felt that their older children are mature and therefore prepared for transcendent mediation more than with their young children.

A more sophisticated data analysis was applied in two other studies on different samples of kindergartners (Tzuriel & Ernst, 1990) and second graders (Tzuriel & Weiss, 1998a). In each study we used a different DA measure (the CATM and CITM) and a different set of predictive distal factors (SES and Mothers' IQ in one, and mother's acceptance/rejection attitudes and child's personality in the second). In both studies we used a SEM to test a theoretical model of the effects of distal and proximal factors on cognitive modifiability. The SEM analysis is considered in the literature to support causal inferences (Joreskog & Sorbom, 1984). Figures 8.1 and 8.2 respectively present the schematic model of the study and the empirical findings of the first study (Tzuriel & Ernst, 1990). Figures 8.3 and 8.4 respectively present the schematic model and the empirical findings of the second study (Tzuriel & Weiss, 1998a). The relative effects of the distal and proximal factors will be discussed in the next section. In this section we will focus on the specific MLE criteria that predict cognitive modifiability.

In the first study (Tzuriel & Ernst, 1990) a sample of kindergartners (n = 48) were given the CATM test and RCPM tests prior to observation of the mother–

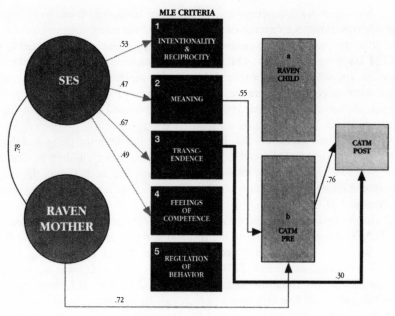

Figure 8.2. Empirical findings of the effects of distal and proximal factors on cognitive modifiability (Tzuriel & Ernst, 1990). (Reproduced by permission from *The Journal of Mediated Learning and Cognitive Education, 1*, 119–135.)

child MLE interactions. The sample was composed of children of high, medium, and low SES; there were 16 children in each SES level. The mother–child interactions were videotaped in two distinct situations, free play and structured (see description in methodological section above) and analyzed later by the OMI.

The findings showed that the MLE criterion of *Transcendence* predicted the CATM Post-Teaching score whereas the MLE criterion of *Meaning* predicted the CATM Pre-Teaching score. The RCPM score (static) did not predicted the child's Post-Teaching score. These findings were explained by referring to the nature of both the specific MLE criteria and the specific cognitive task in each testing phase. *Mediation for Meaning*, which involves labeling of information, was crucial for first encounters with information such as the analogies presented to children in the CATM Pre-Teaching phase. This result supports the idea that the children whose mothers used high a level of mediation for Meaning (e.g., characterized mainly by labeling of objects) internalized this specific mechanism of mediation and therefore performed better on the CATM Pre-Teaching phase. The initial performance on the CATM task requires labeling of the major dimensions, hence the importance of mothers' mediation for meaning.

Mediation for Transcendence, on the other hand, was found to be important when performance depends on learning of abstract rules, cognitive strategies, and principles such as those taught in the Teaching phase and later tested in the CATM Teaching phase. Thus, children whose mothers used a high level of mediation for Transcendence internalized this specific mechanism and used it later in other learning contexts where they needed this type of mediation. These results support the *specificity* (Wachs, 1992) of the MLE criteria as predictors of cognitive outcomes.

Tzuriel and Weiss (1998a, b) reported similar findings using a different DA measure—the CITM—and a different sample—older children in Grade 2 (n = 54). Two types of analyses were used to study the prediction of the cognitive modifiability by the mother–child MLE interaction: a hierarchical regression analysis and SEM.

In the first analysis Tzuriel and Weiss (1998b) controlled the variance of the Pre-Teaching score and used the residual variance as predictor of the Post-Teaching score. The first step predictor was the CITM Pre-Teaching (which can be considered as the low ZPD level) and the second step was the mother's five MLE criteria. Thus, the variance contributed by the MLE interactions to the children's Post-Teaching score (which can be considered as the high ZPD after the Teaching phase given within the DA process) can be considered to be relatively "free" of the effects of initial cognitive performance. One of the advantages of using a hierarchical regression approach with DA data is that it is possible to get indications about the extent to which MLE interactions (or other variables) predict the Post-Teaching performance above and beyond the initial manifested performance. After controlling for the Pre-Teaching score, the residual variation can accurately reflect the effects of mediational criteria. In other words, the contribution of MLE to Post-Teaching, after "washing out" the Pre-Teaching effects, can reflect the "net" effect of mediation on children's cognitive modifiability.

The findings of the first step showed that 18% of the Post-Teaching score was explained by the Pre-Teaching score ($\beta = .43$, $p < .01$). In the second step, two MLE criteria have emerged as significant predictors: Regulation of Behavior ($\beta = .36$, $p < .01$) and Transcendence ($\beta = .21$, $p < .05$) in addition to the Pre-Teaching score ($\beta = .39$, $p < .01$). The three variables explained 42% of the variance and the change from the first to the second step was 24%. These findings showed clearly that the higher the mothers' mediations for *Transcendence* and *Regulation of Behavior*, the higher the change in children's cognitive performance following the mediation within the DA testing situation. The emergence of Transcendence and Regulation of Behavior as significant predictors should be explained not only by the specific MLE criteria but also by the type of the DA task given. These MLE criteria reflect a typical interaction in which the mother mediates rules and principles combined with monitoring and organizing of the child's behavior. Detailed task analysis of the CITM problems reveals that successful performance requires a systematic exploratory behavior, planning, hypothetical thinking, applications of rules, and generalization of principles. These functions are perceived to be dependent not only on adequate internalization of general mediational processes, but more specifically on self-regulatory and control of behavior and application of generalized principles and rules—processes that correspond to the mediational criteria found to be most predictive. It seems that these two MLE components, acquired during normal mother–child interactions, were assimilated by the children and equipped them with the thinking tools and learning mechanisms that are required later in other tasks and learning settings. When similar mediation for Transcendence and Control of Behavior are provided in other learning situations, these children can retrieve their previous mediational mechanisms, apply them efficiently with different tasks, and modify their cognitive structures.

The data were further analyzed using SEM analysis (Tzuriel & Weiss, 1998a), which also includes the distal factors. The schematic model is presented in Figure 8.3 and the empirical findings in Figure 8.4.

The schematic model shown in Figure 8.3 portrays all possible causal effects; the heavy line from MLE criteria to CITM Post-Teaching scores represents the main hypothesis of the MLE theory i.e., MLE processes conceived as proximal factors explain individual differences in cognitive modifiability.

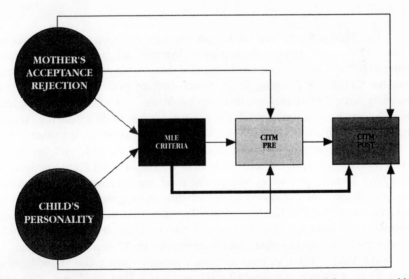

Figure 8.3. A schematic SEM analysis of the effects of distal and proximal factors on cognitive modifiability (Tzuriel & Weiss, 1998a). (Reproduced by permission from *Early Childhood and Parenting, 7,* 79–99.)

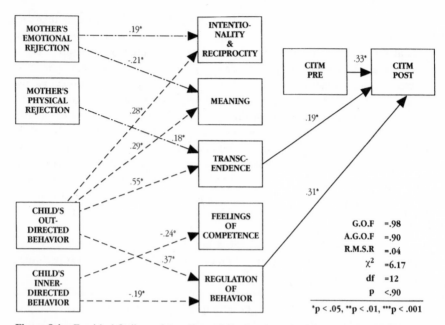

Figure 8.4. Empirical findings of the effects of distal and proximal factors on cognitive modifiability (Tzuriel & Weiss, 1998a). (Reproduced by permission from *Early Childhood and Parenting, 7*, 79–99.)

Two SEM analyses were carried out based on two theoretical models. Comparison of the two analyses allowed us to determine which of them provides a better fit to the theoretical model. In the first analysis the only outcome measure was the CITM Pre-Teaching score, which in turn predicts the CITM Post-Teaching score. In this analysis, no direct prediction of the CITM Post-Teaching by other variables was introduced. The exogenic factors of the model (i.e., factors that influence other factors but are not explained by others) were the mothers' *emotional* and *physical acceptance/rejection* attitudes and the children's *inner-* and *out-directed* behavior (see discussion in next section). The MLE criteria were the endogenic factors (i.e., factors that, on one hand, are influenced by the mothers' acceptance/rejection and children's personality factors, but on the other hand, influence the CITM Pre-Teaching score). The maximum number of paths (or *df*) amounts to 55, however, based on the MLE theory and the derived model, only 38 parameters have been estimated, which leaves us with 12 degrees of freedom.

The results of this analysis revealed a relatively low adjusted goodness of fit of .72 (root mean square residual = .11) and a χ^2 (17) of 30.39 ($p < .03$) which indicates lack of compatibility of the proposed theoretical model to the empirical model. What is important to emphasize here is that this first model did not reveal significant predictions of cognitive scores (CITM Pre-Teaching) by the mothers' MLE criteria, although the mothers' rejection/acceptance and children's personality factors explained the MLE scores. *Modification indices of the SEM, however, indicated that the model should include direct effects of MLE criteria on the CITM Post-Teaching score.*

In the second analysis, an improved model was tested according to which the CITM Post-Teaching score was predicted directly by the endogenic and exogenic factors, in addition to being predicted by the CITM Pre-Teaching score. In this analysis 43 parameters have been estimated, which leaves us with 12 degrees of freedom. The SEM results of this analysis are presented in Figure 8.4. It should be noted that for the sake of clarification only the significant effects are presented (with b = .15 or higher). The overall explained variance of the *CITM-Post-Teaching* score in the model was 44%.

It is seen in Figure 8.4 that, the CITM Post-Teaching score (representing the upper level of Vygotsky's ZPD) was significantly predicted by mediations for Transcendence and for Regulation of Behavior, whereas none of the MLE criteria predicted the CITM Pre-Teaching score (representing the lower level of Vygotsky's ZPD). It is plausible to assume that the performance on the CITM Post-Teaching is composed of two components: (1) learning of principles, rules, and strategies of problem solving and (2) the initial performance on the CITM test. Thus, the first component of the children's performance on the CITM Post-Teaching was explained mainly by the mothers' mediations for Transcendence and Regulation of Behavior, both reflect a typical MLE interaction in which the mother is involved in mediating rules and principles and monitoring the flow of the children's behavior. Detailed task analysis of the CITM problems reveals that successful performance requires a systematic exploratory behavior, planning, hypothetical thinking, applications of rules, and generalization of principles. These functions are perceived to be dependent not only on adequate internalization of general mediational processes, but more specifically on self-regulatory and control of behavior and application of generalized principles and rules— processes that correspond to the mediational criteria found to be most predictive. It seems that these two MLE components, acquired during normal mother–child interactions, were assimilated by the children and equipped them with the thinking tools and mechanisms that are required later in other tasks and learning settings. When similar mediation for Transcendence and Regulation of Behavior are provided in other learning situations, these children can retrieve their previous mediational experiences, apply them efficiently with different tasks, and modify their cognitive structures. The second component that explained the CITM Post-Teaching score was the initial performance on the very same test given before the teaching phase.

The importance of mediation for Transcendence in predicting children's cognitive modifiability has emerged in two other studies on young children

(Tzuriel & Hatzir, 1999; Tzuriel & Weitz, 1998). In the first study, Tzuriel and Weitz (1998) investigated the effects of mother–child MLE interactions on children's cognitive modifiability in a group of VLBW ($n = 26$) and normally birth weight (NBW; $n = 30$). All children were in regular education and were observed interacting with their mothers at the age of 5–8 years. The children were administered several standardized tests as well as DA tests (the CATM and the Complex Figure). A hierarchical regression analysis was used in which MLE scores predicted the children's cognitive modifiability after controlling for the Pre-Teaching and Group (VLBW versus NBW) variables. The findings for mothers MLE showed that in Step 1 (of the hierarchical regression analysis) the CATM Pre-Teaching score predicted 38% of the variance ($\beta = .62$, $p < .001$). In Step 2 the variable of Group was introduced, but it did not add significantly ($\beta = .17$) to the prediction. In Step 3, where all five MLE criteria entered the equation, only Mediation for Transcendence emerged as a significant predictor ($\beta = .21$) of the Post-Teaching score. In other words, the findings showed that after controlling for the Pre-Teaching and Group variables, the Post-Teaching scores were significantly predicted by Mediation for Transcendence. These findings were repeated with both the CATM and the Complex Figure. Further results of this study are discussed in the next-to-last section in relation to the effects of MLE on cognitive modifiability with high-risk groups.

An important question raised recently concerns the effects of parental mediation strategies on children's cognitive modifiability among mothers versus fathers and among sons versus daughters (Tzuriel & Hatzir, 1999). The effect of gender of parent and child was investigated with a sample of 60 kindergartners (30 boys and 30 girls) who were drawn from 61 kindergartens. In order to control for parent–child-rearing experience, all children were the firstborn in families of no more than two children. Each child participated in two sessions one with father and one with mother (each session was composed of free play and structured conditions). The sessions were videotaped and analyzed using the OMI (Klein, 1988). The order of the two situations as well as the order of father-first or mother-first interactions were counterbalanced. The children were administered the following tests sequentially: Vocabulary (WISC-R), RCPM, CATM, and Complex Figure. Dynamic tests were given after static tests to avoid teaching effects on static tests.

In the first step of analyses children's cognitive modifiability indices were computed using a regression analysis in which the Post-Teaching residual score of the DA test was taken after controlling for the Pre-Teaching effect. Stepwise regression analyses were then used (one for each parent) where the criterion variables were the residual Post-Teaching scores (of the CATM and the Complex Figure) and the predicting variables were the MLE criteria of mothers and fathers. The findings showed that mothers' mediation for Transcendence and Intentionality and Reciprocity significantly predicted children's cognitive modifiability as indexed by two different measures, the CATM (Method 2 of scoring) ($R^2 = .33$) and the Complex Figure (Accuracy + Location score) ($R^2 = .27$). Comparison of prediction pattern of fathers' mediation to mothers' mediation revealed a similar pattern for both parents. Fathers' mediation for Transcendence and Intentionality and Reciprocity significantly predicted children's cognitive modifiability as measured by the Complex Figure (Accuracy + Location score) ($R^2 = .27$). On the CATM (Method 2 of scoring) only mediation for Transcendence predicted children's cognitive modifiability ($R^2 = .18$).

The relationship between MLE interactions and children's cognitive ability was also studied by Zambrana-Ortiz and Lidz (1995) on a sample of Puerto Rican Head Start preschool children using static tests. Each child–parent dyad was videotaped in free play and structured teaching situations. The interactions were analyzed later using Lidz's (1991) MLE Rating Scale. The children's cognitive performance was tested with Spanish versions of the PPVT-R (Dunn & Dunn, 1981) and the Vineland Adaptive Behavior Scale (Sparrow, Balla, & Cicchetti, 1984). The results showed significant correlations between total and specific MLE scores and children's cognitive performance. The authors did not suggest explanations for the observed relationship between specific MLE criteria and total or specific subscales of the PPVT-R and the Vineland Adaptive Behavior Scale.

All studies clearly indicate (see also Table 8.2) that from all mediation criteria, Mediation for Transcendence has emerged as the most powerful predictor of cognitive modifiability. The findings support the hypothesis that mother–child mediations were internalized and used later on in other learning contexts.

The generalizability of these findings should be taken with some caution as they might reflect, at least partially, the compatibility between task characteristics and the context of mother–child mediation. In all studies the DA tests used (CATM, Complex Figure, and CITM) require mental strategies and cognitive functions that are similar to the MLE strategies that the mothers used in their interactions within the structured situation. One would like to know whether different MLE criteria would evolve as predictive in different situations or as a function of the specific domain tested.

Relative Prediction of Cognitive Modifiability by Distal and Proximal Factors

The relative prediction of children's cognitive modifiability by distal and proximal factors was examined in three studies (Tzuriel & Ernst, 1990; Tzuriel & Hatzir, 1999; Tzuriel & Weiss, 1998a) using different DA measures and different ages. In two studies the SEM analysis was applied, in each study, however, a different set of distal factors was used. The overall findings of these studies indicate clearly that the children's Post-Teaching scores were predicted only by

the proximal factor of parent–child MLE scores whereas the distal factors predicted none of the children's Post-Teaching scores.

The main hypothesis of the studies was that MLE interaction, as a proximal factor, has direct effect on the child's cognitive performance, especially on
indices of cognitive modifiability and that distal factors will not explain the cognitive factors. The schematic model and the findings of the first study (Tzuriel &
Ernst, 1990) are presented in Figures 8.1 and 8.2. The schematic model in Figure
8.1 depicts all possible influences of distal factors (Mothers' IQ and SES Level)
on proximal factors (five MLE criteria) and the effects of both the distal and proximal factors on children's CATM Pre- and Post-Teaching scores. The sample consisted of mothers from low, medium, and high SES groups and their children who
were at kindergarten age ($n = 48$). Each mother–child dyad was videotaped while
interacting in two separate conditions, free play and structured. The interactions
were analyzed later using Klein's (1988) OMI. The children were given RCPM
(Raven, 1956) and the CATM, the latter being a DA measure.

The data were analyzed using SEM with a LISREL approach (Joreskog &
Sorbom, 1984). The findings show that the CATM Post-Teaching score was
explained by Mediation for Transcendence whereas none of the distal factors used
(Mothers' SES and Mothers' IQ) explained the children's Post-Teaching scores
(see Figure 8.2). It is interesting to note here that the RCPM score (static) was
found to be isolated from the rest of the variables—it was not predicted or predict
other variables in the model. The findings related to the effects of distal on proximal factors will be discussed in the next section.

In the second study (Tzuriel & Weiss, 1998a) on a sample of second graders
($n = 54$), the main dependent variables were the Pre-Teaching and Post-Teaching
scores of the CITM. The findings of this study show (see Figure 8.4) that the
Post-Teaching scores were explained by two of the MLE criteria (Transcendence
and Regulation of Behavior) whereas none of the distal factors explained the Post-
Teaching scores (or the Pre-Teaching scores). The effects of the distal factors on
the proximal factors (MLE interactions) will be discussed separately in the next
section. The finding of both studies confirm the hypothesis that the proximal
factors (MLE processes) predict children's cognitive modifiability whereas the
distal factors did not predict children's cognitive modifiability.

An intriguing issue studied recently was the MLE patterns of mothers and
fathers toward their sons and daughters and the differential effects of both on
children's cognitive modifiability (Tzuriel & Hatzir, 1999). The prediction of children's cognitive modifiability by fathers' and mothers' mediation was discussed
in an earlier section. The focus of the present discussion is on the relative effects
of distal and proximal factors on cognitive modifiability. In this specific study
the distal factors under investigation were the *parents' gender, SES level,* and
the amount of time parents spend with their children during the week. The SES
level was composed of a score based on parents' level of occupation, years of

education, and area of living. The parents were either low, middle, or high SES, 20 subjects in each. All parents received the Time Budget Questionnaire (Katz, 1992) to measure the amount of time each parent was either present or in some activity with his or her child during the last 2 days and the last weekend. As previously mentioned in detail the children's cognitive modifiability was computed first as the residual of the CATM Post-Teaching score after controlling for the variance contributed by the CATM Pre-Teaching score.

In order to test the relative effects of distal and proximal factors a hierarchical regression approach was carried out with the children's cognitive modifiability index (computed previously) as the criterion variable. The hierarchical regression included five steps. In the first and second steps of the regression the children's initial intellectual level (measured by the Vocabulary subscale from WISC-R and the RCPM) and SES level were introduced in that order. In the third step the time budget variable entered the equation. In the fourth step the fathers and mothers MLE-Total scores entered, and in the fifth step the interactions of MLE by Children's Intellectual Level and MLE by SES Level were introduced.

Two hierarchical analyses were carried out, one for the CATM and one for the Complex Figure test. The findings on the CATM test showed that in the first and second steps the RCPM ($\beta = .32$, $p < .05$) and the SES level ($\beta = .27$, $p < .05$) contributed significantly to the prediction of cognitive modifiability. The time budget variable did not enter the equation in the third step. As expected, in the fourth step, mothers' MLE-Total was significantly predicting the children's cognitive modifiability ($\beta = .22$, $p < .05$). In the fifth step, there is an interaction of Fathers' MLE by Children's Intellectual Level ($\beta = -.36$, $p < .01$). The meaning of this interaction is that the lower the children's intellectual level the higher they benefit from fathers' mediation. The total variance of all factors that explain individual differences in cognitive modifiability in the last step was 32%.

The hierarchical regression analysis of the cognitive modifiability on the Complex Figure revealed similar results to those found for the CATM. In the first and second steps the RCPM ($\beta = .33$, $p < .05$) and the SES level ($\beta = .24$, $p < .05$) contributed significantly to the prediction of cognitive modifiability. In the third step the time budget variable contributed negatively to the prediction of cognitive modifiability ($\beta = -.23$, $p < .01$). This last result is related to the fact that mothers of low SES spend more time with their children than mothers of high SES. In the fourth step both mothers' MLE-Total ($\beta = .21$, $p < .05$) and fathers' MLE-Total ($\beta = .36$, $p < .05$) were significantly predicting the children's cognitive modifiability. In the fifth step, an interaction of Mothers' MLE by Children's Intellectual Level ($\beta = -.40$, $p < .01$) predicted the children's cognitive modifiability. The meaning of this interaction is that the lower the children's intellectual level the higher they benefit from mothers' mediation. The total variance of all factors that explain individual differences in cognitive modifiability in the last step was 49%. The findings of Tzuriel and Hatzir (1999) support strongly the idea that the distal factor of time parents spend with their children is not sufficient to explain children's cognitive modifiability. The strongest factor was as expected the parents' mediation, both that of fathers and of mothers. It seems that the role of fathers in developing their children's cognitive modifiability and learning skills is no less important than the mothers' role. Also, it is important to note that the lower the child's intellectual level the higher is the impact of the parent's mediation in determining the child's cognitive modifiability.

In conclusion, the results of the analyses comparing distal and proximal factors validate the MLE theory. The proximal factors (i.e., MLE processes) explained individual differences in children's cognitive functioning, whereas the distal factors (i.e., SES level, child's personality, mother's rejection/acceptance, time parents spend with their children) did not have a direct effect on children's cognitive factors.

These findings are interpreted as indicating the hypothesized close relationship between adults' mediation and their children's *ZPD* upper level (Vygotsky, 1978)—indicated by the Post-Teaching score. These findings also validate what both Vygotskian researchers and Feuerstein's DA-approach followers have argued (Tzuriel, 1992a), namely, that the initial cognitive performance of a child does not often reveal the child's potential, i.e., his or her ability to modify cognitive structures. The specificity of the differential predictions (Wachs, 1992) of the children's Pre- and Post-Teaching scores in different tasks by different criteria, further validates the MLE theory as well as the efficiency of the DA approach in developmental studies.

The Relation between Distal Factors and Mother–Child MLE Strategies

The study of the relation between distal and proximal factors is not directly related to our discussion of DA, but because of its relevance to the MLE theory and explanatory importance, it was decided to discuss the topic here. The relation between distal factors and mother–child MLE interactions was examined four studies (including the two SEM studies reported above). The variables selected to represent distal factors were mother's SES and IQ (Tzuriel & Ernst, 1990), mother's acceptance/rejection attitudes toward the child and the child's personality characteristics (Tzuriel & Weiss, 1998a), cultural background and cultural task-orientation (Tzuriel, Kaniel, & Yehudai, 1994), and time parents spend with their children. The findings in general revealed significant prediction of MLE processes by the various distal factors.

One of the important questions raised frequently in research is the effect of parents' SES level and their IQ on their interactions with children and consequently on children's intellectual development. Tzuriel and Ernst (1990) studied this question on a sample of kindergartners and their mothers. The sample was randomly selected from low-, medium- and high-SES groups, with equal number of mother–child dyads ($n = 16$) in each group. In this study (see Figure 8.2), mothers' SES level explained four of the MLE strategies whereas mothers' intelligence as measured by the Raven's Progressive Matrices (Raven, 1956) did not explain any of the MLE criteria. One of the implications of the last finding is that intervention programs to develop mothers' mediational strategies should not be limited by their level of intelligence, at least not within the average-low range.

The effects of distal factors on MLE processes were investigated further with another set of variables: mothers' emotional attitudes toward their children and the children's personality characteristics (Tzuriel & Weiss, 1998a). This study was based on Tzuriel's (1991a) transactional model of the relations among MLE processes, cognitive modifiability, and motivational and emotional factors. The emotional–motivational factors are conceived of as essential factors that, together with MLE processes, codetermine the development of cognitive modifiability. Symbiotic attachment to a mother figure, for example, or passive–fatalistic tendencies, interfere with the children's *accessibility to mediation* and lead consequently to deficient levels of cognitive modifiability. On the other hand, tendencies for intrinsic motivation, self-determination, an optimistic view of life, basic trust, and harmonious relations with one's parents enhance MLE processes.

Efficient mediation generated by an adult can facilitate motivational and affective processes such as arousal of exploration, seeking of challenges, feelings of competence, and feelings of warmth towards the mediator. The arousal of motivational–affective processes can, in turn, encourage the mediator to maintain his or her mediational efforts, improve their quality, and adjust them to the changing mediated individual. From a transactional point of view, the mediational efforts are calibrated to the children's modifiability, which in turn depends on the initial mediation. In other words, while the adult's mediation is conceived of as a major causative factor of children's motivational–emotional orientation and cognitive modifiability, the children's responses can also be conceived of as influencing, in a cyclical way, the adult's mediation. Clinical experience in both assessment and treatment has shown that motivational–emotional processes are inherently related to cognitive modifiability and vice versa (Tzuriel, 1991a, Tzuriel et al., 1988). Support for this model can be found in Rutter's (1981) argument that lack of warmth or rejection of the child, strongly affect children's deviant behavior and consequently the parents attempts to mediate to their children. Studies with infants have shown that strength of attachment was related to mothers' responsiveness to their infants (Schaffer & Emerson, 1964) and to their infants' signals (Ainsworth & Bell, 1970).

Based on the SEM model presented by Tzuriel and Weiss (1998a) the effects of mothers' emotional attitudes and children's personality orientations on mother–child MLE interactions were studied with a sample of mother–child dyads (26 boys and 28 girls). All children were second graders (32 boys and 28 girls), ranging in age from 7 : 4 years to 8 : 2 years. The children were randomly selected from two classes; all came from a heterogeneous socioeconomic background. The children and their mothers were videotaped in free play and structured situations; the interactions were analyzed later with the OMI. The children were administered the Parent Acceptance-Rejection Questionnaire (PARQ; Rohner, 1978), the Personality Assessment Questionnaire (PAQ; Rohner, 1978), and the CITM (a DA test). The PARQ is a self-report instrument designed to measure children's perceptions of parental acceptance–rejection attitudes. It contains four scales: (1) Warmth/Affection, (2) Aggression/Hostility, (3) Neglect/Indifference, and (4) Rejection (undifferentiated). The PAQ is a self-report instrument composed of seven scales: (1) Hostility/Aggression, (2) Dependency, (3) Negative Self-Esteem, (4) Negative Self-Adequacy, (5) Emotional Unresponsiveness, (6) Emotional Instability, and (7) Negative Worldview. The PAQ was constructed as a complementary measure of the PARQ so that parental attitude can be studied with regard to child's personality.

The two scales used to measure mothers' acceptance/rejection attitudes (PARQ) and children's personality dimensions (PAQ) contained 12 subscales. In order to "economize" the analyses and reduce the number of variables that can enter the SEM, within the restrictions of the ratio of number of variables by sample size, the mothers' acceptance/rejection attitudes and the children's personality dimensions were factor analyzed. The findings revealed two high-order factors for the mothers' attitudes: *Physical Rejection* and *Emotional Rejection*, and two high-order factors for the children's personality dimensions: *Inner-directed* and *Other-directed*. These factors were used in further analyses.

Canonical correlations that were carried out between the PAQ and PARQ scales support the factor analysis findings of the existence of two high order factors in each scale. The first canonical correlation (Rc = .67, p < .001) shows that the PARQ scales related to mothers' *emotional rejection* (i.e., Warmth/Cold and Neglect/Apathy) were correlated mainly with the PAQ scales that reflect children's *inner-directed* behavior (i.e., Negative Self-Adequacy, Negative Self-Esteem, Emotional Responsiveness, and Negative Worldview). The second canonical correlation (Rc = .59, p < .001) shows that the PARQ scales, indicating mothers' *physical rejection* (i.e., Hostility/Aggression), were correlated mainly with the PAQ scales that reflect children's *Other-directed* behavior (i.e., Hostility/Aggression, Emotional Inconsistency). The effects of children's personality and mothers' acceptance–rejection attitudes on mother–child MLE interactions and the combined effects of both on cognitive modifiability were investigated using SEM. Based on MLE theory it was hypothesized that children's personality factors and mothers' emotional attitudes, as distal factors, will specifically affect the MLE processes but not the children's cognitive functioning. The schematic SEM model of this study and the empirical findings are shown in Figures 8.3 and 8.4.

The findings regarding our discussion revealed that all MLE criteria were predicted by mothers' acceptance–rejection and the children's personality dimensions (distal factors). These distal factors did not explain any of the children's cognitive factors. These findings coincide with previous results with kindergartners and first graders (Tzuriel 1996a; Tzuriel & Eran, 1990; Tzuriel & Ernst, 1990) and confirm Feuerstein's MLE theory. The most important conclusion of this study was that while children's personality characteristics and mothers' acceptance–rejection attitudes do not directly affect cognitive performance of the children, they do influence them via MLE processes.

One of the most intriguing findings was that the *inner-directed* behavior predicted negatively two MLE criteria: Feelings of Competence and Control of Behavior, whereas *other-directed* behavior predicted *positively* four MLE criteria: Intentionality/Reciprocity, Meaning, Transcendence, and Regulation of Behavior. These findings indicate that the inner-directed child is "penalized" twice, first by having the personal self-imposed restrictions (Dependency, Emotional Instability), and second by the relative lack of mediations on the mothers' side. On the other hand, the Other-directed child seems to be more noticeable and therefore gets more mediation from the mother. In other words, while the Other-directed behavior can be conceived as a "cry" for help, the inner-directed behavior is more silent and therefore ignored. The specificity of these results is promising in terms of their theoretical and practical implications for theory development and intervention procedures.

The use of SEM seems to be most adequate for validation of MLE theory as causal relations can be inferred without having to apply an experimental design. Personality and emotional factors are not always given to experimental manipulation, multiphase modeling is often not easily subjected, if impossible, to experimental manipulation, and the accumulated effects of several factors are frequently contaminated by the artificiality of the experimental conditions. For further research, however, we propose to combine both experimental and SEM approaches to cross-validate the MLE theory.

Further support for the relationship between MLE processes and emotional processes was reported by Tal and Klein (1996) who investigated the relationship of mother–child MLE interactions to the quality of attachment of the mother–child dyad and the effects of modification of parental mediation on infant's attachment to parents. The subjects were 99 pairs of mothers and their infants, all from a low-SES urban community. The subjects were randomly assigned to experimental or control groups and videotaped in free play situation before the start of the intervention program. The intervention consisted of 11 training sessions in which the videotaped sessions were discussed with each mother on the basis of MLE criteria. The mothers in the experimental group were taught how to mediate to their children during the training sessions. The trainers focused on the mothers' observational skills and sensitive interactions with their infants. The control mothers participated in a program that included training for the analyses of developmental factors. An outcome measure of mother–infant attachment was based on sessions of the Strange Situation procedure (Ainsworth, Belhar, Waters, & Wall, 1978). The mother-infant interactions were videotaped during 10 minutes of free play when the infants were 1 month old and at the end of the program at 13 months old. The quality of mediation was assessed using OMI (Klein, 1988). The findings showed that *secure attachment* was related to mothers' reciprocity with their infants' behavior and to mothers' mediation for Feelings of Competence.

One of the intriguing questions explored recently is related to the effects of gender of both parents and children on mediation strategies and the differential effects of fathers and mothers on intellectual development of their children. The contribution of fathers to the intellectual development of their children has been studied extensively only in the last two decades. Previously, most research focused on the influence of mothers on their children's cognitive development. The neglect of the role of the father derives from social and psychological theories that emphasize the mothers' role. The fathers' role was conceived as instrumental whereas the mothers' role was expressive. Recent technological changes have led to changes in perception of parents' roles. The relatively reduced investment by women in the care of the home and children, and the greater involvement of men in child-rearing have changed the research priorities.

Various studies in the last 20 years demonstrated that fathers are more involved in taking care of their children than in the past, that the style of their interaction with their children differs from that of the mothers, and that they have direct and indirect influence on children's intellectual development. The effects of parents' mediation patterns and the time they spent with children were studied on a sample kindergartners ($n = 60$) and their parents (Tzuriel & Hatzir, 1999). All children were firstborn in families of no more than two children. The age range of the children was between 54 and 68 months. The parents' sample was composed of low, medium, and high SES, 20 families in each level. The study revealed that both parents showed a similar profile of mediation to their sons as well as to their daughters. The mothers, however, showed significantly higher mediation for *Meaning* and *Feelings of Competence* than did the fathers.

Prediction of Cognitive Modifiability in High-Risk Groups

A crucial question posed by many researchers with children at risk is the extent to which mother–child interactions compensate for the negative effects of children's predisposition or detrimental environmental conditions. This question was investigated in two studies, one with a group of 5- to 8-year olds who were

VLBW (<1250 grams)(Tzuriel & Weitz, 1998). This group ($n = 26$) was compared with a children's group ($n = 30$) who were normal birth weight (NBW). The two groups were matched on the variables of age, sex, and parents' educational and professional level, which constitute their SES. Mother–child interactions were videotaped in free play and structured situations and analyzed later using the OMI.

The two groups were administered the following static tests: Concept Formation and Vocabulary subscales from the WISC-R (Wechsler, 1991), Visual-Motor Integration (Beery, 1982), Draw-a-Person (Goodenough, 1926), and Auditory Sequential Memory Test from the ITPA (Kirk, McCarthy, & Kirk, 1968) and two DA measures: the CATM and the Complex Figure. Preliminary factor analysis on the static test scores yielded two high-order factors: (1) Visual-Motor and (2) Verbal Ability and Memory factors. The findings of the static tests showed a different correlational pattern between the MLE scores and cognitive scores in the two groups. For example, the high-order factor of Verbal Ability and Memory was correlated positively with Mediation for Transcendence in the VLBW group ($r = .44$, $p < .01$) as compared with a negative correlation in the NBW group ($r = -.11$, $p = $ ns). Fisher-Z analyses showed significant differences between the two correlations ($Z = 2.04$, $p < .05$). Thus, Mediation for Transcendence is more associated with development of verbal ability and memory skills in the VLBW group than in the NBW group. This finding seems reasonable as Mediation of Transcendence involves more than other MLE criteria the use of verbalization, hence the development of Verbal Ability and Memory factor in the child. These results should be interpreted cautiously with respect to causal inference of MLE as a determinant of cognitive ability. It might well be that mothers of VLBW children tend to use more Mediation for Transcendence to children who *initially* showed a higher level of cognitive ability.

The DA findings were analyzed by a series of hierarchical regression analyses. The CATM (or Complex Figure) Post-Teaching score was taken as a first step predictor, Group as a second step predictor, MLE Criteria as third step predictors, and the Group by MLE Criteria interactions as last step predictors.

The findings, based on a hierarchical regression analysis, showed that the CATM and Complex Figure Post-Teaching scores, indicating the individual's cognitive modifiability, were significantly predicted by the MLE criteria of Transcendence after controlling for the Pre-Teaching and Group variables. Thus, the higher the mother's Transcendence the higher is the Pre- to Post-Teaching improvement. This result is similar to previous results using the CATM (Tzuriel & Ernst, 1990) or the CITM (Tzuriel & Weiss, 1998a).

Of most importance to our discussion on high-risk groups are the interactions of Group by MLE Criteria. The objective of including this step in the analysis was to investigate whether the effect of mother's mediation on the child's cognitive modifiability was differential by group. The findings revealed a complex differential predictive pattern in both groups: positive prediction in the NBW group and negative in the VLBW group. The opposite predictive pattern was found for two criteria: Intentionality and Reciprocity and Feelings of Competence (findings differ somewhat for the different criterion predicted variables).

The findings showed an interaction of Group × Intentionality and Reciprocity ($\beta = .31$) which explained 7% of the variance. This interaction indicates that in the NBW group, as expected, the higher the mother's MLE scores, the higher the child's cognitive modifiability. In the VLBW group, an opposite prediction pattern was found: the higher the mother's MLE score, the *lower* the child's cognitive modifiability. We interpreted this finding as an indication of the circular nature of MLE processes and children's cognitive modifiability. In the NBW group the higher the mother's mediation, as reflected in Intentionality and Reciprocity, the higher the child's ability to change following a mediational experience in a different context such as a DA situation. On the other hand, among the VLBW group, the lower the child demonstrates cognitive modifiability, the higher the efforts the mother has to invest to focus her child to pay attention to stimuli. Thus, the relation between MLE and cognitive modifiability should be conceived as a circular process. It is true that MLE is positively related to children's cognitive modifiability, as was shown among the NBW group. However, among high-risk children such as the VLBW group, the child's cognitive modifiability is negatively related to the amount of mediation required. Mothers in this group demonstrated higher mediational efforts with children with low cognitive modifiability than mothers of children with relatively high cognitive modifiability. It is plausible to assume that within this group the mothers of low cognitive modifiability children perceive their children as more vulnerable and therefore "invest" more efforts when interacting with their children than mothers of children who are relatively more modifiable.

Separate analyses were carried out in this study on children's MLE scores (mother's mediation to the child and child's mediation to the mother were recorded separately in each observation). The findings for children's MLE revealed, similar to mothers' MLE, that in Step 3 Transcendence significantly ($\beta = .32$) added (10%) to the prediction of the Post-Teaching scores (in Steps 1 and 2 the variables of Pre-Teaching and Group were introduced, respectively; the findings have been presented earlier in this chapter). In Step 4 two interactions were found to be significant predictors: Group × Transcendence ($\beta = .33$) and Group × Regulation of Behavior ($\beta = .24$); both contributed an additional 7% to the overall variance.

Similar to the findings on mothers' MLE, the findings on children's MLE show that children who use more Transcendence in their interactions (e.g., use more rules and principles) are more cognitively modifiable in another context. The two Group × MLE criterion interactions showed a complex pattern. In the

NBW group, the higher the children's Intentionality and Reciprocity (e.g., focusing their mothers) and the lower their Regulation of Behavior (e.g., inhibiting their mother's behavior), the higher is their cognitive modifiability. Children in this group who are more task oriented and less manipulative and dominant when interacting with their mothers showed higher cognitive modifiability in a different learning context than children who tend to use less focusing behavior and more regulation of their mothers.

The findings for the NBW children were in correspondence with the main hypothesis of MLE theory; the higher the mediation mothers reveal in their interactions with their children, the higher the children's Post-Teaching performance on cognitive tasks. The findings for the VLBW children, on the other hand, seem, at first glance, to be contrary to what is hypothesized by MLE theory. In order to explain the findings it is suggested that some clarification of MLE theory be made. Although generally, MLE is considered to be a proximal factor for children's cognitive modifiability in some cases the child's initial level dictates the parental MLE approach. In this case children with high-risk conditions and low level of cognitive modifiability trigger their mothers to provide higher levels of MLE, a response that can be considered as a compensating effort from the mothers side for the difficulties experienced by the child. *Thus, we should look on MLE not only as an independent parental interaction mode that is necessary for the development of cognitive modifiability, but also as a behavioral parental response to the child's initial difficulties.* As a matter of fact Feuerstein himself emphasized the reciprocal nature of the MLE interactions, suggesting that parents calibrate their mediational efforts to the child's difficulties. One could predict that without the extra mediational efforts given to the VLBW children by their mothers the children's cognitive level might be much lower than what has been revealed. Certainly more research of an experimental nature is required to verify the directionality of effects in the two groups.

One of the intriguing issues regarding the MLE processes is their effect on cognitive modifiability across different cultural groups, e.g., the Ethiopian Jewish immigrants to Israel. This issue is intimately related to the distinction made by Feuerstein and Feuerstein (1991) between *cultural difference* and *cultural deprivation*. Cultural difference exists when the individual is exposed to MLE processes the content of which is different from that of the culture in which he or she is living. Cultural deprivation results when individuals do not have adequate MLE within their own culture. According to Feuerstein's approach MLE, which explains the individual's development of cognitive modifiability, does not depend on the content embodied in the culture but on the quality of the interaction between mediators and learners. In line with MLE theory the *culturally different* individuals are those who may manifest certain deficient cognitive functions, but are expected to overcome them rather quickly and/or with less mediational efforts. This occurs because the MLE they have received prepared them to be more modifiable. The *culturally deprived* individuals, on the other hand, have a relatively reduced modifiability, which is a result of the insufficient mediation on a proximal level.

The Ethiopian immigrants, on arriving in Israel, had to overcome a gap of civilization and information of several hundred years, in order to adapt to Israeli society (Kaniel et al., 1986). Leaving an illiterate society where their "rich" culture was transmitted orally, they have to go through rapid change and adjust to differences in both material and symbolic tools (Cole & Griffin, 1980). Based on what we knew about the Ethiopian immigrants to Israel we expected a significant relation between children's cognitive modifiability by mother–child MLE interactions. This relation was explored on a sample of mother–child dyads ($n = 20$) of Ethiopian immigrants to Israel; all children were girls between 5 and 6 years old (Tzuriel, Kaniel, & Yehudai, 1994). Mother–child interactions were observed in two free play situations, one with Western-oriented and the other with Ethiopian-oriented characteristics. In this study we used the CITM and the CPM. The Teaching phase within the CITM included teaching of task-specific strategies, self-regulation of impulsive behavior, planning, systematic exploratory behavior, hypothesis testing, and inferential thinking. The CPM, which is a static psychometric test, was given in a standard way before and 1 week after administration of the CITM. Positive changes on the CITM and the CPM were considered as indications of *near* and *far* transfer of learning, respectively. Mothers were divided into low, medium, and high mediators in each of the Western and Ethiopian interactive situations. The CITM and CPM scores were analyzed by ANOVA of Mediation Level by Time (3×2); separate analyses were carried out on Western and Ethiopian MLE scores. The findings revealed a significant interaction of Mediation Level by Time ($F (2, 17) = 8.02$, $p < .004$) only on the CPM in the Ethiopian situation. These findings indicate that children of mothers who demonstrated a high level of mediation in Ethiopian tasks showed higher improvement (12.17 to 17.17) on the CPM than children of mothers who had medium (10.67 to 13.33) or low (13.12 to 14.37) MLE scores. The lack of significant findings on the CITM could be attributed to the ceiling effect of the CITM Post-Teaching scores (all subgroups reached a ceiling level of 35 points or more out of 37 maximal score). The lack of clear cross-cultural validation with these specific Ethiopian immigrants might be attributed partially to two interrelated factors. First, the Ethiopian mothers were more sensitive to the experimental procedures (i.e., exposure to videotaping) and therefore did not reveal their typical MLE interactions. Second, Ethiopian mothers tend to express their mediation nonverbally and in real life situations (Klein, 1996). In any case, this ad hoc explanation calls for additional studies in which mediations are also observed under natural conditions and compared with the seminatural conditions that are used in our studies.

Prediction of Children's Cognitive Scores by MLE Interactions in Free Play versus Structured Situations

As mentioned above the context of mediation was hypothesized to trigger different styles of mediation as well as to predict differentially the children's cognitive performance. The free play situation was created by giving mothers and their children some cookies, colorful booklets, games, coloring materials, and other materials to play with, but no clear instructions were given as to the specific interaction. This situation represents a frequent interactional pattern characterized by spontaneity, divergent thinking, lack of a specific task, and relative lack of goals or externally imposed demands and structure. Such MLE interactions are most likely to occur in free play situations at home or in kindergarten. The structured situation, on the other hand, represents conditions in which a caregiver is engaged in activity aimed at teaching a child how to perform a task, solve a problem, or convey information and teach rules and principles. In all of these activities the mediating adult must structure the situation, using planning and higher level of thinking. The structured situation, on the other hand, was manipulated by giving mothers specific cognitive tasks to teach their children, although no instruction was given as to how to solve the problems. The differences between the two learning contexts were investigated in two studies (Tzuriel, 1996, Tzuriel & Weiss, 1998a). In both studies MLE in the structured situation has emerged as more powerful in the prediction of a child's cognitive performance than MLE in the free play situation. The first study (Tzuriel, 1996) was carried out with kindergartners and used the CATM test, the MLE scores in the structured situation predicted the children's Pre-Teaching ($R = .36$, $F(1, 46) = 7.03$, $p < .01$) and Post-Teaching scores ($R = .50$, $F(1, 46) = 15.05$, $p < .0003$). This result was observed despite the smaller variance of MLE scores in the structured than in the free play situation.

Prediction of the CATM scores by specific MLE categories revealed that Feelings of Competence in the structured situation was the most powerful MLE category in predicting both the Pre-Teaching ($R = .46$, $F(1, 34) = 9.11$, $p < .005$) and Post-Teaching ($R = .47$, $F(1, 34) = 9.78$, $p < .004$) scores. None of the free play scores has emerged as significant in predicting the children's performance before or after the mediation phase of the DA procedure. The second study (Tzuriel & Weiss, 1998a) was carried out with older children (Grade 2) and another cognitive task as criterion variable (the CITM). The findings were similar to the first study in regard to the predictive power of the MLE scores in the structured situation. However, unlike the first study, only the Post-Teaching scores have emerged as significantly predicted by the MLE scores. Correlational analyses showed zero correlations of mothers' MLE with the CITM Pre-Teaching scores in the free play and structured situations (.00 and −.01, respectively) as compared with correlations with the CITM Post-Teaching scores ($R = .28$, $p <$

.05 and $R = .43$, $p < .002$, respectively) and with the CITM-Transfer scores ($R = .26$, $p < .01$ and $R = .41$, $p < .002$, respectively).

A hierarchical regression analysis was carried out with the CITM Post-Teaching score as the predicted variable, the CITM Pre-Teaching score as a first step predictor, and the mothers' MLE scores in free play and structured situations as second step predictors. The findings showed that in Step 1 the CITM Pre-Teaching score correlated .43 ($p < .01$) and explained 18% of the variance. In the second step only mothers' MLE score in the structured situation entered the equation ($R = .45$, $p < .001$) in addition to the CITM Pre-Teaching score ($R = .43$, $p < .001$). The two variables explained 38% of the variance and the change from first to second steps was 20%. Thus, the higher the mothers' mediations in the structured situation, the higher is the improvement in children's cognitive performance following a mediational phase within the testing situation. As mentioned above, the hierarchical regression analysis approach allows better indications of cognitive modifiability than other correlational approaches, since it shows the unique variance contributed by MLE after "washing out" the variance contributed by the dynamic assessment Pre-Teaching scores and Group.

The results of these two studies support the hypothesis that MLE processes in the structured situation are more powerful in predicting children's cognitive modifiability, and that they reveal more of the mothers' MLE interactional pattern than do MLE interactions in the free play situation. A possible explanation for these findings is that MLE in structured situations, *because of its active and demanding nature*, highlights better the quality of the mother–child interactions as a determinant of cognitive development than does the simpler MLE in a free play situation. Another possible, complementary explanation is that mediation given within the DA procedure of the predicted cognitive variable (CATM or CITM tasks) is more similar to the MLE aspects tapped in the structured mother–child interaction than it is to those of free play situations. This correspondence of MLE in structured situations with a child's functioning in cognitive tasks and the tendency of Post-Teaching scores to be more highly predicted by the MLE interaction scores than Pre-Teaching scores, confirm that the effect of mediation is particularly noticeable at the upper level of the ZPD.

9

Use of Dynamic Assessment in Evaluation of Cognitive Education Programs

THE RATIONALE OF USING DA FOR EVALUATION OF COGNITIVE EDUCATION PROGRAMS

An efficient way to evaluate the effects of cognitive education programs aimed at development of learning and thinking skills is by DA. The argument is that if the declared objective of the intervention is teaching children "how" to learn and how to benefit from mediation, then the criterion outcome measures should be assessed in a dynamic way. This means that there must be some opportunity for new learning to take place as part of the assessment. The focus of evaluation should be on change criteria and cognitive modifiability indicators rather than on static measures. It is surprising that many intervention programs aimed at modifying learning skills do not use DA as a primary outcome measure (Tzuriel, 1989a). In the following I describe three cognitive intervention programs: the Bright Start Program, Structured Program for Visual–Motor Integration (SP-VMI), and Peer-Mediation for Young Children (PMYC). All programs were designed for young children. In each program one of the goals was to develop children's learning potential and therefore a DA approach was applied in evaluating its effectiveness.

THE BRIGHT START PROGRAM

The Bright Start: Cognitive Curriculum for Young Children Program (Haywood, Brooks, & Burns, 1986, 1992) was designed for preschool children and for children in the early grades of school who experience learning difficulties. The objectives of Bright Start are: (1) to increase the children's learning effectiveness, (2) to develop efficient cognitive processes and thinking skills, and (3) to prepare children for school learning. Bright Start was designed originally for use with normally developing children who were at high risk of school failure, i.e., children from poor families, ethnic minority status, inner-city residence, and sociocultural disadvantage. The target population has been extended to include children who have mild to severe mental retardation, emotional disturbance, autism and "pervasive developmental disorders," neurological and sensory impairments, cerebral palsy, and orthopedic handicaps (Haywood, 1995).

Unlike many other preschool programs, which emphasize development of basic skills, Bright Start is not content oriented. It is focused rather on development of cognitive processes and metacognitive operations that appear to be prerequisite to academic learning in the primary grades. Haywood et al. (1986) have argued that in spite of the proliferation of such programs for kindergartners (e.g., Bereiter & Engelmann, 1966; Gray & Klaus, 1970; Montessori, 1967; Weikart & Schweinhart, 1997), too many children arrive at first grade unprepared to master the primary curriculum, and they often wind up in special education classes. Many of these programs fail to take into account the vast individual differences among preschool children, as well as the basic cognitive functions and transfer skills that are essential for school achievement. Before describing the use of DA to assess the effectiveness of the program, a brief theoretical background of the program is necessary.

Theoretical Background of the Bright Start Program

Bright Start is based on a comprehensive theoretical approach synthesized by its authors from several developmental theories. The main theories are Haywood's transactional view of the nature and development of human ability (Haywood, 1995; Haywood, Brooks, & Burns, 1992; Haywood & Switzky, 1992; Haywood, Tzuriel & Vaught, 1992) and Feuerstein's theory of structural cognitive modifiability (Feuerstein, et al., 1979). Other theoretical sources are Piaget's developmental theory of intelligence and Vygotsky's (1978) sociocultural theory, especially the concept of the ZPD, and the social context for acquisition of cognitive tools. Because of their centrality and contribution to the Bright Start program, the principal points of these theories are briefly described; for a detailed description of Vygotsky's and Feuerstein's theories see Chapters 2 and 3.

Haywood's Transactional View

Haywood's transactional perspective is characterized by several assumptions about the nature of cognitive processes, the nature of intelligence and its development, the role of motivational and affective variables in the development of each, and the nature of cognitive modifiability (Haywood, Tzuriel, & Vaught, 1992). According to Haywood and colleagues, intelligence is perceived as multifaceted and multidetermined (i.e., a result of complex polygenic and experiential factors that affect each other in a transactional way). Thinking and learning processes are codetermined by *native ability* (or "intelligence," which is the commonly used term) and *learned cognitive processes* related to perception, learning, thinking, and problem solving. Even individuals born with high native ability must learn basic cognitive processes to be effective learners and thinkers.

Haywood, Tzuriel, and Vaught (1992) have distinguished sharply between *cognitive processes* and *intelligence*. They have maintained that the questions of whether or not intelligence is modifiable by experience, or to what extent it is modifiable, are less important questions than the history of the well-known debate. According to this view, intelligence alone is never sufficient to understand individual differences in criterion variables such as effectiveness of thinking, learning strategies, problem solving, gathering of information, and applying knowledge. Academic success depends to a large degree on adequate acquisition of cognitive processes. Lack of opportunities to acquire cognitive processes does not destroy intelligence but rather makes manifest performance less efficient.

A crucial component of Haywood's transactional model is *task-intrinsic motivation*, defined as the individual's tendency to seek novel stimuli, explore the environment, engage in tasks for the sake of information processing, and look for challenges and reasonable risk-taking (Haywood, 1968, 1971, 1980; Haywood & Burke, 1977; Haywood & Switzky, 1986, 1992). Task-intrinsic motivation and cognitive development are mutually dependent (Haywood, 1992b) and both influence learning processes and academic success.

Piaget's Developmental Approach

The Bright Start program is usually applied with 3- to 6- year-olds approaching the concrete operational thinking stage of development. This stage is characterized by Piaget (Piaget & Inhelder, 1969) as one in which the operations of classification, class inclusion, understanding of relations (e.g., seriation, transitivity, causality), conservation, and number are developed. Most of the program's activities are designed with the aim of enhancing these operations.

Vygotsky's Sociocultural Approach

Vygotsky's approach is based on the crucial role of adults in developing children's mental operations, Vygotsky emphasized the importance of sociocultural factors, and more specifically the role of adult–child interactions, in development of children's intellectual skills (see detailed discussion in Chapter 2). Vygotsky (1978), and later neo-Vygotskian researchers (e.g., Kozulin, 1990;

Luria, 1976; Wertsch, 1985), suggested that the thinking processes of educationally deprived and culturally different persons could be radically influenced by the introduction of *symbolic psychological tools*. The symbolic psychological tools include writing, numerical, notational, and other sign systems. These psychological tools can turn individuals' experience from immediate to mediated by culturally determined systems of symbols. Vygotsky conceived of the learning process as a process of interaction between individuals and the materials or subject matter, mediated by internalized psychological tools. Thus, sociocultural factors are constantly affecting the learning situations, the available psychological tools, and the agents of their delivery, usually parents, teachers, or more competent peers.

Vygotsky's ZPD construct is of central importance in construction of the Bright Start program and in studies aimed at evaluating its effectiveness. This construct has been defined as the difference between a child's "actual developmental level as determined by independent problem solving" and the higher level of "potential development as determined through problem solving under adult guidance or in collaboration with more capable peers" (Vygotsky, 1978, p. 86). The ZPD, investigated by Vygotsky himself, was further developed by neo-Vygotskian investigators (e.g., Campione & Brown, 1987; Luria, 1976; Rogoff, 1990; Wertsch, 1985). Since the main objective of the Bright Start program is to teach "learning how to learn" skills, it follows that exactly these skills should be assessed as a primary criterion of the program's evaluation.

Feuerstein's MLE Approach

Feuerstein and his colleagues (Feuerstein & Feuerstein, 1991; Feuerstein et al., 1979, 1980, 1988) suggested that MLE processes determine development of cognitive functions. According to this approach, lack of, impaired, or insufficient MLE determines deficient cognitive functions and subsequent failure in general problem solving and school achievement. MLE was defined by several criteria, the most important of which are intentionality and reciprocity, meaning, and transcendence (see Chapter 3 for a detailed description of criteria).

In MLE interactions, a caregiver (e.g., parent or teacher) interposes him or herself between the child and the environment and mediates the environment to the child. Mediation is carried out by a combination of behavior aimed at teaching the child how to register information, elaborate (process) it, and express it adequately. The mediator focuses the child on the crucial aspects of the stimuli (intentionality), adapts the mediation to the child's responses (reciprocity), labels the information and emphasizes its importance and significance (meaning), and transcends the information by applying to it rules, generalizations, and principles that are beyond the here and now.

Modification of the stimuli is carried out either spontaneously (at home or playground) or in a structured way (teaching contexts). In both situations, a major characteristic of MLE is the *development of systematic thinking processes* (cognitive tools in Vygotsky's concepts), which help to direct learning and performance in school situations as well as in other life domains. Similar to Vygotsky's theory, Feuerstein has argued that children gradually internalize the MLE processes, which becomes an integrated mechanism of change within the children. Adequate MLE facilitates the development of various cognitive functions, learning sets, mental operations, and need systems, whereas inadequate MLE is responsible for their lack or impairment. The acquired and internalized MLE processes allow children later to benefit from learning experiences, to use them independently, and to modify their cognitive system. The basic assumption of MLE theory is that *mediation of principles of thinking, learning, and problem solving will eventually prove to be more effective in preparing preschool children for academic and social learning than mere teaching of contents and skills.* The more children experience MLE interactions, the more they are able in the future to learn from direct exposure to formal and informal learning situations, regardless of the richness of stimuli they provide.

Lack of MLE may be attributable to two broad categories: (1) lack of environmental opportunities for mediation and (2) inability of the child to benefit from mediational interactions, which are potentially available. For detailed a description of MLE theory and applications the reader is referred to Chapter 3 and to the relevant literature (e.g., Feuerstein Klein, & Tannenbaum, 1991; Tzuriel 1998, 1999b, 1999d).

Feuerstein has proposed a list of deficient cognitive functions that characterize children who have been deprived of MLE. Examples of deficient cognitive functions include: impulsive and unsystematic exploratory behavior, lack of or impairment in simultaneous consideration of two sources of information, episodic grasp of reality, difficulties in planning behavior, egocentric communication style, and trial and error response style. Those deficient cognitive functions and others are the main target of modification in the Bright Start program.

The Bright Start Goals

Bright Start has, in general, the following goals: (1) development and elaboration of learning skills and basic cognitive functions, especially those necessary to accede to (Piaget's) stage of concrete operations; (2) identification and remediation of deficient cognitive functions; (3) development of task-intrinsic motivation; (4) development of representational thinking; (5) enhancement of learning effectiveness and readiness for school learning; (6) prevention of inappropriate special education placement (Haywood, Brooks, & Burns, 1986, 1992).

The Bright Start Components

Bright Start has five components whose combination is essential for effective implementation of the program: understanding of the theoretical base, the mediational teaching style, the seven cognitive "small-group" curriculum units, a cognitive mediational behavior management system, and a program of parent participation.

(1.) Haywood, Brooks and Burns (1992) conceive the understanding of the theoretical basis of the program as a crucial aspect of successful application of the program as well as any other educational program. The reason is that teachers are confronted with thousands of situations where they have to overcome difficulties that were not specified previously. Understanding of the theoretical guidelines would help them to find a creative solution that is in line with the theory.

(2.) The mediational teaching style is characterized by mediating to the children basic thinking skills, generalized meanings of the children's experiences, and the children's own metacognitive processes. Haywood, Brooks, and Burns (1992) consider the mediational teaching style to be the most important and distinguishing characteristic of teachers' behavior. Teachers with a mediational style help children to examine their own interactions and evaluate their compatibility with MLE criteria. The type of questions asked in process-oriented lessons differs from the type of questions asked in content-oriented lessons. For example, in structured activities teachers try to elicit evidence of systematic thinking (e.g., "Give me a reason why we should first examine the picture, and then describe it"), use process-oriented questioning ("Why do you think it's better to look from this side first?"), and accept children's responses while challenging their answers and requiring justification ("That's a very good answer, but can you tell me why it is correct?"). By using a mediational teaching style the teachers facilitate children's understanding of the generalized meaning of their experiences, efficient strategies of gathering information and its elaboration, systematic thinking processes, and accurate communication strategies.

(3.) The third Bright Start component is the cognitive–mediational behavior management. This component refers to application of the mediation principles to behavior problems that arise either in teaching sessions or in social interactions within the kindergarten. The teacher might encourage self-regulation of the children by asking them to think first about a reaction before they actually respond, to anticipate verbally an answer before giving the answer, think about reasons or motives for their behavior or others' behavior, suggest alternative responses, weigh advantages and disadvantages of possible courses of action, and mentally represent others' reactions to their choice.

(4.) The fourth Bright Start component, which constitutes the core of the program, is the "small-group" instructional units, used to instruct children. The small-group units address fundamental aspects of preschool children's cognitive functioning. Each lesson of these units is taught in groups of four to six children, for a period of about 20 minutes each day. During each lesson the teacher facilitates discussion about the activities in the lessons. The small group units are: Self-Regulation, Quantitative Relations, Comparison, Role Taking, Classification, Sequences and Patterns/Seriation, and Letter-Shape Concepts/Distinctive Features.

In the Self-Regulation unit, for example, children are presented with activities that deal with cues that help to monitor fast versus slow behavior. The teacher might present a stimulus (e.g., picture, hand movement, or a rhythm on a small drum) and ask the children to walk slowly or quickly in response to the stimulus. In more advanced lessons children are presented with symbols and abstract cues that inform the children how to self-regulate their behavior. After each activity the teacher tries to elicit meaningful examples of the cognitive principle(s) acquired. The examples are based on the children's experiences at home, in the kindergarten, or the playground. For recent detailed descriptions of the program and its components see Haywood (1995) and Haywood, Brooks, and Burns (1992).

Evaluation of the Bright Start Program

The efficacy of the Bright Start program has been studied in several countries, including the United States, Canada, France, Belgium, and Israel. In some studies a DA approach was applied, whereas in others only standardized tests or Piagetian-type tasks were applied. Haywood et al., (1986) studied it first in the United States with two groups of preschool children: mentally retarded (MR) children ($n = 27$) with a mean IQ of 58.85 and "high-risk" low-SES children ($n = 48$) with a mean IQ of 89.48. Both groups received Bright Start for 7 months and were tested before and after the program on the McCarthy Scales of Children's Abilities (McCarthy, 1972). The McCarthy Scales yield a General Cognitive Index as well as specific scores on Verbal, Perceptual Performance, Memory, and Motor abilities. Other tests included the Stencil Design Test (Arthur, 1947), adapted by Burns (1991) for administration as a standard test and as a DA. The last test was important for tapping mental representation skills, systematic exploratory behavior, planning, and control of impulsiveness; all are cognitive functions, which were emphasized throughout Bright Start. A control group of "high-risk" children ($n = 44$) with a mean IQ of 91.45 participated in a noncognitively oriented "Project Head Start" program. The findings showed that the MR and the "high-risk" Bright Start groups gained 12 and 9 points, respectively, on the General Cognitive Index, as compared with a gain of 1 point for the control group. The "high-risk" group showed significant improvement on three of the four scales of the McCarthy (Quantitative, Perceptual Performance, and

Memory), and the MR group gained significantly on all four (including the Verbal subscale). The MR children doubled their performance on the Stencil Design Test from pre- to posttest, but the gain in the experimental "high-risk" group did not differ from that found in the control group. Haywood et al. (1986) suggested that this task is sensitive to maturational changes and therefore the gains could not be attributed to treatment effects.

These findings on the McCarthy Scales were replicated by Canadian investigators (Samuels et al., 1992) on a socially heterogeneous group of preschool children who were diagnosed as learning disabled, MR, and emotionally disturbed. The Bright Start children improved their performance significantly from pre- to posttreatment on the McCarthy Scales, on a test of expressive language, and on the Peabody Developmental Motor Scale as compared with a comparison group (who received a "good non-cognitively oriented preschool program"). Other results indicated that children whose parents participated in the program "often" showed more gains on some measures than did children whose parents participated "seldom" or "not at all." Also, a higher percentage of the Bright Start children were subsequently assigned, through independent assessment, to "regular" classes, whereas most of the comparison children were assigned to special education classes following their kindergarten year.

Studies in Belgium (Vanden Wijngaert, 1991; Warnez, 1991) have also shown remarkable cognitive improvement among young deaf children and those with significant language delays. These studies, however, had no control or comparison groups, and their results can be interpreted only within the framework of other studies.

Paour, Cebe, Lagarrigue, and Luiu (1993) have applied Bright Start partially in France with immigrant, low-SES disadvantaged children. The Bright Start children were compared with control children of low- and high-SES groups. The experimental children received only two small group units during the year: Self-Regulation and Comparison. All children were tested extensively at the end of the year using various tests including psychometric tests, Piagetian tasks, achievement tests, metacognitive tasks, and an intrinsic motivation measure. The experimental group scored higher than did the control group on almost all of the cognitive measures, and on some measures, even higher than the control high-SES group. When the groups were compared on metacognitive tasks, the low-SES experimental children scored higher than did their parallel control children. Findings from the achievement tests showed that the experimental children scored higher on general information, as well as on a reading task, especially on a list of "difficult" words. This last result was interpreted to mean that Bright Start enhanced application of systematic cognitive strategies in order to process novel information. A follow-up study carried out 2 years after the end of the program showed clear superiority of the experimental group over the control group in reading and in math. This last result lends support to the hypothesis that cognitive education programs may facilitate the development of cognitive processes that are then generalized to the learning of academic subjects. In all of the studies mentioned above, with all of their importance, no attempt was made to assess the intervention outcomes by DA measures. In the following studies carried out at Bar-Ilan University, a DA component was introduced together with static standardized tests.

Bright Start was studied in Israel with disadvantaged kindergartners and their teachers (Tzuriel et al., 1998, 1999). The major objectives of these studies were: (1) to assess the effects of the program, applied with kindergarten disadvantaged children, on learning, transfer, and task-intrinsic motivation; (2) to determine whether there are generalized effects of the program on reading comprehension and math skills in Grade 1; and (3) to explore the effects of using the program on mediated learning strategies of kindergarten teachers. In the following section the Israeli studies are described in regard to the effects of Bright Start on children's cognitive functioning and cognitive modifiability, academic achievements in school, task-intrinsic motivation, and mediational style of the teacher.

The Effects of Bright Start on Children's Cognitive Functioning

In the first study (Tzuriel et al., 1999) a sample of kindergartners who had Bright Start in their classrooms ($n = 82$) was compared to a group of children ($n = 52$) who received a basic skills program, using both static and dynamic tests. The static tests were the RCPM (Raven, 1956), the Cognitive Development subtest (from the Preschool Diagnostic Advancement Test; Simpson, 1985), and the Knowledge of Numbers subtest (from the Adelphi Parent Administered Readiness Test; Klein, 1982).

Two DA instruments were administered before and after the intervention: the CATM (Tzuriel & Klein, 1985) and the Complex Figure (Tzuriel & Eiboshitz, 1992). For a detailed description of these instruments the reader is referred to Chapter 6. In addition, both groups received, at the end of the program, a Self-Regulation task and Knowledge of Numbers subtest (from the Adelphi Parent Administered Readiness Test). In order to avoid interference of the static tests with the effects of mediation given in the DA measures, the static tests were always given first, followed by the dynamic ones.

It should be noted that the experimental group had an initial disadvantage in relation to the comparison group. Unfortunately, there was no possibility of random assignment of children in each class to experimental and comparison groups without raising resentment from parents. It would also have been confusing to the kindergarten teacher who would have had to implement both programs within one class. We had to rely, therefore, on supervisors' assessments of children's background as a basis for equating the treatment groups. This eventually proved to be not completely accurate. The initial cognitive scores on the dynamic tests and the RCPM serve therefore as our baseline for comparison of improvements as a function of treatment.

The Bright Start program was applied for 10 months, during which the experimental children received five of the seven small-group units: Self-Regulation, Quantitative Relations (Number Concepts), Comparison, Classification, and Role-Taking. The small-group lessons were taught three times a week, each session for a period of 20 minutes, for a total of 60 minutes per week, and a total number of 32 hours for the academic year. The comparison group was given the basic skills program during the academic year and the teachers were visited periodically to observe their skills based program.

All experimental teachers participated in a preliminary 5-day teacher-training workshop, and later during the year were observed and supervised by a program supervisor for 2 hours each week. The supervision included modeling of the mediational teaching style by the supervisor. In addition there were six group meetings to discuss special topics and problems that arose during the year. In addition to the intervention with the kindergartners themselves, a parent participation component was also applied. Eight parent meetings were carried out to explain the program's objectives, teach mediational strategies and their use with the children at home, and deal with specific learning and behavior problems.

At the end of the program all children were given the following tests: RCPM, Cognitive Development, Knowledge of Numbers, CATM (Pre-Teaching, Teaching, and Post-Teaching phases), Complex Figure, and the Mazes Test of Task-Intrinsic Motivation (Delclos & Haywood, 1986).

The findings on the static tests revealed a significant Group by Time interaction on the Cognitive Development test, indicating that the Bright Start children improved their performance more than did the comparison group from pre- to postintervention. Evaluation based on the CATM, which is a DA measure, was divided into two parts. The first was the group comparison on Set A (Pre-Teaching) scores given before and after the intervention. This can be considered as a static test score as no mediation was given. Since the CATM is scored by two methods—"all or none" and "partial credit"—and both scores are derived from the same measure, data on these scores were analyzed by a repeated measures MANOVA of Treatment (experimental versus comparison) by Time (pre- versus postintervention) (2×2). The findings revealed an overall significant Treatment by Time interaction. Univariate analyses showed that both Method 1 ("all-or-none") and Method 2 ("partial credit") contributed significantly to the overall interaction. On both measures the experimental group showed higher pre- to postintervention improvement than did the comparison group. Thus, in two independent cognitive measures (Cognitive Development and CATM-Set A), the Bright Start group showed significantly greater pre- to posttreatment improvement than did the comparison group.

The second group comparison was on CATM Pre- and Post-Teaching scores *given at the end* of the intervention, using the CATM as a full DA task. A MANOVA of Treatment (experimental versus comparison) by Phase (Pre- versus Post-Teaching) revealed an overall significant Treatment by Phase interaction indicating, unexpectedly, that the comparison group improved more than did the experimental group from the Pre- to Post-Teaching phases of the DA. Univariate analyses showed that both, Methods 1 and 2 contributed significantly to this interaction. Thus, although the experimental children showed higher pre- to post-intervention improvements on the CATM administered in a static way, they did not benefit from the mediation given within the test as much as the comparison group did. These results could suggest that the experimental group could not yet totally overcome their initial disadvantage, and in spite of the cognitive education program they did not transfer the learning principles and strategies that were taught during the program. An alternative explanation is that the comparison group may have had the most "room" to change because they had not systematically been exposed to mediation strategies before and their scores on the unassisted task were still low.

The findings from the Complex Figure test were impressive in view of the fact that the visual–motor aspects of the test were remote from the intervention activities within the Bright Start. The Complex Figure was administered as a DA measure before and after the intervention. In order to avoid a ceiling effect at the end of the intervention the easier version (A) of the Complex Figure test was administered before the intervention and the difficult version (B) was administered in the postintervention phase. Each administration included Pre- and Post-Teaching scores on both Copy and Memory phases. A repeated measures MANOVA of Treatment (experimental versus comparison) by Time (pre- versus postintervention) by Pre-Post-Teaching by Phase (Copy versus Memory) ($2 \times 2 \times 2 \times 2$) was carried out on the original Complex Figure scores. The dependent variables were composed of (1) Accuracy + Location and (2) Organization scores. The findings revealed an overall significant Treatment by Time interaction. Univariate analyses showed that this interaction was contributed significantly by Accuracy + Location. This result indicates that while the experimental group increased its overall performance from pre- ($M = 33.94$) to postintervention ($M = 48.52$), the comparison group showed a decrease from pre- ($M = 42.93$) to postintervention ($M = 39.99$). The significance of the greater gains of the experimental children should also be evaluated in relation to the fact that Bright Start was not fully implemented with the experimental group. Only five of the seven small-group units were implemented, in some units only about 70% of the lessons were used, and each small group had to participate in small-group lessons once every 2 days. The experimental children received during the 10-month intervention period only 32 hours of small-group cognitive teaching. Also, the parent participation component was implemented in a limited way and its effectiveness within the overall intervention efforts is doubtful. Thus, the cognitive gains shown by the experimental group above those of the comparison group are all the more impressive.

Given that MLE processes were central in the program, it was expected that children would show higher skills of "learning to learn" than would those in a comparison group. A follow-up study was carried on both groups in Grade 1, using achievement tests of reading comprehension and math. These tests were administered in addition to DA and static tests. All tests were administered 1 year after the children had left the program and entered first grade in school.

The results of the follow-up study confirmed the effectiveness of Bright Start in developing learning skills. The Bright Start children scored higher than did the comparison children not only in the Pre-Teaching phase of the DA tests, but also in the Post-Teaching phase. In spite of the fact that both groups received the same amount of teaching (mediation) within the DA procedure, the Bright Start group continued to show superiority over the comparison group.

The original DA scores (CATM and Complex Figure) were analyzed by MANOVA with repeated measures nested design of Treatment (experimental versus control) by Grade (end of kindergarten versus first grade) by Pre-Post-Teaching ($2 \times 2 \times 2$), the last two variables were within-groups variables.

The findings for the CATM showed significant Treatment by Grade interaction ($F(2, 69) = 5.53$, $p < .0001$). This result indicates that while at the end of the kindergarten the comparison group scored somewhat higher than the experimental group, in the follow-up phase the experimental group was significantly higher than the comparison group. Univariate analyses indicated that the superiority of the experimental group was uniquely contributed by both Method 1 ($F(1, 70) = 11.16$, $p < .001$) and Method 2 ($F(1, 70) = 8.78$, $p < .004$). The two-way interaction was modified by a three way interaction of Treatment by Grade by Pre-Post-Teaching ($F(2, 69) = 4.27$, $p < .02$). Univariate analyses revealed that both Method 1 ($F(1, 70) = 8.41$, $p < .005$) and Method 2 ($F(1, 70) = 7.55$, $p < .008$) contributed significantly to the interaction. The triadic interaction of method 1 is presented in Figure 9.1. Findings of Method 2 are similar to those of Method 1 and therefore are not presented in a figure. For comparative reasons the CATM scores at the start of the program are also plotted. The figure, however, is based only on students who participated in the follow-up.

The CATM findings (Figure 9.1) show that the experimental children made higher improvement on the CATM Pre-Teaching (A) from preintervention (K-Pre-A) to postintervention (K-Post-A) phase. The findings also show that while at the end of the program (kindergarten) the comparison children improved their performance from the Pre- to Post-Teaching phase of the DA test more than did the experimental children, in the follow-up year the trend was reversed. The experimental group showed in the follow-up phase higher improvement from Pre- to Post-Teaching than did the comparison group. This result was interpreted as

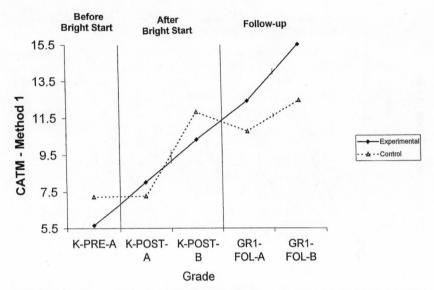

Figure 9.1. CATM scores ("none-or-all"—Method 1) before the intervention, after the intervention, and in Grade 1 (follow-up). (Reproduced by permission from Tzuriel, D., et al. (1999). The effectiveness of Bright Start Program in kindergarten on transfer abilities and academic achievements. *Early Childhood Research Quarterly, 14,* 111–141.)

an indication for a "snowball" effect of the "learning to learn" treatment. According to the "snowball" effect, treatment effects gain power with time without any additional treatment, which is to be expected when the treatment is designed to enhance "learning to learn" skills.

A second set of analyses was carried out on cognitive modifiability indices that were based on the residual Post-Teaching scores after controlling for the Pre-Teaching score. A MANOVA of Treatment by Grade (2 × 2) applied on the CATM Post-Teaching residual scores revealed a significant overall interaction of Treatment by Grade ($F(2, 69) = 10.08, p < .0001$). This finding indicates higher improvement of the cognitive modifiability scores in the experimental than in the comparison group, from kindergarten to first grade. Univariate analyses showed that the interaction was uniquely contributed by variance of both, Method 1 ($F(1, 70) = 20.43, p < .0001$) and Method 2 of scoring ($F(1, 70) = 15.92, p < .0001$).

The Complex Figure data were analyzed similarly to the CATM data by a repeated measures MANOVA. The independent variables were Treatment (experimental versus comparison), Time (pre- versus post-intervention), Pre-Post-Teaching, and Phase (Copy versus Memory). The dependent variables were scores of Accuracy + Location and Organization. The findings revealed an

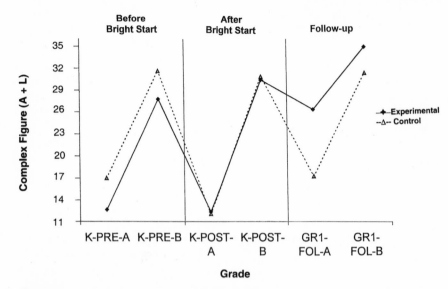

Figure 9.2. Complex Figure scores (Accuracy + Location) before the intervention, after the intervention, and in Grade 1 (follow-up). (Reproduced by permission from Tzuriel, D., et al. (1999). The effectiveness of Bright Start Program in kindergarten on transfer abilities and academic achievements. *Early Childhood Research Quarterly, 14*, 111–141.)

overall significant Treatment by Time interaction ($F(2, 114) = 3.39, p < .04$). Univariate analyses showed that the interaction was contributed significantly by Accuracy + Location score ($F(1, 115) = 4.57, p < .04$). The findings are presented in Figure 9.2.

Figure 9.2 shows that while the experimental group increased its overall performance from pre- ($M = 33.94$) to postintervention ($M = 48.52$) the comparison group showed a decrease from pre- ($M = 42.93$) to postintervention ($M = 39.99$). It should be noted here that a more difficult version of the Complex Figure was administered in the post-intervention phases. The results of the Complex Figure test (Figure 9.2), reveal a combination of both developmental and intervention effects. As can be seen, the comparison group showed, at the start of the program, higher performance than did the experimental group on the Pre-Teaching phase of the test. The initial superiority of the control group over the experimental group continued after the Teaching phase as shown in the Post-Teaching score on the Accuracy + Location component. The picture changed, however, at the end of the program, when both groups scored about the same on both Pre- and Post-Teaching phases. It seems that at this stage the experimental children closed the initial gap with their control counterparts. The closing of the gap phenomenon was extended further in the follow-up phase. The experimental group not only functioned initially higher than the comparison group, but also remained higher in the Post-Teaching phase. Thus, an initial tendency for superiority of the comparison group was not only overcome at the end of the program but was actually reversed, with the children who had received the cognitive education treatment showing superiority over the comparison group.

The similar findings from the Complex Figure test (Figure 9.2) further support the CATM findings (Figure 9.1). It should be noted that Bright Start does not include any specifically *visual–motor* exercises. Rather, the whole program is based on visual presentation of stimuli, discussion of strategies for solving problems, metacognitive processes, verbal dialogues, social interactions, and analyses of situations and problems. In spite of the verbal–logical nature of the program, the most impressive results are those found on the Complex Figure test.

The replication of results on both tests, which represent different cognitive domains, might suggest that, unlike skills-based programs, the treatment effects of cognitive education programs could be integrated within individuals' cognitive systems and become structural (durable) only after a certain "incubation" period. In other words, contrary to the "decay" phenomenon characterizing evaluations of general content-based programs, treatment effects of cognitive education programs need time to be fully infused into individuals' cognitive system. A simple explanation is that in cognitive education, children acquire and elaborate more effective processes for learning, but then need time to go out and do some learning, exercising their recently acquired learning skill.

The effects of Bright Start were investigated in another study (Tzuriel et al., 1998) in which only two small-group units were applied: Seriation and Classification. A sample of 51 kindergartners was randomly assigned to experimental ($n = 25$) and control groups ($n = 26$). The age range of the whole sample was 47 to 63 months, and the mean age of the experimental and control groups was 56.52 months ($SD = 5.18$) and 57.78 months ($SD = 5.80$), respectively. The experimental children came from three kindergartens located in low-socioeconomic areas as defined by the Israeli Ministry of Education. The comparison children came from two kindergartens located in similar low-socioeconomic areas. Most parents in the experimental (71%) and comparison (64%) groups had only 8 years of formal education. All control children participated in a skills based program that emphasized basic academic skills such as reading, writing, and math. The teachers of the control group were involved during the year in the assessment process and were aware of the fact that their program and the children's achievement were being observed and evaluated.

The criterion measures included both static and DA measures. The static tests were: the Cognitive Development subtest, the Visual Memory subtests (taken from the Preschool Diagnostic and Advancement Test; Simpson, 1985), and Knowledge of Numbers and Concept Formation subtests (taken from the Adelphi Parent Administered Readiness Test, Klein, 1982). The Cognitive

Development tasks included concept formation, two-way classification, and perceptual matching of quantities. The Visual Memory tasks included sequential memory of objects, sequential memory of geometric shapes, and organization of patterns from memory. Knowledge of Numbers is composed of items relating to understanding of basic quantitative concepts, conservation of number, and simple addition and subtraction. Concept Formation is composed of items in which the child is asked to mark an exceptional picture presented among four pictures.

The DA measures were the CATM and Complex Figure tests (see description in Chapter 6). All of the children were given the static tests, before and after the cognitive education intervention. The DA tests, however, were given only after the intervention. In order to avoid contamination of the static tests with the effects of mediation of cognitive and test-taking processes, the static tests, at the end of the intervention, were given first, followed by the DA tests.

The Bright Start program was applied for 3 months, during which the experimental children received the Seriation (Patterns and Sequences) and Classification small-group units. There were 20 lessons in Seriation and 22 lessons in Classification. Each small group was composed of 5 or 6 children. The small group units were taught three times a week, each session lasting 20 minutes, for a total of 60 minutes per week. The total number of hours of cognitive small-group lessons for the whole intervention was 14. The experimental teachers were supervised during the intervention period in three individual sessions and seven group sessions, each session lasting 1 hour. The control group was given a basic skills program designed by the Ministry of Education during the intervention period, using the same procedure of three times a week, each session lasting 20 minutes. This program was aimed at acquiring basic concepts of color, shape, number, space, and visual—motor coordination. These teachers were visited periodically to observe their skills based program.

A series of Treatment by Time (2×2) ANOVAs carried out on the static test scores revealed significant interactions for Visual Memory and Concept Formation. The interactions on Visual Memory indicate that while both groups were about the same before the intervention, the experimental group made greater improvement and scored higher at the end. For Concept Formation, the control group scored higher than the experimental group before the intervention but the gap was closed after the intervention and both groups scored about the same.

The findings on the DA measures, given at the end of the intervention, showed that the control group had lower scores than did the experimental group on both Pre- and Post-Teaching tests. In order to compare Pre- and Post-Teaching improvements in both groups, the data were analyzed by a series of Group by Time repeated measures ANOVA (2×2). The independent variables were Treatment (Bright Start versus Basic Skills) and Time (Pre-Post-Teaching), the second variable being a within-groups variable.

The analyses revealed significant Treatment main effects on the CATM (Methods 1 and 2 of scoring) and the Complex Figure (Accuracy + Location and Organization scores). These main effects indicate that the experimental group scored higher on both tests than the control group at the end of the intervention. Our main interest, however, was in the cognitive modifiability represented by the pre- to postteaching improvement. The ANOVAs revealed significant interactive effects of Treatment by Time on both the CATM scores (Methods 1 and 2 of scoring) and the Complex Figure score (Accuracy + Location). These findings indicate that on all of these measures, the experimental group made greater changes from pre- to postteaching than did the control group. Of most importance are the results of the Complex Figure, which requires fine visual–motor integration skills. This type of skill is not part of the Bright Start program, which is heavily based on verbal interactions, but was emphasized in the basic skills program of the control group.

The Effects of Bright Start on Task-Intrinsic Motivation and Self-Regulation

The Bright Start goals included enhancement of task-intrinsic motivation and metacognitive processes. The effects of Bright Start on these nonintellective aspects were tested in two studies (Tzuriel et al., 1998, 1999). In the first study (Tzuriel et al., 1998) the Picture Task-Intrinsic Motivation test (Haywood, 1971) was administered at the end of the intervention. The test was designed to assess children's tendency to engage in tasks for their own sake. The test is composed of a set of 20 pairs of pictures, each pair representing two different activities. In each item the subject is asked to choose the activity he or she likes more and then give a reason for the choice. The child is given a list of 10 reasons to select from, of which 5 represent a task-intrinsic motive (e.g., challenge, curiosity, aesthetics) and 5 represent a task-extrinsic motive (e.g., physical safety, familiarity, salary). The original test, which included 20 items, was administered in a previous study (Tzuriel & Klein, 1983) to a sample of kindergartners ($n = 413$). The findings revealed significant item discrimination indices only for 12 items; those items were selected for further analysis. Findings on the Picture Task-Intrinsic Motivation task showed that the experimental group scored about the same ($M = 5.50$, $SD = 1.93$) as the control group ($M = 5.92$, $SD = 2.49$) before treatment. After treatment, the experimental group had increased their score ($M = 7.16$, $SD = 2.01$) more than had the control group ($M = 6.42$, $SD = 2.06$). An ANOVA of Treatment by Time (2×2) showed a significant interaction, indicating higher increase in task-intrinsic motivation in the experimental than in the control group.

In the second study (Tzuriel et al., 1998) the Mazes Test of Task-Intrinsic Motivation (Delclos & Haywood, 1986) and a self-regulation task were administered. The Mazes Test was designed by Delclos and Haywood to assess willingness to do mental work in the absence of any requirement to do it, that is, motivation to engage in tasks for their own sake and as their own reward. The task is composed of a set of four mazes. In each maze the subject traces the path until he or she comes to a "goal," where there is a choice of entering the goal and thereby ending engagement with the task (and any requirement for further work) or beginning work on the next maze in the sequence. The number of mazes chosen (total = 4) and the efficiency (number of correct decisions per minute of engagement with the task) are taken as indications of task-intrinsic motivation.

The findings indicated, as expected, at the end of the program, higher task-intrinsic motivation and self-regulation in the experimental than in the control group. The experimental group chose significantly more mazes ($M = 3.05$, $SD = 1.23$) than did the control group ($M = 2.43$, $SD = 1.40$) on the Mazes Test, indicating a higher tendency to do challenging mental work as its own reward ($t (108) = 3.05$, $p < .003$). Analysis of the answers given to the Self Regulation Task revealed that the experimental children gave significantly ($p < .05$) more answers indicating knowledge of rules as their first response or reached an answer after short mediation than did the control group.

The results of both studies showed that the program's effectiveness was not limited to the cognitive realm but was accompanied by changes in the experimental children's tendency to be more intrinsically motivated and have more self-regulation over their behavior than the control children. It seems that the emphasis given in Bright Start to self-directed activities, expressing of personal views, exploration of alternative solutions, reflective thinking, and task-intrinsic motivation, paid off in long-term gains in both cognitive competence and task-intrinsic motivation. The findings of both studies are consistent with Feuerstein's conceptualization of *structural cognitive modifiability*, according to which there is a strong tendency for changes in one of the individual's system components to be "diffused" and to affect the whole. Thus, changes in the motivational aspects affect cognitive aspects and vice versa. The data accord quite nicely as well with Haywood's "motivational theory of cognition" (Haywood, 1992b; Haywood & Burke, 1977; Haywood & Wachs, 1981), in which intervention at either the motivational or the cognitive level of functioning can influence the development of the other in a transactional way.

The Effects of Bright Start on School Achievements

The effects of Bright Start on school achievements were studied by testing the children in a follow-up study (Tzuriel et al., 1999) in Grade 1. The children were administered popular group tests of reading comprehension and math. The findings showed a small, insignificant superiority of the experimental over the comparison group. These findings should be considered in regard to three factors: (1) the nature of the intervention given to the comparison children (basic-skills program specifically geared toward reading and arithmetic), (2) the initial superiority of the comparison over the experimental children, and (3) the strength of the Bright Start implementation in this study. The last factor seems to be crucial, as the program was not implemented ideally using all small-group units, with the original suggested intensity. After all, the core of the program, the small-group units, was implemented only for 32 hours during the year. In spite of the combination of all factors, the experimental group showed somewhat better achievement than the comparison group, and at least had closed the gap that was present initially between the two groups.

The Effects of Bright Start on Modifying Teachers' Mediational Style

One of the phenomena found frequently in implementation of Bright Start is the change in the teachers' mediation style. Tzuriel et al. (1998) investigated the extent to which teachers who apply the Bright Start program for a year, absorbed the principles of the program and actually applied them in their classrooms. Failure to ensure teachers' actual implementation of the core principles of educational programs has been identified as a major reason for the difficulties encountered in demonstrating the effectiveness of even well-known and respected programs. In Bright Start, as in several other structured cognitive curricula, quite special teacher–learner interactions, characterized as "mediated learning," constitute a critical element; in fact, the success of such curricula undoubtedly depends on the teachers' understanding and implementation of the principles and techniques of mediated interactions with the learners.

In this study a sample of 11 kindergarten teachers were trained in Bright Start for 1 year and assigned to kindergartens designated for implementation of the Bright Start program. These teachers comprised the experimental group; all of them were active teachers at the year of the study. The experimental teachers were sampled based on preliminary selection of several kindergartens considered by the Ministry of Education in Israel to have a high proportion of socially disadvantaged and high-risk children and therefore requiring application of Bright Start. A group of control teachers ($n = 11$) was selected from neighborhoods of similar socioeconomic level. The control teachers were pair-matched with the experimental teachers based on years of education, children's families' socioeconomic level, and years of experience in teaching. Training of experimental teachers included a preliminary workshop of 20 hours during 1 week, application of the program for 10 months and supervised training during the year for 1 hour each week. A sample of 220 children was selected for the observation of MLE processes at the end of the intervention. Each teacher was asked to choose from his or her kindergarten 10 children, 5 considered by him or her as functioning on a low level and 5 as functioning on a high level. Thus, the number of children in each of the Treatment groups was 110 ($2 \times 5 \times 11$). Each teacher was asked to teach the group a specific subject given to him or her by the investigators. The teaching sessions were videotaped and later analyzed for mediated learning criteria, using the Observation of Mediation Instrument (Klein, 1988). The findings revealed the experimental teachers to be significantly higher on mediation for transcendence than the control teachers.

Conclusion of Evaluation of Bright Start Studies

The main objectives of the studies on Bright Start were to assess the effectiveness of the program on the children's cognitive modifiability and "learning how to learn" skills, the mediational teaching style of teachers, and children's task-intrinsic motivation and self-regulation. The findings in general confirm our expectations about the program's effectiveness as well as the efficacy of DA measures in revealing children's cognitive modifiability as a function of the cognitive intervention. Children participating in the Bright Start program showed greater improvements on both static-standardized tests and DA tasks than did comparable children who did not receive this program. Of special interest are the DA results, which indicate that the experimental groups benefited more from the mediation given to them within the testing situation than did the control children. The significance of the greater gains of the experimental children should be evaluated in relation to two facts; first, that Bright Start was not fully implemented with them, and second, that the cognitive domains tested were not directly related to the program's activities.

The similar findings from both DA measures, the Complex Figure and the CATM, strengthen our hypothesis about the effects of Bright Start on development of learning skills. The replication of results on both tests might suggest that, unlike skills-based programs, the treatment effects of cognitive education programs can be integrated across skills domains within individuals' cognitive systems. It should be noted that Bright Start does not include any specifically visual–motor exercises. Rather, the whole program is based on visual presentation of stimuli, discussion of strategies for solving problems, metacognitive processes, verbal dialogues, social interactions, and analyses of situations and problems. In spite of the verbal–logical nature of the program, the experimental children could generalize from the mediational experiences and therefore benefited more than the control children from the mediation.

It should also be noted that the changes found on the DA tests should not be interpreted as permanent changes. These changes point to the fact that if sufficient mediation is given in the future to children they will be better prepared to take advantage of the mediation given to them, and even will help them to mediate to themselves in some circumstances.

The findings on the task-intrinsic motivation measures indicate, as expected, that the pre- to postintervention changes were not limited to the cognitive realm but were accompanied by a tendency to be more intrinsically motivated. The experimental groups' tendency toward higher intrinsic motivation, after implementation of the program, can be attributed to the Bright Start emphasis on self-directed activities, expression of personal views, exploration of alternative solutions, reflective thinking, and task-intrinsic motivation produced by the children's perception of their own increased competence.

The motivational findings support the structural cognitive modifiability theory (Feuerstein et al., 1979, 1980) according to which there is a tendency for changes in one of the individual's system components to be "diffused" and to affect the whole. Thus, changes in the motivational aspects affect cognitive aspects and vise versa. The data accord quite nicely as well with Haywood's "motivational theory of cognition" (Haywood, 1980, 1992b; Haywood & Burke, 1977; Haywood & Wachs, 1981), in which intervention at either the motivational or the cognitive level of functioning can influence the development of the other in a transactional way.

The results of the evaluation studies support the argument that DA measures should be used to assess cognitive intervention programs. Previous studies have shown similarly that DA was useful when applied in cognitive education programs aimed at teaching "how to learn" with adolescents (Tzuriel & Alfassi, 1994) or preschool children (Tzuriel & Eiboshitz, 1992). Our argument is that *if the declared goal of the intervention is to teach children how to learn, the outcome measures should tap precisely that goal.* It is surprising therefore to find that many intervention programs aimed at modifying learning skills do not apply DA as a primary outcome measure.

THE STRUCTURED PROGRAM OF VISUAL MOTOR INTEGRATION (SP-VMI)

Other evidence for the utility of DA use in cognitive intervention programs is reported by Tzuriel and Eiboshitz (1992) in regard to the SP-VMI.

Description of the SP-VMI

The objectives of the SP-VMI are to develop visual–motor integration skills that are related to writing and reading abilities. These skills are composed of hand–eye coordination, organization and understanding of written symbols in two-dimensional space. In developing the SP-VMI, the authors relied on three types of theories: (1) visual–motor development theories (Gesell, 1940; Kephart, 1968; Piaget, 1964), (2) theories that emphasize the need for visual–motor mastery as a basic preschool skill, and (3) MLE theory (Feuerstein et al., 1979, 1980).

According to Piaget the developing child learns first to manipulate three-dimensional objects using the principles of assimilation and accommodation. The child then gradually moves to two-dimensional stimuli using the same principles, thus enhancing transfer from one phase to another. Piaget emphasized the assimilation of experience and the transfer of acquired principles to new experiences. In the SP-VMI program these operations are used in combination with MLE criteria, especially those related to activation of metacognitive processes.

In practice the child is asked to copy prearranged three-dimensional patterns or sequences (i.e., sequences of colored plastic pins), to continue these sequences according to the respective principles, and to immediately transfer these patterns into a two-dimensional modality using a restricted space (i.e., a notebook page). Using Kephart's (1968) terminology, the child is developing skills of control over a small space by manipulating three- and two-dimensional objects. Unlike Piaget's and Kephart's conceptions, which conceive of development as a spontaneous process with relatively no involvement of guiding adults, in my approach, based on MLE theory and Vigotskian concepts the adult is more active in modifying and enhancing the child's development. The adult, usually the parent or teacher, monitors the child's learning processes in various ways, including the metacognitive processes and the nonintellective factors, untill the child shows independence in self regulating his or her learning process. The metacognitive strategies refer mainly to an analysis of errors and response style (i.e., analytic versus global, impulsive versus reflective), modeling of specific techniques, and comparing the child's performance to previous own behavior and to the teacher's behavior.

Operative Principles of the SP-VMI Implementation

The SP-VMI is based operationally on the following operative principles:

- The program's phases are congruent with the perceptual–motor developmental stages.
- The visual–motor tasks are constructed in a gradual way so that level of difficulty increases by small steps. This graduation guarantees opportunities for success and enhancement of feelings of competence.
- The teaching process is based on the MLE criteria. The main criteria that are used are Intentionality and Reciprocity, Meaning, Transcendence, Feelings of Competence, and Regulation of Behavior. The combination of these criteria within the teaching process was found effective in several programs with infants and toddlers (Klein, 1996), schoolchildren (Shamir & Tzuriel, 1999; Tzuriel, 1999b), and adolescents (Feuerstein et al., 1980; Tzuriel & Alfassi, 1994).

- The instructions and models of operation administered in the program to the children are simple, structured, and continuously modeled.

From a practical point of view the SP-VMI implementation depends on three elements:

- *The physical conditions.* The physical conditions are arranged so that the lessons are carried out with small groups in the kindergarten. The lessons are carried out in an adjacent room or a separate corner within the kindergarten.
- *Modes of operation.* The teacher uses modeling, full verbalization of the task components and activities (i.e., verbal description of directions and use of spatial orientation concepts), error analysis, and reasoning and justification of the visual–motor performance. Toward the end of each session, after the structured tasks, the children are encouraged to replace the materials and allowed a free-drawing activity for relaxation.
- *Teaching materials.* The teaching materials include small colored blocks, plastic board with holes and plastic pins that can be inserted, pencils, colored crayons, and blank papers.

Evaluation of the SP-VMI

The effectiveness of the SP-VMI was investigated using both static and DA instruments on a sample of kindergartners children. The sample was comprised of a group of disadvantaged ($n = 60$) and special education ($n = 30$) children attending integrated kindergartens. Half of each group was randomly assigned to an experimental group ($n = 45$) and the other half was assigned to a control group ($n = 45$). The special education children were characterized as having adequate learning potential, but for various reasons had learning difficulties, developmental delays, and/or behavior problems. Because of their difficulties they were given educational support within an integrative kindergarten setting. They were not labeled on purpose at this age, but toward the end of the year and before school assignment they are diagnosed and labeled. The special education children usually receive individual tutoring for 2–3 hours a week by a special education teacher to prepare them for school.

The experimental children received the program for about 3 months, three sessions each week, each session lasting 20 minutes, and a total of $11\frac{1}{2}$ hours of intervention. Different static visual–motor tests and one DA measure, the Complex Figure test–version for young children were administered to the whole sample before and after the intervention. For the purpose of this study two versions of the Complex Figure test were developed. The second version was more difficult than the first one and was given after the intervention to avoid a ceiling effect (the two versions are presented in Chapter 6).

The data were analyzed by a repeated measures MANOVA of Treatment (experimental versus control) by Type of Child (Disadvantaged/Special Education) by Time (pre/post Intervention). The dependent variables were the static test scores and the Complex Figure Pre- and Post-Teaching scores (the scores of both before and after the intervention were used). The results indicated an overall significant Treatment by Time interaction with a canonical correlation of .93. The findings showed pre- to postintervention improvement of the experimental over the control group on most static tests and on the Complex Figure measures (Copy-II and Memory-II). On all of the static measures the experimental group scored about the same as the control group before the intervention, but higher after the intervention. On the Complex Figure both groups scored about the same before the intervention but after the intervention, the experimental group showed an increase whereas the control group showed a *decrease*. This last result was explained by the more difficult version of the Complex Figure given after the intervention. It is interesting to note that only the Post-Teaching scores of the Complex Figure test have emerged as significant (Copy-II and Memory-II).

The DA data were further analyzed using Gain Scores on the Complex Figure. A repeated measures MANOVA of Treatment by Time (2×2) was carried out on the Copy and Memory gain Scores. The findings showed very clearly that both groups had similar Gain Scores before the intervention. However, after the intervention the experimental group showed an increase whereas the control group showed a decrease. A univariate analysis showed that the overall significant interaction (canonical correlation = .54) was contributed by both Copy and Memory scores.

The improvement of the experimental group occurred despite the more difficult version of the Complex Figure given at the end of the program. The increase in the Gain scores found in the experimental group was interpreted as improvement in the children's cognitive modifiability or their "learning how to learn." The decrease of the Gain scores in the control group strengthens the hypothesis that the differences are due to treatment effects. It seems that in spite of the more difficult task given at the end of the intervention, the experimental group improved their skills of how to benefit from the mediation provided within the testing situation. The control group, in spite of their maturity ($5\frac{1}{2}$ months older at the end of intervention) and of their previous learning of the Complex Figure task (at the start of the intervention) did not know how to use and benefit from the mediation given to them. The decrease in the control group can be attributed mainly to the more difficult task given at the end of the program. The results deriving from the DA measure, in addition to verifying the MLE theory and the effects of MLE within the SP-VMI, shed a unique light on the effects of the cognitive intervention program that could not be achieved with static test scores.

THE PEER MEDIATION WITH YOUNG CHILDREN (PMYC) PROGRAM

The PMYC program is a novel intervention paradigm based on the socio-cultural theory of Vygotsky and the MLE theory of Feuerstein. The objectives of the PMYC program, developed recently at Bar-Ilan University (Shamir & Tzuriel, 1999; Tzuriel & Shamir, 1999) are as follows:

- To enhance a mediating teaching style among young children in Grade 3
- To develop the learning skills and cognitive modifiability of young mediators
- To facilitate performance and learning skills of young children who are mediated by their experienced mediator peers

In the following, a brief description of the PMYC program is given followed by a presentation of a study aimed at evaluation of the PMYC program and validation of the peer-mediation model.

Characteristics of the PMYC Program

Previous research on peer tutoring and peer collaboration was focused on separate aspects of the interaction such as structure of the tutorial interaction, specific tutor behaviors, degree of student's regulation of the learning process, and status within the tutor–tutee relationship (i.e., Rogoff, 1990). In many studies only one or two of the above aspects were studied. Unlike the peer tutoring or peer collaboration approaches, four points characterize the peer-mediation approach.

- The peer mediation approach is based on a comprehensive theoretical model, which combines cognitive and emotional components. These components are entailed in the mediated learning experience criteria.
- The peer mediation approach goes beyond content domains and contexts of learning and can be applied with problem solving tasks as well as with school subject matters.
- The mediation procedures used in the peer mediation program are, on one hand, structured and theoretically guided, but on the other hand, contain creative ways for mutuality between the mediator and the learner. The mediator can modify his or her mediation as a response to changes in the learner's behavior.
- The status of the mediator differs from that of the learner—the mediator, as a more experienced individual, has an active-modifying role in the interaction. The peer-mediation approach has the advantage of both

the experience of an older mediating peer and the collaboration of an almost same age peer that participate in the teaching interaction.

The PMYC is composed of three components:

*   *Teaching* young children in Grade 3 the basic principles of mediation.
*   *Observing* and discussing a didactic movie, which demonstrates mediation processes with young children (in the movie, each of the first five MLE criteria is presented using an actual learning event).
*   *Practicing* of mediation principles with peers using both a multimedia program and a conventional interactive teaching.

Evaluation of the PMYC Program

The PMYC was evaluated in a study using a sample of young third graders (n = 89) who were randomly assigned to experimental (n = 43) and control (n = 46) groups (Shamir & Tzuriel, 1999); For each mediator-child in third grade a younger learner-child in first grade was matched. The matching was carried out based on the intellectual level of the mediator and the learner, as measured by standardized tests. Following the PMYC program each pair was involved in a teaching session in which the mediator has to teach his or her younger peer how to solve seriational problems using the "Think-in-Order" multimedia program (Tzuriel & Shamir, in press). The objectives of the study were as follows:

*   To investigate the effects of the PMYC program on mediation teaching style of both the third grade mediators and first grade learners.
*   To investigate the effects of the PMYC program on cognitive modifiability of both the third grade mediators and first grade learners. The cognitive modifiability was measured by DA measures administered after the teaching session to mediators and learners in the experimental and control groups.
*   To investigate the effects of the intellectual level of the mediator and the intellectual level of the learner on the mediation process.
*   To investigate the prediction of children's cognitive modifiability (both mediators and learners) by the mediational style and intellectual level of the mediators and learners.

The sample consisted of 178 pupils (89 pairs); half of them were mediators (in Grade 3) and and the other half (in Grade 1) were learners. The mediators and learners came from six classes (three third grade and three first grade) in a primary school. The mediator group was composed of 50 boys (56.2%) and 39 girls (43.8%). The learner group was composed of 41 boys (46.1%) and 48 girls (53.4%). The mediator and learner groups were each divided into two subgroups of high and low cognitive level, based on their scores on the RSPM (third-grade mediators) or the RCPM (first-grade learners). Each high- and low-functioning mediator was matched with a high- and low-functioning learner in a counterbalanced design.

The study's procedure was composed of four stages:

Stage 1—Administration of initial cognitive tests. The mediators were administered the RSPM and the learners were administered the RCPM. In addition, the learner group was administered the Pre-Teaching CSTM test. The CSTM Pre-Teaching will be compared later to the CSTM Post-Teaching, which followed the peer-mediation stage.

Stage 2—Application of the PMYC program. In this stage the mediators in the experimental group participated in the PMYC program whereas the mediators in the control group received an intervention aimed at emphasizing the importance of peer interaction. In the second part of this stage both the experimental and control mediators received a demonstration of the "Think-in-Order" multimedia program and practiced some of the items. The "Think-in-Order" program is a multimedia program based on the CSTM (Tzuriel, 1995b; Tzuriel & Shamir, in press). The purpose of the demonstration and practice of the "Think-in- Order" program was to familiarize the mediators with the program's features and the procedures of teaching. It should be noted that both the experimental and control children received the same preparation for teaching of the program. The main difference between the two groups was participation in the PMYC program.

Stage 3—Videotaping of peer-mediation interaction. In this stage the experimental and control children were involved in peer-mediation interaction where the mediators were required to teach their young counterparts the mediation phase of the "Think-in-Order" program. The interactions were videotaped for 30 minutes and analyzed later using the OMI (Klein, 1988) with some adaptations for young children. Each child (teachers and learners) was given a score on each of the following MLE criteria: Intentionality and Reciprocity (focusing), Meaning (affecting), Transcendence (expanding), Feelings of Competence (rewarding), and Regulation of Behavior. The reliability of the MLE interaction scores was examined by two raters who observed the videotapes and rated each child using the OMI. The interrater reliability coefficients on a separate sample of children ($n = 10$) were between .85 and .95 for the different criteria.

Stage 4—Testing of cognitive modifiability. The mediators in both the experimental and control groups were administered the Analogies subtest from the CMB (Tzuriel, 1995a, 2000d, see Chapter 6). The CMB Analogies Subtest, which is a dynamic test, was administered in order to examine the effects of the PMYC program on the mediators' cognitive modifiability. Learners in both the experimental and control groups were administered the Post-Teaching phase of the CSTM test. The improvement on the seriational tasks was measured by comparing the CSTM Pre-Teaching score (given in Stage 1) to the Post-Teaching score (given in Stage 4).

The MLE scores were analyzed by a MANOVA of Treatment (experimental/control) by Mediators' Cognitive Level (high/low) by Learners' Cognitive Level (high/low) ($2 \times 2 \times 2$). The findings clearly indicate that the mediation level of the children in the experimental group was significantly and uniquely higher than the mediation level of the children in the control group on each of the five MLE criteria (see Figure 9.3). Separate analysis on the learners mediation scores revealed similar results. The last finding is intriguing because the learners, who did not participate in the PMYC program, showed higher scores than their control counterparts as a result of being taught by their peers who learned how to mediate.

As can be seen in Figure 9.3 the highest group differences were found in the criteria of Feelings of Competence, Regulation of Behavior, and Transcendence. These findings shed light on the spontaneous mediation style of 8-year-olds (third graders), who usually do not get direct intervention to develop their mediation teaching style. Children at this age might show spontaneously some indications for intentionality and maybe a low and negligible level of other mediations, as evidenced in the control group. However, after being exposed to the MLE principles in a structured way and practice them during the short supervised PMYC intervention, a dramatic change was found in their mediational teaching style. They used more principles and generalizations (transcendence), more rewarding and feelings of success (competence) with their peers, and more help to to regulate and organize their peers' behavior adapting it to the task demands. The regulation of behavior was expressed by slowing down the process of task execution ("stop and think"), suggesting planning before performance, looking

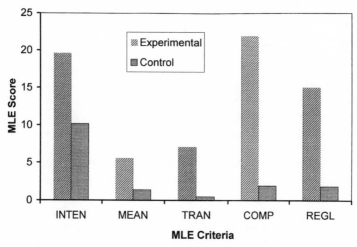

Figure 9.3. Mediators' MLE scores during peer-mediation in the experimental and control groups.

for stages of implementation ("what comes first?"), and checking the solution for mistakes.

One of the questions of the study was whether the mediation teaching style of mediators and learners depend on their cognitive level. In other words, the question is whether a certain match between the cognitive levels of the mediator and that of the learner produces the most efficient mediation style. Vygotsky (1978) himself claimed that learning and cognitive change are more effective when the learner interact with a more experienced adult or peer. Tudge (1992) have documented that peer learning is an effective means to improve cognitive growth of young children, especially when one child is more advanced, cognitively, than the other (Tudge, 1999). Both researcers, however, did not refer to the differential effects of the cognitive level of the mediator or the learner on the learning outcomes. This question was examined by two MANOVA's of Treatment × Mediator's Cognitive Level × Learner's Cognitive Level (2 × 2 × 2), carried out on mediator's and on learner's Total MLE scores. The findings showed no significant interactions for either the mediator's or the learner's scores.

This question was investigated further by comparing two subscores of *Giving* versus *Requesting* of mediation. The findings indicated two significant and complementary interaction patterns, which reflect mutuality between Requesting of Mediation for Meaning from the learner's side and Giving of Mediation for Meaning from the mediator's side. (1) In the low-functioning learners group, *Giving* of Mediation for Meaning was higher among experimental than among control mediators. (2) In the low-functioning learners group, *Requesting* of Mediation for Meaning was higher among learners taught by experimental mediators than among learners taught by control mediators. These mutuality between Giving and Requesting of Mediation for Meaning shows that mediators in the experimental group spontaneously adapted their mediation to the cognitive level of the learners, and that their mediation was reciprocated by the low-functioning learner. Similar kind of mutuality was found in previous mother–child MLE interactions (Tzuriel, 1999; Tzuriel & Eran, 1990; Tzuriel & Ernst, 1990; Tzuriel & Weiss, 1998a; Tzuriel & Weitz, 1998).

These findings suggest that the mediators in the experimental group not only learned how to mediate better but also internalized the mediation mechanisms and used them differentially with peers of high versus low cognitive ability. In some intuitive and sensitive way the experimental children could adjust their mediation efforts to the level of the child they were teaching. Also, it seems that better mediatuion does not necessarily relate to the cognitive level of the teacher.

The second part of the study was related to the effects of the PMYC program on children's cognitive performance and cognitive modifiability of the mediators and the learners. The effects of treatment on cognitive modifiability of the teachers and learners are shown in Figures 9.4 and 9.5.

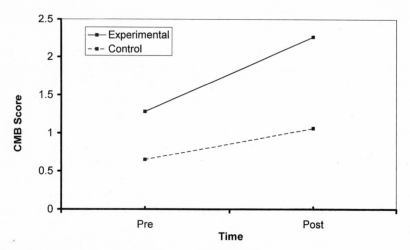

Figure 9.4. Pre- and Post-Teaching scores of mediators (Grade 3) on the CMB Analogies subtest in the experimental and control groups.

The mediators in the experimental group (see Figure 9.4) showed significantly higher Pre-Teaching scores than the control children. Furthermore, a significant interaction of Treatment (experimental/control) by Time (Pre/Post) indicated that the experimental group made higher improvement from Pre- to Post-Teaching than the control group. These findings clearly indicate that the effects of the PMYC were transferred beyond the mediational domain. The

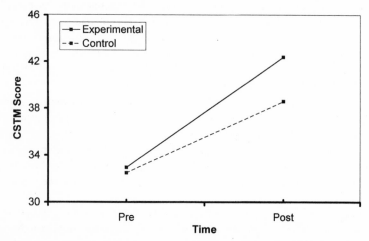

Figure 9.5. Pre- and Post-Teaching scores of learners (Grade 1) on the CSTM test in the experimental and control groups.

mediators in the experimental group not only used higher level of mediation in their interaction with their younger peers but could also use their refined mediation skills to perform better on an abstract cognitive test such as the CMB Analogies and benefit more from the mediation given to them within the DA test than their control counterparts. It should be emphasized that the higher performance and improvement on the DA measure shown by the experimental mediators was beyond the cognitive and behavioral domain taught during the PMYC program.

The findings in the learner group were even more intriguing (See Figure 9.5). Experimental learners (i.e., they were mediated by their peers in the experimental group but actually did not receive the program) showed about the same level of performance on the CSTM Pre-Teaching test as control learners (i.e., they were mediated by their peers in the control group). However, on the Post-Teaching test the experimental learners showed significantly higher scores than the control learners. This finding is impressive in view of the fact that the mediation session of the first grade learners with their third grade peers was only about an hour. Thus, the effects of the PMYC program were transferred not only to the cognitive modifiability domain of the mediator who participated in the program but also affected the cognitive modifiability of the learner who was not part of the program but was mediated by a peer who participated previously in the program.

10

Epilogue

This epilogue will consider two episodes experienced by me while giving workshops as a DA trainer. These episodes exemplify dilemmas in real life situations and conflicts that psychologists and educators who practice DA might encounter. Subsequent sections of this chapter discuss issues that are related to use of DA in different settings, unresolved research questions, and varied applications of DA. The chapter concludes with questions and issues that derive from MLE theory, which is one of the bases for the DA approach presented in this book. Although those issues are not directly related to DA, they are nevertheless within the scope of DA and relate to the subjects discussed in this book.

CROSS-CULTURAL DILEMMAS OF PRACTICING COGNITIVE EDUCATION

A few years ago I was invited to South Africa to consult and to give a series of workshops on DA and cognitive intervention. One of the workshops was for a group of leaders in education who came from different regions of the country. During this workshop I demonstrated an assessment of a few children using some of the DA instruments for young children. In a discussion that followed the demonstration a difficult question was raised by one of the participants: "Why should we adopt a cognitive education approach, which emphasizes the Western type of thinking?" The emphasis on cognitive strategies, systematic exploratory behavior, analytic perception, planning, and logical thinking seemed to that person to oppose his tribal tradition of sharing, associative, and spontaneous thinking. The ideas of change, cognitive modifiability, innovation, and creativity were perceived as a menace to the tradition of oral teaching, rote learning, and the values of sharing and collective knowledge that he grew up with and knew best. Paraphrasing, his question came down to: "Aren't you, the cognitive education people, trying to patronize others by suggesting a more 'efficient' way of learning and thinking, so different from the familiar system of thinking that has worked well for us for many centuries?" The cognitive education strategies were clearly perceived as a menace.

I tried to answer this dilemma in a mediational way by asking questions. "Suppose you have to have a brain operation. Would you trust someone from your tribe to do it, or a brain surgeon who has the education, practice, and experience gained with the help of the so-called Western type of thinking?" "If you want your people to have their equal share in society as pilots, engineers, or bank managers, what kind of thinking processes do you think they need?"

At this point I gave my personal story which expresses my personal philosophy. My father, who was born in 1907 in Yemen, grew up in a traditional simple society with no technological development (i.e., there was no electricity, cars, or running water at home). Nevertheless, he comes from a rich Jewish culture, which emphasizes a tradition of learning, noble interpersonal relationships, education for deep human values, enthusiasm in worshipping God, beautiful customs; yearnings for Zion expressed in daily prayers, singing, and dancing. The culture he comes from was traditional, conservative, and continuous, with a central theme of perseveration of the status quo, and conscious transmission of culture from one generation to the next. When he was exposed to the "Western" type of thinking he had to adjust, in a very short time, to a technological, open, and constantly changing society that differs from his in terms of content and experience, and in terms of structure and form.

I adopted many of my father's "Oriental" and traditional values, customs, and an "Oriental" thinking style. However, when I am conducting research, analyzing test findings, reporting the end results of my studies, or planning my travel schedule, I adopt the "Western" type of thinking. I believe that different cultural orientations can be integrated, each living in peace with the other without losing its identity. A person can move flexibly from one orientation to another based on the requirements of the context and situation. The need for this flexibility applies to a variety of populations who, for socio-historical reasons live as subcultures within a broad culture, and whose members might be penalized by inadequate diagnostic procedures or inappropriate teaching strategies.

The second episode took place in upstate New York (USA). The experience I had there brought me to sharpen my ideas regarding the DA strategies I have developed and application of cognitive education strategies. Within the context of demonstration of DA of young children, I had to assess a 5- or 6-year-old hyperactive child, using the CATM test. One of the child's most severe problems was his impulsive motor approach. When presented an analogy problem, using the CATM blocks, he was immediately grabbing another block to complete the problem without trying to process the dimensions of the problem, anticipate the solution verbally, and chose the right block. One of the intervention strategies I used was to hold his hands on the table, let him absorb the details, verbalize the information, define and verbally anticipate the required block, and only then choose the block from the pile. A few weeks later, when I asked for a feedback from the psychologists who participated in the DA workshop (for most of them this was their first encounter with a dynamic/interactive approach), I got a surprising response: "You were too physical with the child." When I asked the workshop organizer "What is the meaning of 'too physical'?" the answer was "physical" in the sense of having been too rough in my efforts to restrain and then reorient the child.

In the United States, there are certain rules restricting teachers and psychologists from touching their students. My attempts and hopes to help the child to control his impulsivity by holding his hands and then, perhaps, teaching him how to self-regulate his behavior by holding back his hands by himself, were perceived as opposing the child's welfare.

Both examples represent the dilemma that we face in our day-to-day experiences with children, parents, and teachers. Some of our cognitive educational ideas and techniques are not so self evident to others.

WHY IS IMPLEMENTATION OF DA DIFFICULT?

Although there is ample evidence that cognitive educational theories and practice have come to the forefront of people's awareness and become more popular than in the past, there are some unresolved dilemmas that should be countered and dealt with. One of them is a question that has puzzled me for many years: Why is it that ideas that seem to me full of common sense are so difficult to be accepted and/or implemented? For example, the idea that measures of modifiability are more closely related to teaching processes by which the child is taught how to process information, than they are to standardized conventional measures of intelligence seems to me to be very attractive, yet is rarely adopted in practice. In other words, the mediational strategies used within the DA procedure are more closely related to learning processes in school and to other life contexts than are conventional static methods. Why then is this practice not more prevalent and popular?

The efficacy of DA has been proven by many researchers such as Brown, Budoff, Campione, Carlson, Elliott, Feuerstein, Guthke, Hamers, Haywood, Hessels, Kaniel, Lidz, Resing, Sternberg, Swanson, Tzuriel, Vygotsky, Wiedl, and many others. But despite the many studies in the last two decades, DA has still to prove itself as an efficient method of assessment. Does DA carry with it some difficulties to some people that overcome the common sense of its use? This question transcends the specific context of DA as it has implications for adopting a cognitive education approach in classroom teaching. Does implementation of cognitive education strategies and programs, beyond the practical aspects of

funding and training, carry with it a menace to some people? Are cognitive education programs that emphasize cognitive processes (rather than content) perceived suspiciously, and if so, why? The answer to these questions might lie in
some of the validation questions and unresolved issues that are discussed below.

SOME UNRESOLVED ISSUES

In spite of the efficacy of DA there are some unresolved problems that are
related to cost-effectiveness, level of training, reliability and validity, and continuity between assessment and intervention. The cost-effectiveness considerations
relate to the fact that DA takes much more time to administer than static tests,
and it requires more skill, better training, more experience, and greater investment of efforts. School psychologists and policymakers may ask themselves "how
can we afford testing a child for 6–8 hours when the case load is high and the
time required for DA exceeds the maximal 2–3 hours given for each case?"
Policymakers will surely ask why they should invest in methods that require several times as many hours from the psychologists as do present methods. More
evidence should be presented for the effectiveness of DA, especially in relation
to popular criterion measures of school achievements (i.e., reading comprehension, math). The answer lies in what one considers being the major goal of the
assessment. If the goal is to provide a quick and an economical device to scan
the child's current difficulties and to predict his or her future performance, then
static tests are more useful than DA tests. If the goal is to reveal the child's learning potential and learning processes and, as a result, to prescribe specific learning strategies, then DA seems to be a better approach. To some degree the goal
of the DA approach is to refute the prediction of the static test approach.

The distinction between the static and DA goals derives from different
philosophical perspectives. Some authors referred to the differences between the
static and DA approaches as those between *passive-acceptant* versus *active-
modifying* approaches, respectively (Feuerstein et al., 1979).

The challenge of DA, then, is to be certain that the information derived is
worth the investment required to get it, and that the information is then used in
a way that results in educational benefits for the tested child. Proponents of DA
frequently mention the argument that society at large and the individual, in particular, benefit in the long run (and often in the short run) from DA. A short,
"instant" assessment might be cheaper in the short run but superficial, wasteful,
and less effective in the long run. DA, on the other hand, is lengthier and more
expensive but provides in-depth and qualitatively better results, which ensure
accurate future intervention procedures. Psychologists, educators, and policymakers should be convinced first that the information derived from DA is worth
the investment required to get it, and that the information acquired will then be

used in a way that will have an impact on specific learning strategies and academic achievements.

IS COGNITIVE MODIFIABILITY GENERALIZED ACROSS DOMAINS?

Several intriguing issues raised so far have opened a new field for further research. One of the main issues is *to what extent cognitive modifiability is generalized across domains*. This issue not only has theoretical importance but carries with it practical implications for designing of tests and mediational procedures. In several studies carried out in the laboratory of Bar Ilan University, we found that different measures of cognitive modifiability did not correlate significantly at kindergarten age, but with increasing age there was a tendency for increased correlations; a phenomenon that is attributed to the development of metacognitive skills with age. The increasing metacognitive processes helped children to benefit from mediation in one domain and transfer whatever has been learned to another domain. Metacognitive processes had a consolidating effect by "bridging" cognitive modifiability across different domains.

PREDICTION OF SCHOOL ACHIEVEMENTS BY DA VERSUS STATIC MEASURES

Another important issue refers to prediction of academic achievements by DA versus static tests. The results of several studies support the argument that DA measures are more accurate than static measures in evaluation of cognitive intervention programs (Guthke & Wingenfeld, 1992; Tzuriel, 1989a, 1992a, 1998; Tzuriel et al., 1999), especially when the aim is to evaluate "learning how to learn" skills and cognitive modifiability. My argument is that *if the declared goal of the intervention is to teach children how to learn, the outcome measures should tap precisely that goal*. The outcome measures should be assessed dynamically; change criteria and cognitive modifiability indicators should be the focus of evaluation. It is surprising, therefore, why many intervention programs aimed at modifying learning skills do not use DA as a primary outcome measure.

One of the practical problems that we often encounter when testing children from a different culture is how to differentiate, on an individual level, between those who manifest low level of functioning as a result of *cultural difference* and those whom also have experienced *cultural deprivation*. These two concepts were discussed in Chapter 3. In this respect, the DA approach offers an alternative, which is superior over the static approach not only for its differential diagnostic value but also for its potential prescriptive remediation of deficiencies and enhancement of learning processes. On a broader sociohistorical scale it can open opportunities for investigating cognitive change processes as a function of specific mediational procedures, implementation of learning contexts, and use of mental operations across cultures. What is important is not so much *what* children know or do but rather *how* they learn, and how they modify their cognitive structures as a function of mediational processes. Most important in further research is for researchers to look at children's cognitive modifiability indices as a function of specific cultural components that enhance mediation and change processes within families, classrooms, and more extensively in broader social circles. DA has much to offer examiners who want to understand what is limiting the child's performance and what may be helpful for facilitating higher levels of performance (Elliott, 1993; Feuerstein et al., 1979; Haywood, 1997; Tzuriel, 1997a, 1998, 2000c).

RELIABILITY OF DA

A major unresolved issue that should be further researched is the *reliability* of DA. One of the objectives of DA is to change the individual's cognitive functioning within the testing context so as to produce internal "unreliability." Reliability can be assessed then by interrater comparisons (Tzuriel, 1992b). The psychometric properties of the tests can be examined by group administration of the DA measures as actually was done by several researchers (Kaniel et al., 1991; Tzuriel, 1998; Tzuriel & Feuerstein, 1992; Tzuriel & Schanck, 1994). The group DA results, besides providing information about the psychometric properties of the tests, have been found to be crucial for indicating prescriptive teaching and educational strategies for the integration of students into educational systems.

Interrater agreement of DA tests has been studied intensively by Samuels et al. (1989) and Tzuriel and Samuels (2000), with learning disabled and educable mentally handicapped children. The authors showed, for example, that the overall interrater percentage of agreement for rated *deficient cognitive functions* was 87.6 and 91.6% for *type of mediation*. For different cognitive tasks, a different profile of deficient cognitive functions has been observed and different types of mediation can be applied. In spite of these findings more research is needed to verify the reliability of judgments made with DA procedures.

VALIDITY OF DA

Validity is a major concern for any test, especially for DA, which claims to be a more accurate measure of learning potential than static tests. Validation of DA is much more complex than validation of a static test, for several reasons.

First, DA claims to have a broader scope of goals such as assessing initial performance, deficient cognitive functions, type, and amount of mediation, nonintellective factors, and different parameters of modifiability. Each of these dimensions requires a different criterion; some of them might overlap. Second, many concepts within the MLE theoretical framework applied extensively in assessment and intervention still require empirical validation (e.g., the distinction among deficient cognitive functions of the input, elaboration, and output phases of the mental act). It is important to validate which deficient cognitive functions are more easily observed than others are, and in what kind of task domain.

One of the problems in validating DA is the need to develop a criterion variable that is derived from a cognitive intervention. The criterion validity of DA should be tested against criteria that match the nature of the testing, namely, with changes in other domains (e.g., school achievements, cognitive changes on other tests). This requires implementing a cognitive education program that is aimed at bringing about these changes. This point has been discussed previously in relation to the use of DA measures in cognitive education programs (Tzuriel, 1989a, 2000c). Because a main objective of many programs is to teach children how to learn and to be independent in developing their learning potential, it follows that exactly this ability of learning how to learn should be assessed as a primary effect in a program's evaluation. Unfortunately, not many studies concentrate on this aspect of validity. Many investigators have used standard normative tests of general intelligence to assess children's stores of knowledge, and they have sometimes regarded the results as indicators of learning potential.

The main validation of DA should refer to prediction of aspects that are not predicted by static test results. Future research should tap questions such as the effects of failure and success in test items on subsequent performance, the effects of nonintellective factors on cognitive change, and the utility of specific mediation strategies on both specific cognitive and motivational factors.

A major criticism of DA relates to the relatively high prediction of school achievement by static test scores. Some new evidence shows however that DA scores are more predictive of school achievement than are static test scores (i.e., Guthke et al., 1997, Hessels, 1997; Resing & Van Wijk, 1996; Tzuriel, 2000c, 2001b; Tzuriel et al., 1999). The literature is replete with evidence showing a strong relation between IQ and school achievement. For example, Fraser, Walberg, Welch, and Hattie (1987) carried out a meta-analysis based on 2575 studies, to support the relationship between IQ and academic achievement. The massive data set in this case showed a familiar IQ–achievement correlation of .71. This means that nearly 50% of the variance in learning outcomes for students was explained by differences in psychometric IQ. This is indeed a crowning achievement for psychometrics. My argument is that although no one argues that ability is uncorrelated with achievement, three extremely important questions remain: What happened to the other 50% of the achievement variance? When IQ predicts low achievement, what is necessary to defeat that prediction? What factors influencing the unexplained variance can help us to defeat the prediction in the explained variance?

The theories and research evidence presented in this book validate DA as a useful approach for measuring children's cognitive abilities, especially their cognitive modifiability. In Chapters 7–9 I tried to demonstrate the utility of DA findings in three major domains: educational, developmental, and intervention. Current research in these areas shows that children's performance in a DA context is a more accurate indicator of their learning potential than performance on a standardized static test.

One of the repeated findings was that the lower the initial cognitive performance level of the child, the more effective is the mediation given in DA for modifying the child's performance. Studies with various groups of children (i.e., regular school children, deaf children, mentally handicapped children, children from disadvantaged families, minority children, and learning disabled children) have shown higher predictive value of school performance than standard static tests. Similarly, DA was found to be most useful when applied in cognitive education programs aimed at teaching children systematic data gathering, problem solving strategies, and learning "how to learn."

The use of DA in different settings and groups has proved its efficiency not only as an evaluation tool but also as a powerful intervention procedure. The integrative blend of assessment and intervention is novel in view of the fact that over so many decades each activity was separated, conceptually and methodologically. Another aspect of DA is that it offers an optimistic view of the individual as a problem-solving thinker, who possesses much higher ability than what is manifested in other testing approaches.

Haywood and Tzuriel (1992a) have concluded in their epilogue on DA that in spite of the remaining difficult problems and unresolved issues,

> interactive approaches to psychoeducational assessment appear to offer useful and even rich alternatives to standardized, normative assessment. The DA approaches appear to offer the possibility of more adequate assessment of handicapped persons (e.g., mentally retarded, sensory impaired, emotionally disturbed persons) and persons with learning disabilities, than do standardized, normative tests. They appear also to offer the possibility of some solution to "nondiscriminatory" assessment and educational programming for persons in minority ethnic groups and those in "transcultural" status: immigrants and those with language differences. (pp. 56–57)

Grigorenko and Sternberg (1998), in their extensive review of dynamic testing, concluded that it is difficult to argue that DA "clearly has proved its usefulness and has shown distinct advantages over traditional static testing relative to the resources that need to be expanded" (p. 105). They admit, however, that DA has suggested interesting paradigms as well as promising findings, and that in the future DA will prove to be a valuable resource to the psychological profession. They suggested that in order to make DA studies more compelling certain requirements are needed. One of these requirements is definition of DA as an independent tradition in the psychology of testing, in terms of better distinction of goals and methodologies. On a small-scale level the requirements are to conduct studies with larger populations, to validate DA against educational and professional criteria, and to replicate findings beyond different laboratories and specific methodologies.

My conclusion, based on educational and intervention research with young children is more positive than Grigorenko and Sternberg's conclusion. Some of this research was probably not familiar to them as well as developmental research that provides further support for the utility of the DA (a detailed review of the developmental line of research is given in Tzuriel, 1999a, and in Chapter 8 of this book). I believe that DA has already established itself as a separate branch in the psychology of assessment, especially among circles that are involved in the practice of education than among circles that are research oriented. I agree, though, with their requirements for defining DA as an independent tradition in the psychology of testing, in terms of better distinction of goals and methodology, and in regard to the need for studies with larger populations, validation of DA against educational and professional criteria, and replication of findings beyond different laboratories and specific methodologies.

THE NEED FOR A TRANSACTIONAL ECOLOGICAL MODEL IN MEDIATED LEARNING INTERACTIONS

MLE has been conceptualized so far as a determinant of cognitive development, especially of cognitive modifiability. It seems to me, however, that the time is ripe for extending the concept to a more complex transactional–ecological model. In this model, we should take into account the reciprocal nature of MLE, cognition, and emotion as well as treating MLE as only one component within a holistic framework. This is especially important because of the danger of overextending the presumed influence of MLE and attributing overly many cognitive and noncognitive effects to MLE.

Overgeneralization of MLE theory to explain too many phenomena may bring about only the devaluation of the theory. It is most important now that the effects of MLE are established, to delineate the conceptual limits of the theory. The term *transactional* rather than *interactional* is meant to emphasize the idea of the mutual effects of MLE and cognitive functioning. Wachs and Plomin (1991) defined interaction as involving different individuals differentially reacting to similar environments, whereas transaction implies effects that are differential both for individuals and for environments. Tzuriel (1991a) conceptualized interaction as characterized by relative simplicity and transience of effects, whereas the transactional process is dialectically *circular* with a continual change and adjustment of factors. This dialectical circularity poses a real challenge for theory development and methodology, but with recent advances in technology and statistical analyses it can be handled efficiently. We should be aware that there is a possibility that children's cognitive functioning might influence parental MLE strategies, and that the circular relation depends on broader family, social, and cultural contexts.

Similar conceptions have been discussed in Bronfenbrenner's (1979) ecological approach and by Super and Harkness (1986) who also proposed the concept of *developmental niches*. Some evidence for the effects of age, context, severity of child's problems, and cultural background has been reported in Chapter 8. The affective and motivational processes of children and their parents are also very important—as prerequisite factors in determining the nature of MLE processes, children's cognitive modifiability, and the nature of their reciprocal effects.

THE FAMILY AS A MEDIATIONAL UNIT

Another issue is the number of mediating agents within the family. Most research has focused on the interaction of a child with one person, usually the mother; only rarely do observations consider a child's multiple relationships with the father, grandparents, siblings, and other members of the child's extended social world. The usual focus on dyadic interactions derives not only from the need for simplicity, but from the assumption that this type of interaction is the ideal, unique prototype, of a child's interactions with familiar others. Rogoff (1990) has challenged this idea by suggesting the concept of *apprenticeship*. According to this concept, children's development occurs as they participate in organized sociocultural activities in a process resembling an apprenticeship. This mediated apprenticeship process involves shared problem solving, focus on routine activities, supportive structuring of the novice's efforts, and gradual transfer of responsibility from mediator(s) to child.

While most investigators so far have looked into the role of mothers in the child/adult interaction, the role of the family as a total mediating unit has been neglected. Research findings indicate that even in the first months of life, fathers and mothers engage in different styles of interactions with their infant. In general, fathers' interactions are characterized by play activities, whereas mothers' interactions are characterized by child-care activities (Bornstein & Lamb, 1992). Families, for example, usually differ in the "normative mediational scripts" they have or activate in their daily interactions. These scripts depend, in turn, on larger cultural norms and styles of mediation. Normative mediational scripts refer to the parental mediational patterns developed within each family that are intimately related to the family's unique norms. In some families a spontaneous automatic mediational chain of activity is triggered in response to a child's behavior, whereas in other families the same type of behavior passes unnoticed. What makes some families more mediational than others? What are the influences of life events, family structure, and cultural background?

Clinical experience has shown that some individuals exhibit a natural talent for efficient mediation, in spite of the fact that they have never been exposed to the MLE concept. It is likely that they learned to be efficient mediators via the modeling process encountered during their formative years of development. The question is whether there is also some inherited component for this talent. Greenberg (1993), basing his discussion on an ethological theory, suggested that individuals have differential needs to mediate, and that such needs operate like other organismic needs such as eating, breathing, or processing information. This idea raises the question of whether there are prerequisite factors for becoming an efficient mediator. This question is of most importance in intervention programs in which parents or teachers are being trained to be mediators.

DOES QUANTITY OF INTERACTIONS TRANSFORM INTO QUALITY?

MLE processes are considered to be a qualitative aspect of parent–child interactions. If children experience some requisite amount of this interaction, their development is secured. The problem is that many children do not have enough time to spend with their parents in order to benefit from the qualitative interaction that may be offered. Some children have many interactions but those interactions may be deficient in terms of their quality, while other children may experience high-quality interactions but fewer of them. The question is, where can we draw the line between a small amount of interactions (quantity) but saturated with MLE interactions (quality) and a large amount of interactions but diluted in terms of the MLE given? This question is of utmost importance for parents who are frequently occupied with their careers and cannot spend enough time with their children. A study carried out in our laboratory at Bar-Ilan University focused around this question and also the complementary question of how much and what type of mediation is given by mothers and fathers to sons versus daughters (Tzuriel & Hatzir, 1999).

DOES MLE PROCESS TRANSFER ACROSS CONTEXTS?

Another most intriguing question in MLE intervention programs is the transfer of treatment effects through circular influence. One can think here of the analogy of the process of osmosis, according to which there is a tendency for a liquid to be diffused through a membrane—which typically separates a solvent and a solution—and finally equalize the concentrations. In intervention programs with parents, there are several steps of transfer of MLE principles from parents to targets (i.e., the children). The main objective, usually, in teaching MLE processes to parents is to give them as tools to use with their children, with the aim to bring about better cognitive performance and academic success in children. The phases of transmission are depicted in Figure 10.1.

Each step carries with it some reduction of the initial intervention power. The question is how to facilitate the intervention. What other ingredients are required to catalyze the mediational process?

Figure 10.1. Flowchart of the effects of intervention with parents on children's functioning.

THE QUESTION OF THE OUTCOME MEASURES

The issue of criterion measures is of utmost importance. One of the main objectives in MLE is to develop "learning-to-learn" skills. The outcome measures, therefore, should tap exactly that characteristic, that is, the criterion measure must be a measure of change, rather than a static test performance. Unfortunately, not many studies concentrate on this aspect of validity.

CAN WE PREDICT COGNITIVE MODIFIABILITY?

One of the basic dilemmas in the field of cognitive modifiability is related to the dialectical position of the structural cognitive modifiability theory in regard to the issue of predictability. On one hand, it is assumed that an adequate experience with mediated learning prepares the individual to benefit from learning in the future. The basic distinction between distal and proximal factors suggests that adequate or inadequate cognitive development depends on MLE processes. This means that we can predict learning processes by the type and amount of mediation previously given to the individual. On the other hand, cognitive changes are conceived as self-perpetuating, autonomous, and self-regulatory. Once an individual acquires the capacity for change it is difficult, if not impossible to predict the "trajectory" of his or her development. The question is, how can we integrate scientific requirements for predictability within a theory that is based on unpredictability of changes?

References

Ainsworth, T., Belhar, M., Waters, E., & Wall, S. (1978). *Patterns of attachment: A psychological study of the strange situation.* Hillsdale, NJ: Erlbaum.

Ainsworth, T., & Bell, S. M. (1970). Attachment, exploration, and separation: Illustrated by the behavior of 1-year-olds in a strange situation. *Child Development, 41,* 49–67.

Arthur, G. (1947). *Stencil Design Test 1 of the Arthur Point Scale of Performance Tests.* New York: Psychological Corporation.

Ashman, A. F. (1992). Process-based instruction: Integrating assessment and instruction. In H. C. Haywood & D. Tzuriel, (Eds.), *Interactive assessment* (pp. 375–396). Berlin: Springer-Verlag.

Barr, P., & Samuels, M. (1988). Dynamic assessment of cognitive and affective factors contributing to learning difficulties in adults. *Professional Psychology: Research and Practice, 19,* 6–13.

Bee, H., Barnard, K., Eyres, S., Gray, C., Hamond, N., Spietz, A., Snyder, C., & Clark, B. (1982). Prediction of IQ and language skills from parental status, child performance, family characteristics, and mother infant interaction. *Child Development, 53,* 1134–1156.

Beery, K. E. (1982). *Revised administration, scoring, and teaching manual for the developmental test of visual-motor integration.* Cleveland, OH: Modern Curriculum Press.

Belsky, J., Goode, M. K., & Most, R. K. (1980). Maternal stimulation and infant exploratory competence: Cross-sectional, correlational, and experimental analyses. *Child Development, 51,* 1168–1178.

Bereiter, C. (1963). Some persisting dilemmas in the measurement of change. In C. W. Harris (Ed.), *Problems in measuring change* (pp. 3–20). Madison: University of Wisconsin Press.

Bereiter, C., & Engelmann, S. (1966). *Effectiveness of direct verbal instruction on IQ performance and achievement in reading and arithmetic.* Champaign, IL: Academic Preschool.

Berk, L. E., & Spuhl, S. T. (1995). Maternal interaction, private speech, and task performance in preschool children. *Early Childhood Research Quarterly, 10,* 145–169.

Biemans, H. J. A., & Simons, P. R. J. (1996). Contact 2: A computer-assisted instructional strategy for promoting conceptual change. *Instructional Science, 24,* 157–176.

Binet, A., & Simon, T. (1916). *The development of intelligence in children.* Vineland, NJ: Publications of the Training School at Vineland. Reprinted by Williams Publishing Co., Nashville, TN, 1980.

Bleichrodt, N., Drenth, P. J. D., Zaal, J. N., & Resing, W. C. M. (1984). *Revisie Amsterdamse Kinder Intelligentietest [Revised Amsterdam Child Intelligence Test].* Amsterdam: Swets & Zeitlinger.

Bolig, E. E., & Day, J. D. (1993). Dynamic assessment and giftedness: The promise of assessing training responsiveness. *Roeper Review, 16,* 110–113.

Boreland, J. H., & Wright, I. (1994). Identifying young, potentially gifted, economically disadvantaged students. *Gifted Child Quarterly, 38,* 164–171.

Bornstein, M. H. (1985). How infant and mother jointly contribute to developing cognitive competence in the child. *Proceedings of the National Academy of Sciences USA, 82,* 7070–7073.

Bornstein, M. H. (1988). Mothers, infants, and the development of cognitive competence. In H. E. Fitzgerald, B. M. Lester, & M. W. Yogman (Eds.), *Theory and research in behavioral pediatrics,* (Vol. 4, pp. 67–99). New York: Plenum Press.

Bornstein, M. H. (1989a). Between caretakers and their young: Two modes of interaction and their consequences for cognitive growth. In M. H. Bornstein & J. S. Bruner (Eds.), *Interaction in human development* (pp. 197–214). Hillsdale, NJ: Erlbaum.

Bornstein, M. H. (1989b). Cross-cultural developmental comparisons. *Developmental Review, 9,* 171–204.

Bornstein, M. H., Azuma, H., Tamis-LeMonda, C., & Ogino, M. (1990). Mother and infant activity and interaction in Japan and in the United States: I. A comparative macroanalysis of naturalistic exchanges. *International Journal of Behavioral Development, 13,* 267–288.

Bornstein, M. H., & Lamb, M. E. (1992). *Development in infancy: An introduction* (3rd ed.). New York: McGraw–Hill.

Bornstein, M. H., Miyake, K., & Tamis-LeMonda, C. S. (1986). A cross-national study of infant and mothers activities and interactions: Some preliminary comparisons between Japan and the United States. In *Annual report of the Research and Clinical Center for Child Development.* Sapporo, Japan: University of Hokkaido.

Bornstein, M. H., & Tamis-LeMonda, C. S. (1989). Maternal responsiveness and cognitive development in children. In M. H. Bornstein (Ed.), *Maternal responsiveness: Characteristics and consequences* (pp. 49–61). San Francisco: Jossey–Bass.

Bornstein, M. H., & Tamis-LeMonda, C. (1990). Activities and interactions of mothers and their first-born infants in the first six months of life. *Child Development, 61,* 1206–1217.

Bornstein, M. H., & Tamis-LeMonda, C. S. (1997). Maternal responsiveness and infant mental abilities: Specific predictive relations. *Infant Behavior and Development, 20,* 283–296.

Bowlby, J. (1969). *Attachment and loss: Vol. 1. Attachment.* New York: Basic Books.

Braden, J. (1985). LPAD applications to deaf populations. In D. Martin (Ed.), *Cognition, education and deafness* (pp. 124–128). Washington, DC: Gallaudet College Press.

Bradley, R. H., & Caldwell, B. M. (1984). *Home Observation for Measurement of the Environment (HOME)* (rev. ed.). Little Rock: University of Arkansas.

Brainard, C. J. (1979). *Piaget's theory of intelligence.* Engelwood Cliffs, NJ: Prentice–Hall.

Bronfenbrenner, U. (1979). *The ecology of human development.* Cambridge, MA: Harvard University Press.

Brown, A. L., & Ferrara, R. A. (1985). Diagnosing zones of proximal evelopment. In J. V. Wertsch (Ed.), *Culture, communication, and cognition: Vygotskian perspectives* (pp. 273–305). London: Cambridge University Press.

Bryant, N. R. (1982). *Preschool children's learning and transfer of matrices problems: A study of proximal development.* Unpublished master's thesis, University of Illinois.

Büchel, F. P., Schlatter, C., & Scharnhorst, U. (1997). Training and assessment of analogical reasoning in students with severe difficulties. *Educational and Child Psychology, 14,* 109–120.

Buckingham, B. R. (1921). Intelligence and its measurement: A symposium. *Journal of Educational Psychology, 12,* 271–275.

Budoff, M. (1967). Learning potential among institutionalized young adult retardates. *American Journal of Mental Deficiency, 72,* 404–411.

Budoff, M. (1987). The validity of learning potential assessment. In C. S. Lidz (Ed.), *Dynamic assessment* (pp. 52–81). New York: Guilford Press.

Burns, S. (1991). Comparison of two types of dynamic assessment with young children. *The International Journal of Dynamic Assessment and Instruction, 2,* 29–42.

Campione, J. C. (1989). Assisted assessment: Taxonomy of approaches and an outline of strengths and weaknesses. *Journal of Learning Disabilities, 22,* 151–165.

Campione, J. C., & Brown, A. L. (1987). Linking dynamic assessment with school achievement. In C. S. Lidz (Ed), *Dynamic assessment* (pp. 82–115). New York: Guilford Press.

Campione, J. C., Brown, A. L., Ferrara, R. A., Jones, R. S., & Steinberg, E. (1985). Differences between retarded and non-retarded children in transfer following equivalent learning performance: Breakdowns in flexible use of information. *Intelligence, 9,* 297–315.

Carew, J. V. (1980). Experience and the development of intelligence in young children at home and in day care. *Monographs of the Society for Research in Child Development, 45* (6–7, Serial No. 187).

Carlson, J. S., & Wiedl, K. H. (1992). The dynamic assessment of intelligence. In H. C. Haywood & D. Tzuriel, (Eds.), *Interactive assessment* (pp. 167–186). Berlin: Springer-Verlag.

Case, R. (1978). Intellectual development from birth to adulthood: A neo Piagetian interpretation. In R. S. Siegler (Ed.), *Children's thinking: What develops?* (pp. 37–71). Hillsdale, NJ: Erlbaum.

Clariana, R. B. (1993). The motivational effect of advisement on attendance and achievement in computer-based instruction. *Journal of Computer-Based Instruction, 20,* 47–51.

Clarke-Stewart, K. A. (1973). Interactions between mothers and their young children: Characteristics and consequences. *Monographs of the Society for Research in Child Development, 38* (6–7, Serial No. 153).

Clarke-Stewart, K. A. (1993). *Daycare.* Cambridge, MA: Harvard University Press.

Cole, M. (1990). Cognitive development and formal schooling: The evidence from cross-cultural research. In L. C. Moll (Ed.), *Vygotsky and education* (pp. 89–110). London: Cambridge University Press.

Cole, M., & Griffin, P. (1980). Cultural amplifiers reconsidered. In D. R. Olson (Ed.), *The social foundations of language and thought* (pp. 343–364). New York: Norton.

Collins, W. A. (1984). Commentary: Family interaction and child development. In M. Perlmutter (Ed.), *Parent–child interaction and parent–child relations in child development* (pp. 241–258). The Minnesota Symposia on Child Psychology, Vol. 17. Hillsdale, NJ: Erlbaum.

Cronbach, L. J., & Furby, L. (1970). How should we measure change—or should we? *Psychological Bulletin, 74,* 68–80.

Day, J. D., Engelhardt, J. L., Maxwell, S. E., & Bolig, E. E. (1997). Comparison of static and dynamic assessment procedures and their relation to independent performance. *Journal of Educational Psychology, 89,* 358–368.

Day, J. D., & Hall, L. K. (1987). Cognitive assessment, intelligence, and instruction. In J. D. Day & J. G. Borokowsky (Eds.), *Intelligence and exceptionality: New directions for theory, assessment, and instructional practices* (pp. 57–80). Norwood, NJ: Ablex.

Dearborn, W. F. (1921). Intelligence and its measurement. *Journal of Educational Psychology, 12,* 210–212.

Delclos, V. R., & Haywood, H. C. (1986). *Mazes Test of Task-Intrinsic Motivation.* Unpublished manuscript, Vanderbilt University, Nashville, TN.

Deutsch, R. (1998). *A tripartite model of mediator, task and student.* Unpublished manuscript, BINOE, London.

Dunn, L. M., & Dun, L. M. (1981). *Peabody Picture Vocabulary Test-Revised.* Circle Pines, MN: American Guidance Service.

Elliott, J. (1993) Assisted assessment: If it is dynamic why is it so rarely employed? *Educational and Child Psychology, 10,* 48–58.

Elliott, J., & Lauchlan, F. (1997). Assessing potential—The search for the philosopher's stone. *Educational and Child Psychology, 14,* 6–16.

Embretson, S. E. (1992). Measuring and validating cognitive modifiability as ability: A study in the spatial domain. *Journal of Educational Measurement, 29,* 25–50.

Farran, D. C., & Ramey, C. T. (1980). Social class differences in dyadic involvement during infancy, *Child Development, 51*, 254–257.

Ferrara, R. A., Brown, A. L., & Campione, J. C. (1986). Children's learning and transfer of inductive reasoning rules: Studies in proximal development. *Child Development, 57*, 1087–1099.

Feuerstein, R., & Feuerstein, S. (1991). Mediated learning experience: A theoretical review. In R. Feuerstein, P. S. Klein, & A. Tannenbaum (Eds.), *Mediated learning experience (MLE)* (pp. 3–52). London: Freund.

Feuerstein, R., Klein, P. S., & Tannenbaum, A. (Eds.) (1991). *Mediated learning experience (MLE)*. London: Freund.

Feuerstein, R., Rand, Y., Haywood, H. C., Kyram, L., & Hoffman, M. B. (1995). *Learning Propensity Assessment Device-manual*. Jerusalem: The International Center for the Enhancement of Learning Potential.

Feuerstein, R., Rand, Y., & Hoffman, M. B. (1979). *The dynamic assessment of retarded performers: The learning potential assessment device: Theory, instruments, and techniques*. Baltimore: University Park Press.

Feuerstein, R., Rand, Y., Hoffman, M., & Miller, R. (1980). *Instrumental enrichment*. Baltimore: University Park Press.

Feuerstein, R., Rand, Y., Jensen, M. R., Kaniel, S. & Tzuriel, D. (1987). Prerequisites for assessment of learning potential: The LPAD model. In C. S. Lidz (Ed.) *Dynamic assessment*, (pp. 35–51), New York: Guilford Press.

Feuerstein, R., Rand, Y., & Rynders, J. E. (1988). *Don't accept me as I am*. New York: Plenum Press.

Flor-Maduel, H. (2001, June). *Prediction of Emergent Literacy by Analogical Thinking Modifiability Among Kindergarten Children*. Paper presented at the 8th Conference of the International Association for Cognitive Education, Jyvaskyla, Finland.

Fraser, B. J., Walberg, H. J., Welch, W. W., & Hattie, J. A. (1987). Synthesis of educational productivity research. *International Journal of Educational Research, 11*, 145–252.

Frisby, C. L., & Braden, J. P. (1992). Feuerstein's dynamic assessment approach: A semantic, logical and empirical critique. *Journal of Special Education, 26*, 281–301.

Gal'perin, P. Ya. (1966). K Ucheniui ob interiorizatsii [Toward the theory of interiorization]. *Voprosy Psikhologii, 6*, 20–29.

Gamlin, P. (1989). Issues in dynamic assessment/instruction. *The International Journal of Dynamic Assessment and Instruction, 1*, 13–25.

Garrison, S. J. (1996). Influence of metacognitive prompting on learning with computer-mediated problem sets, *Dissertation Abstracts International, 57/08–A*.

Gentner, D., & Markman, A. B. (1997). Structure mapping in analogy and similarity. *American Psychologist, 52*, 45–56.

Gessel, A. (1940). The first five years of life. New York: Harper and Brothers.

Ginsburg, H. (1977). *Children's arithmetic: The learning process*. Princeton, NJ: Van Nostrand.

Goswami, U. (1991). Analogical reasoning: What develops? A review of research and theory. *Child Development, 62*, 1–22.

Goswami, U., & Brown, A. L. (1989). Melting chocolate and melting snowman: Analogical reasoning and causal relation. *Cognition, 35*, 69–95.

Gottfried, A. W. (1984). *Home environment and early cognitive development*, Orlando, FL: Academic.

Greenberg, K. H. (1990). Mediated learning in the classroom. *International Journal of Cognitive Education and Mediated Learning, 1*, 33–44.

Greenberg, N. (1993, July). *The ethology of teaching*. Paper presented at the Fourth Conference of the International Association for Cognitive Education, Nof-Ginossar, Israel.

Grigorenko, E. L., & Sternberg, R. J. (1998). Dynamic testing. *Psychological Bulletin, 124*, 75–111.

Gupta, R. M., & Coxhead, P. (Eds.) (1988). *Cultural diversity and learning efficiency: Recent developments in assessment,* London: NFER–Nelson.

Guthke, J. (1982). The learning test concept—an alternative to the traditional static intelligence test. *The German Journal of Psychology, 6,* 306–324.

Guthke, J. (1992). Learning tests: The concept, main research findings, problems, and trends. In J. S. Carlson (Ed.), *Advances in cognition and educational practice* (Vol. 1A, pp. 213–233). Greenwich, CT: JAI Press.

Guthke, J., & Al-Zoubi, A. (1987). Kulturspezifische differenzen in den Colored Progressive Matrices (CPM) und in einer Lerntestvariante der CPM. [Specific cultural differences in the Colored Progressive Matrices and in a CPM learntest variant]. *Psychologie in Erziehung und Unterricht, 34,* 306–311.

Guthke, J., Beckmann, J. F., & Dobat, H. (1997). Dynamic testing—problems, uses, trends and evidence of validity. *Educational and Child Psychology, 14,* 17–32.

Guthke, J., & Gitter, K. (1987). Zur Vorhersagbarkeit der Schulleistungsentwicklung in der Unter- und Mittelstufe auf Grund von Status und Lerntestresultaten in der Vorschulzeit [Predictability of the development of school achievement in elementary and middle school levels based on preschool learning test results]. In: Rektor der Universität (Ed.), *Risikobewältigung in der lebenslangen psychischen Entwicklung* (pp. 71–74). *Proceedings of the Third Baltic Sea Symposium on Clinical Psychology.* Rostock: Wilhelm-Pieck Universität.

Guthke, J., & Lehwald, G. (1984). On component analysis of the intellectual learning ability in learning tests. *Zeitschrift fûlr Psychologie, 192,* 3–17.

Guthke, J., & Stein, H. (1996). Are learning tests the better version of intelligence tests? *European Journal of Psychological Assessment, 12,* 1–13.

Guthke, J., & Wingenfeld, S. (1992). The learning test concept: Origins, state of the art, and trends. In H. C. Haywood & D. Tzuriel (Eds.), *Interactive assessment.* (pp. 64–93). Berlin: Springer-Verlag.

Hamers, J. H. M., Hessels, M. G. P., & Van Luit, J. E. H. (1991). *Learning potential test for ethnic minorities. Manual and test.* Amsterdam: Swets & Zeitlinger.

Hamers, J. H. M., Sijtsma, K., & Ruijssenaars, A. J. J. M. (Eds.) (1993). *Learning potential assessment.* Amsterdam: Swets & Zeitlinger.

Haywood, H. C. (1968). Motivational orientation of overachieving and underachieving elementary school children. *Journal of Personality, 30,* 63–74.

Haywood, H. C. (1971). Individual differences in motivational orientation: A trait approach. In P. I. Day, D. E. Berlyne, & D. E. Hunt (Eds.), *Intrinsic motivation: A new direction in education* (pp. 113–127). New York: Holt, Rinehart, & Winston.

Haywood, H. C. (1980). Motivational influences on learning and performance in disadvantaged youth. In S. Adiel, H. Shalom, & M. Arieli (Eds.), *Fostering deprived youth and residential education* (pp. 69–80). Tel Aviv: Mabat (in Hebrew).

Haywood, H. C. (1988). Dynamic assessment: The Learning Potential Assessment Device. In R. L. Jones (Ed.), *Psychoeducational assessment of minority group children: A casebook* (pp. 39–63). Richmond, VA: Cobb & Henry.

Haywood, H. C. (1992a). Interactive assessment: A special issue. *Journal of Special Education, 26,* 233–234.

Haywood, H. C. (1992b). The strange and wonderful symbiosis of motivation and cognition. *International Journal of Cognitive Education and Mediated Learning, 2,* 186–197.

Haywood, H. C. (1993, November). *Interactive assessment: Assessment of learning potential, school learning, and adaptive behavior.* Invited paper, Ninth Annual Learning Disorders Conference, Harvard Graduate School of Education, Cambridge, MA.

Haywood, H. C. (1995, November). *Cognitive early education: Confluence of psychology and education.* Paper presented at the Second International Congress on Psychology and Education, Madrid, Spain.

Haywood, H. C. (1997). Interactive assessment. In R. Taylor (Ed.), *Assessment of individuals with mental retardation* (pp. 108–129). San Diego: Singular Publishing Group.

Haywood, H. C., Brooks, P., & Burns, S. (1986). Stimulating cognitive development at developmental level: A tested non-remedial preschool curriculum for preschoolers and older retarded children. In M. Schwebel & C. A. Maher (Eds.), *Facilitating cognitive development: Principles, practices, and programs* (pp. 127–147). New York: Haworth Press.

Haywood, H. C., Brooks, P. H., & Burns, S. (1992). *Bright Start: Cognitive curriculum for young children.* Watertown, MA: Charles Bridge Publishers.

Haywood, H. C., & Burke, W. P. (1977). Development of individual differences in intrinsic motivation. In I. C. Uzgiris & F. Weizman (Eds.), *The structuring of experience* (pp. 235–263). New York: Plenum Press.

Haywood, H. C., & Menal, C. (1992). Cognitive-developmental psychotherapy: A case study. *International Journal of Cognitive Education and Mediated Learning, 2,* 43–54.

Haywood, H. C., & Switzky, H. (1986). Intrinsic motivation and behavior effectiveness in retarded persons. In N. R. Ellis & N. W. Bray (Eds.), *International review of research in mental retardation* (Vol. 14, pp. 1–46). Orlando, FL: Academic Press.

Haywood, H. C., & Switzky, H. N. (1992). Ability and modifiability: What, how, and how much? In J. S. Carlson (Ed.), *Cognition and educational practice: An international perspective* (pp. 25–85). Greenwich, CT: JAI Press.

Haywood, H. C., & Tzuriel, D. (1992a). Epilogue: The status and future of interactive assessment. In H. C. Haywood & D. Tzuriel (Eds.), *Interactive assessment* (pp. 504–507). Berlin: Springer-Verlag.

Haywood, H. C., & Tzuriel, D. (Eds.) (1992b). *Interactive assessment.* Berlin: Springer-Verlag.

Haywood, H. C., Tzuriel, D., & Vaught, S. (1992). Psychological assessment from a transactional perspective. In H. C. Haywood & D. Tzuriel (Eds.), *Interactive assessment* (pp. 38–63). Berlin: Springer-Verlag.

Haywood, H. C., & Wachs, T. D. (1981). Intelligence, cognition, and individual differences. In M. J. Begab, H. C. Haywood, & H. Garber (Eds.), *Psychosocial influences in retarded performance. Vol. 1. Issues and theories in development* (pp. 95–126). Baltimore: University Park Press.

Hessels, M. G. P. (1997). Low IQ but high learning potential: Why Zeyneb and Moussa do not belong in special education. *Educational and Child Psychology, 14,* 121–136.

Hessels, M. G. P., & Hamers, J. H. M. (1993). A learning potential test for ethnic minorities. In J. H. M. Hamers, K. Sijtsma, & A. J. J. M. Ruijssenaars (Eds.), *Learning potential assessment* (pp. 285–312). Amsterdam: Swets & Zeitlinger.

Holyoak, K. J., & Thagard, P. (1995). *Mental leaps: Analogy in creative thought.* Cambridge, MA: MIT Press.

Holyoak, K. J., & Thagard, P. (1997). The analogical mind. *American Psychologist, 52,* 35–44.

Jeffrey, I. (1997, July). *The Cognitive Modifiability Battery—Assessment and Intervention: Clinical perspectives of a language therapist.* Paper presented at the 6th Conference of the International Association for Cognitive Education (IACE), Stellenbosch, South Africa.

Jeffrey, L., & Tzuriel, D. (1999). *The Cognitive Modifiability Battery (CMB): Applications of a dynamic instrument in speech language therapy.* Unpublished paper, School of Education, Bar-Ilan University, Ramat Gan, Israel.

Jensen, M. R. (2000). The mindladder model: Using dynamic assessment to help students learn to assemble and use knowledge. In C. S. Lidz & J. Elliott (Eds.), *Dynamic assessment: Prevailing models and applications* (pp. 187–227). Greenwich, CT: JAI Press.

Joreskog, K. G., & Sorbom, D. (1984). *LISREL VI: Analysis of linear structural relationships by the method of maximum likelihood.* Chicago: National Educational Resources.

Kagan, J. (1965). Individual differences in the resolution of response uncertainty. *Journal of Personality and Social Psychology, 2,* 154–160.

Kahn, R., & King, S. R. (1997). Dynamic procedures for assessing children's cognitive and emotional strengths and needs. *Journal of Cognitive Education, 6,* 101–114.

Kaniel, S., & Tzuriel, D. (1992). The mediational approach in assessment and treatment of borderline psychotic adolescents. In H. C. Haywood & D. Tzuriel (Eds.), *Interactive assessment* (pp. 399–418). Berlin: Springer-Verlag.

Kaniel, S., Tzuriel, D., Feuerstein, R., Ben-Shachar, N., & Eitan, T. (1991). Dynamic assessment, learning, and transfer abilities of Jewish Ethiopian immigrants to Israel. In R. Feuerstein, P. S. Klein, & A. Tannenbaum (Eds.), *Mediated learning experience* (pp. 179–209). London: Freund.

Kao, M. T., Lehman, J. D., & Cennamo, K. S. (1996). Scaffolding in hypermedia assisted instruction: An example of integration. In *Eric Document Reproduction Service* No. ED397803.

Katy, A. (1992). Tarbut hapnai bisrael: Tmurot bidfusei hapailut hatarbutit 1970–1990, [Leisure culture in Israel: Changes in cultural activity patterns 1970–1990]. Jerusalem: Gutman Institute.

Katz, M., & Buchole, E. (1984). Use of the LPAD for cognitive enrichment of a deaf child. *School Psychology Review, 13,* 99–106.

Kaufman, A. S., & Kaufman, N. L. (1983). *Kaufman Assessment Battery for Children: Administration and scoring manual.* Circle Pines, MN: American Guidance Service.

Keane, K. J., & Kretschmer, R. E. (1987). Effect of mediated learning intervention on cognitive task performance with a deaf population. *Journal of Educational Psychology, 79,* 49–53.

Keane, K., Tannenbaum, A., & Krapf, G. F. (1992). Cognitive competence: Reality and potential in the deaf. In H. C. Haywood & D. Tzuriel (Eds.), *Interactive assessment* (pp. 300–316). Berlin: Springer-Verlag.

Kephart, N. C. (1968). Learning ability: An educational adventure. Danville, IL: Interstate.

Kern, B. (1930). *Winkungsformen der Ubung [Effects in training].* Munster, Germany: Helios.

Kester, E. T., Peña, E. D., & Gillam, R. B. (in press). Outcomes of dynamic assessment with culturally and linguistically diverse students: A comparison of three teaching methods. *Journal of Cognitive Education and Psychology.*

Kidron, R. (1989). *Basic tasks in math: Diagnostic didactic system* (4th ed.). Tel Aviv: Nitzan.

Kingma, J. (1983). Seriation, correspondence, and transitivity. *Journal of Educational Psychology, 75,* 763–771.

Kingma, J., & Reuvekamp, J. (1984). The construction of a developmental scale for seriation. *Educational and Psychological Measurement, 44,* 1–23.

Kirk, S. A., McCarthy, J. J., & Kirk, W. D. (1968). *Illinois Test of Psycholinguistic Abilities.* Urbana, IL: The University of Illinois Press.

Klein, P. S. (1982). *Adelphi Parent Administered Readiness Test (APART).* New York: Grant.

Klein, P. S. (1988). Stability and change in interaction of Israeli mothers and infants. *Infant Behavior and Development, 11,* 55–70.

Klein, P. S. (1991). Improving the quality of parental interaction with very low birth weight children: A longitudinal study using a mediated learning experience model. *Infant Mental Health, 12,* 321–337.

Klein, P. S. (Ed.) (1996). *Early intervention: Cross-cultural experiences with a mediational approach.* New York: Garland.

Klein, P. S., & Aloni, S. (1993). Immediate and sustained effects of maternal mediating behaviors on young children. *Journal of Early Intervention, 17,* 1–17.

Klein, P. S., & Hundeide, K. (1989). *Training Manual for the MISC (More Intelligent and Sensitive Child) Program.* Sri Lanka: UNICEF.

Klein, P. S., Raziel, P., Brish, M., & Birnbaum, E. (1987). Cognitive performance of 3-year olds born at very low birth weight. *Journal of Psychosomatic Obstetrics and Gynecology, 7,* 117–129.

Klein, P. S., Wieder, S., & Greenspan, S. I. (1987). A theoretical overview and empirical study of mediated learning experience: Prediction of preschool performance from mother—infant interaction patterns. *Infant Mental Health Journal, 8,* 110–129.

Koszalska, T. A. (1999). *The relationship between the types of resources used in science classrooms and middle school students' interest in science careers: An exploratory analysis.* Thesis submitted in partial fulfillment of the requirements for the degree of Doctor of Philosophy at the Pennsylvania State University.

Kozulin, A. (1990). *L. S. Vygotsky.* Brighton, England: Harvestor Press.

Kozulin, A., & Presseisen, B. Z. (1995). Mediated learning tools and psychological tools: Vygotsky and Feuerstein's perspectives in study of student learning. *Educational Psychologist, 30,* 67–75.

Lauchlan, F. & Elliott, J. (1997, July). *The use of the Cognitive Modifiability Battery (CMB) as an intervention tool for children with complex learning difficulties.* Paper presented at the 6th Conference of the International Association for Cognitive Education (IACE), Stellenbosch, South Africa.

Leont'ev, A. N. (1968). *Einige aktuelle Aufgaben der Psychologie* [Some current tasks of psychology]. Sowjetwissenschaft. Gesellschaftswissenschaftliche Beiträge.

Leont'ev, A. N., & Luria, A. R. (1964). Die psychologischen Anschauungen L. S. Wygotskis. Einführung. [The psychological views of L. S. Vygotsky. Introduction]. In L. S. Vygotsky: *Denken und Sprechen* (pp. 1–33). Berlin: Akademie-Verlag.

Lidz, C. S. (Ed.) (1987). *Dynamic assessment.* New York: Guilford Press.

Lidz, C. S. (1991). *Practitioner's guide to dynamic assessment.* New York: Guilford Press.

Lidz, C. S. (1995). Dynamic assessment and the legacy of L. S. Vygotsky. *School Psychology International, 16,* 143–153.

Lidz, C. S., Bond, L., & Dissinger, L. (1990). Consistency of mother—child interaction using the mediated learning experience (MLE) scale. *Special Services in the Schools, 6,* 145–165.

Lidz, C. S., & Elliott, J. (Eds.). (2000). *Dynamic assessment: Prevailing models and applications.* Greenwich, CT: JAI Press.

Lidz, C. S., Jepsen, R. H., & Miller, M. B. (1997). Relationships between cognitive processes and academic achievement: Application of a group dynamic assessment procedure with multiple handicapped adolescents. *Educational and Child Psychology, 14,* 56–67.

Lidz, M. C., & Macrine, S. I. (2001). An alternative approach to the identification of gifted culturally and linguistically diverse learners: The contribution of dynamic assessment. *School Psychology International, 22,* 74–96.

Lidz, C. S., & Pena, E. (1996). Dynamic assessment: The model, its relevance as a non-biased approach, and its application to Latino American children. *Language, Speech and Hearing in the Schools, 27,* 367–372.

Lidz, C. S., & Thomas, C. (1987). The Preschool Learning Assessment Device: Extension of a static approach. In C. S. Lidz (Ed.), *Dynamic assessment* (pp. 288–326). New York: Guilford Press.

Luria, A. R. (1976). *The working brain* (B. Haigh, Trans.). New York: Basic Books.

Luther, M., & Wyatt, F. (1989). A comparison of Feuerstein's method of (LPAD) assessment with conventional IQ testing on disadvantaged North York high school students. *Journal of Dynamic Assessment and Instruction, 1,* 49–64.

Lyytinen, P., Rasku-Puttonen, H., Poikkeus, A. M., Laakso, M. L., & Ahonen, T. (1994). Mother–child teaching strategies and learning disabilities. *Journal of Learning Disabilities, 27,* 186–192.

McCarthy, D. (1972). *Manual for the McCarthy Scales of Children's Abilities.* New York: Psychological Corporation.

Mearig, J. S. (1987). Assessing the learning potential of kindergarten and primary-age children. In C. S. Lidz (Ed.). *Dynamic assessment* (pp. 237–267). New York: Guilford Press.

Meili, R. (1965). *Lehrbuch der psychologischen Diagnostik* [Textbook of psychological diagnostics]. Bern: Huber.

Miech, E. J., Nave, B., & Mosteller, F. (1997). On call: A review of computer assisted language learning in US colleges and universities. In R. M. Branch & B. B. Minor (Eds.), *Educational Media and Technology Yearbook, 22,* 61–84.

Minkowich, A. (1976). *Mathematics Readiness Test.* Jerusalem: Ministry of Education Pedagogic Center.

Missiuna, C., & Samuels, M. (1988). Dynamic assessment: Review and critique. *Special Services in the Schools, 5,* 1–22.

Missiuna, C., & Samuels, M. (1989). Dynamic assessment of preschool children in special education with special needs: Comparison of mediation and instruction. *Remedial and Special Education, 5,* 1–22.

Moll, L. C. (Ed.) (1990) *Vygotsky and education: Instructional implications and applications of sociohistorical psychology.* London: Cambridge University Press.

Montessori, M. (1967). *The Montessori method.* Cambridge, Ma: Robert Bentley.

Moores, D. (1985). Reaction from a researcher's point of view. In D. Martin (Ed.), *Cognition, education and deafness* (pp. 224–228). Washington, DC: Gallaudet College Press.

Moss, E. S., & Strayer, F. F. (1990). Interactive problem solving of mothers and gifted and nongifted preschoolers. *International Journal of Developmental Psychology, 20,* 166–179.

Myklebust, H. (1960). *The psychology of deafness.* New York: Grune & Stratton.

Naglieri, J. A., & Das, J. P. (1988). Planning—arousal—simultaneous—successive (PASS): A model for assessment. *Journal of School Psychology, 26,* 35–48.

Olson, S. L., Bates, J. E., & Bayles, K. (1984). Mother–infant interaction and the development of individual differences in children's cognitive competence. *Developmental Psychology, 20,* 166–179.

Olswang, L., & Bain, B. (1996). Assessment information for predicting upcoming change in language production. *Journal of Speech and Hearing Research, 39,* 414–423.

Ortar, G., & Ben-Schachar, N. (1972). *Reading comprehension tests.* Jerusalem: Ministry of Education and Culture.

Paour, J. L. (1992). Induction of logic structures in mentally retarded: An assessment and intervention instrument. In H. C. Haywood & D. Tzuriel (Eds.). *Interactive assessment.* (pp. 119–166), Berlin: Springer-Verlag.

Paour, J. L., Cebe, S., Lagarrigue, P., & Luiu, D. (1993). A partial evaluation of Bright Start with pupils at risk of school failure. *The Thinking Teacher, 8,* 1–7.

Pena, E. D., Gillam, R. B. (2000). Outcomes of dynamic assessment with culturally and linguistically diverse students: A comparison of three teaching methods. In C. S. Lidz & J. Elliott (Eds.), *Dynamic assessment: Prevailing models and applications.* (pp. 543–572). Greenwich, CT: JAI Press.

Pena, E., Quinn, R., & Iglesias, A. (1992). The application of dynamic methods to language assessment: A nonbiased procedure. *Journal of Special Education, 26,* 269–280.

Penrose, L. S. (1934). *Mental defect.* New York: Farrar & Reinehart.

Piaget, J. (1952). *The origins of intelligence.* New York: Norton.

Piaget, J., & Inhelder, B. (1969). *The psychology of the child.* London: Routledge & Kegan Paul.

Price, G. G., Hess, R. D., & Dickson, W. P. (1981). Processes by which verbal-educational abilities are affected when mothers encourage preschool children to verbalize. *Developmental Psychology, 17,* 554–564.

Ramey, C. T., Farran, D. C., & Campbell, F. A. (1979). Predicting IQ from mother–infant interactions. *Child Development, 50,* 804–814.

Rand, Y., & Kaniel, S. (1987). Group administration of the LPAD. In C. S. Lidz (Ed.), *Dynamic assessment* (pp. 196–214) New York: Guilford Press.

Rand, Y., Tannenbaum, A. J., & Feuerstein, R. (1979). Effects of instrumental enrichment on the psychoeducational development of low-functioning adolescents. *Journal of Educational Psychology, 71*, 751–763.

Raven, J. C. (1956). *Guide to using the Colored Progressive Matrices, Sets A, Ab, and B*. London: H. K. Lewis.

Reinharth, B. M. (1989). *Cognitive modifiability in developmentally delayed children*. Unpublished doctoral dissertation, Yeshiva University, New York.

Resing, W. C. M. (1997). Learning potential assessment: The alternative for measuring intelligence? *Educational and Child Psychology, 14*, 68–82.

Resing, W. C. M., & Van Wijk, A. M. (1996). Leerpotentieel: Onderzoekbij allochtone leerlingen uit het basisonderwijs. [Learning potential: Research with minority children in primary education]. *Tijdschrift voor Orthopedagogiek, 35*, 432–442.

Rey, A. (1934). D'un procede pour evaluer l'educabilite [A method for assessing educability]. *Archives de Psychologie, 24*, 297–337.

Rey, A. (1950). *Six epreuves au service de la psychologie clinique*. [Six proofs in service of clinical psychology] Brussels: Establissements Bettendorf.

Rey, A. (1956). *Test de copie et de reproduction de mémoire de figures géométriques complexes* [Test of copying and memory reproduction of geometric figures]. Paris: Centre de Psychologie Applique.

Rey, A., & Dupont, J. B. (1953) Organization de groupes de points en figures geometriques simples. [Organization of groups of dots in simple geometric figures] *Monographes de Psychologie Appliques, 3.*

Richard G. I., & Hanner, M. A. (1987). *Language Processing Test (LPT)*, Moline, IL: Linguisystems.

Rogoff, B. (1990). *Apprenticeship in thinking: Cognitive development and social context*. London: Oxford University Press.

Rogoff, B., & Chavajay, P. (1995). What's become of research on the cultural basis of cognitive development? *American Psychologist, 50*, 859–877.

Rogoff, B., & Morelli, G. (1989). Perspectives on children's development from cultural psychology. *American Psychologist, 44*, 343–348.

Rohner, R. P. (1978). *The warmth dimension: Foundation of parental acceptance-rejection theory.* Newbury Park, CA: Sage.

Rom, A., & Morag, L. (1999). Ma'ase—Mivchan Ibud Safah Dvurah [*Test of Expressive Language Processing*]. Tel Aviv: Niv Etzion College.

Rubinstein, S. L. (1958). *Grundlagen der allgemeinen Psychologie* [Foundations of general psychology]. Berlin: Volk und Wissen.

Ruiz, C. J. (1985). Modificabilidad cognoscitive y irreversibilidad: Un estudio sobre elefecto a mediano plazo del programa enriquecimiento instrumental (Publicacion No. 4) [Cognitive modifiability and irreversibility: A study of the midterm effect of the instrumental enrichment program (Publication No. 4)]. Ciudad de Guayana, Venezuela: Universidad de Guayana.

Rutter, M. (1981). *Maternal deprivation reassessed*. London: Penguin Group.

Samuels, M. T. (1998a). Children's analogical thinking modifiability Test. *Journal of Psychoeducational Assessment, 16*, 270–274.

Samuels, M. T. (1998b). Children's inferential thinking modifiability test. *Journal of Psychoeducational Assessment, 16*, 275–279.

Samuels, M. T., Killip, S. M., MacKenzie, H., & Fagan, J. (1992). Evaluating preschool programs: The role of dynamic assessment. In H. C. Haywood & D. Tzuriel (Eds.), *Interactive assessment* (pp. 251–271). Berlin: Springer-Verlag.

Samuels, M. T., Lamb, C. H., & Oberholtzer, L. (1992). Dynamic assessment of adults with learning difficulties. In H. C. Haywood & D. Tzuriel (Eds.), *Interactive assessment* (pp. 275–299). Berlin: Springer-Verlag.

Samuels, M., Tzuriel, D., & Malloy-Miller, T. (1989). Dynamic assessment of children with learning difficulties. In R. T. Brown & M. Chazan (Eds.), *Learning difficulties and emotional problems* (pp. 145–166). Calgary, Canada: Detselig Enterprises.

Santostefano, S. (1978). *A biodevelopmental approach to clinical child psychology.* New York: Wiley.

Scarr, S. (1981). Testing for children: Assessment and the many determinants of intellectual competence. *American Psychologist, 36,* 1159–1166.

Schaffer, H. R., & Emerson, P. E. (1964). The development of social attachments in infancy. *Monograph of the Society for Research in Child Development, 29,* 94.

Scribner, S. (1984). Studying working intelligence. In B. Rogoff & J. Lave (Eds.), *Everyday cognition: Its development in social context* (pp. 9–40). Cambridge, MA: Harvard University Press.

Sharpe, D. Cole, M., & Lave, J. (1979). Education and cognitive development: The evidence from experimental research. *Monographs of the Society for Research on Child Development, 44* (1–2, Serial No. 178).

Shamir, A., & Tzuriel, D. (1999, June). *Peer-mediation with young children: The effects of intervention on children's mediational teaching style and cognitive modifiability.* Paper presented at the International Conference of the International Association for Cognitive Education (IACE), Calgary, Canada.

Sharoni, V., & Greenfeld, T. (1999). Applications of dynamic assessment and mediated learning principles in a reading remedial workshop: Case study. In D. Tzuriel (Ed.), *Mediated learning experience: Theory, applications and research* (pp. 121–141). Haifa: Ach and the International Center for Enhancement of Learning Potential.

Shochet, I. M. (1992). A dynamic assessment for undergraduate admission: The inverse relationship between modifiability and predictability. In H. C. Haywood & D. Tzuriel (Eds.), *Interactive assessment* (pp. 332–355). Berlin: Springer-Verlag.

Shure, M. B. (1987). Interpersonal problem-solving: A cognitive approach to behavior. In F. Weinert & R. Kluwe (Eds.), *Metacognition, motivation and human understanding* (pp. 191–207). Hillsdale, NJ: Erlbaum.

Sigel, I. (1982). The relationship between parental distancing strategies and the child's cognitive behavior. In L. Laosa & I. Sigel (Eds.), *Families as learning environments for children* (pp. 47–86). New York: Plenum Press.

Silverman, H., & Waxman, M. (1992). Assessing the learning potential of penitentiary inmates: An application of Feuerstein's Learning Potential Assessment Device. In H. C. Haywood & D. Tzuriel (Eds.), *Interactive assessment* (pp. 356–374), Berlin: Springer-Verlag.

Simpson, S. (1985). *Test for Assessment and Advancement of Preschool Children.* Bar-Ilan University, Ramat-Gan, Israel.

Skuy, M., Kaniel, S., & Tzuriel, D. (1988). Dynamic assessment of intellectually superior Israeli children in a low socio-economic status community. *Gifted Education International, 5,* 90–96.

Skuy, M., & Shmukler, D. (1987). Effectiveness of the Learning Potential Assessment Device for Indian and "colored" South Africans. *International Journal of Special Education, 2,* 131–149.

Skuy, M., Visser, L., Hoffenberg, S., & Fridjohn, P. (1990). Temperament and the cognitive modifiability of academically superior adolescents in South Africa. *International Journal of Disability, Development and Education, 37,* 29–43.

Snijders, J. T., & Snijders-Oomen, N. (1970). *Non-verbal intelligence tests for deaf and hearing subjects.* Groningen, Netherlands: Walters-Noordhoff.

Sparrow, S. S., Balla, D. A., & Cicchetti, D. V. (1984). *Vineland Behavior Adaptive Scales.* Circle Pines, MN: American Guidance Cervice.

Spector, J. E. (1992). Predicting progress in beginning reading: Dynamic assessment of phonemic awareness. *Journal of Educational Psychology, 84,* 353–363.

Speece, D. L., Cooper, D. H., & Kibler, J. M. (1990). Dynamic assessment, individual differences, and academic achievement. *Learning and Individual Differences, 2,* 113–127.

Sroufe, L. A. (1995). *Emotional development: The organization of emotional life in the early years.* London: Cambridge University Press.

Sroufe, L. A., & Waters, E. (1977). Attachment as an organizational construct. *Child Development, 48,* 1184–1199.

Super, C., & Harkness, S. (1986). The developmental niche: A conceptualization at the interface of society and the individual. *International Journal of Behavioral Development, 9,* 545–570.

Swanson, H. L. (1995). Using the cognitive processing test to assess ability: Development of a dynamic assessment measure. *School Psychology Review, 24* (4), 672–693.

Tal, C., & Klein, P. S. (1996). *Mediational behavior and attachment in mother-child interactions.* Unpublished manuscript, School of Education, Bar-Ilan University, Ramat Gan, Israel.

Tamis-LeMonda, C. S., & Bornstein, M. H. (1991). Individual variation, correspondence, stability, and change in mother and toddler play. *Infant Behavior and Development, 14,* 143–162.

Tharp, R. G., & Gallimore, R. (1988). *Rousing minds to life.* London: Cambridge University Press.

Tudge, R. H. (1992). Process and consequences of peer collaboration: A vygotskian analysis. *Child Development, 63,* 1364–1397.

Tzuriel, D. (1989a). Dynamic assessment of learning potential in cognitive education programs. *The Thinking Teacher, 5,* 1–4.

Tzuriel, D. (1989b). Inferential cognitive modifiability in young socially disadvantaged and advantaged children. *International Journal of Dynamic Assessment and Instruction, 1,* 65–80.

Tzuriel, D. (1991a). Cognitive modifiability mediated learning experience and affective-motivational processes: A transactional approach. In R. Feuerstein, P. S. Klein, & A. Tannenbaum (Eds.), *Mediated learning experience* (pp. 95–120). London: Freund.

Tzuriel, D. (1991b). *The Children's Inferential Thinking Modifiability (CITM) test: A preschool dynamic assessment measure of learning potential.* Unpublished manuscript, School of Education, Bar-Ilan University, Ramat Gan, Israel.

Tzuriel, D. (1992a). The dynamic assessment approach: A reply to Frisby and Braden. *Journal of Special Education, 26,* 302–324.

Tzuriel, D. (1992b). *The Children's Inferential Thinking Modifiability (CITM) Test—Instruction Manual.* School of Education, Bar-Ilan University, Ramat Gan, Israel.

Tzuriel, D. (1995a). *The Cognitive Modifiability Battery (CMB): Assessment and Intervention—Instruction Manual.* School of Education, Bar-Ilan University, Ramat Gan, Israel.

Tzuriel, D. (1995b). *The Children's Seriational Thinking Modifiability (CSTM) Test—Instruction Manual.* School of Education, Bar-Ilan University, Ramat Gan, Israel.

Tzuriel, D. (1996). Mother-child mediated learning strategies in free-play and structured situations among low, medium, and high-SES levels. *Child Development and Care, 126,* 57–82.

Tzuriel, D. (1997a). A novel dynamic assessment approach for young children: Major dimensions and current research. *Educational and Child Psychology, 14,* 83–108.

Tzuriel, D. (1997b, July). *The Cognitive Modifiability Battery (CMB): Assessment and Intervention.* Presentation at the 6th Conference of the International Association for Cognitive Education (IACE), Stellenbosch, South Africa.

Tzuriel, D. (1998). *Cognitive modifiability: Dynamic assessment of learning potential.* Tel Aviv: Sifriat Poalim (in Hebrew).

Tzuriel, D. (1999a). Dynamic assessment of preschool children: Principles and measures. In D. Tzuriel (Ed.), *Mediated learning experience: Theory, research, and applications* (pp.

182–212). Haifa: Ach Press, Oranim College, and the International Center for Enhancement of Learning Potential (in Hebrew).

Tzuriel, D. (1999b). Parent-child mediated learning transactions as determinants of cognitive modifiability: Recent research and future directions. *Genetic, Social, and General Psychology Monographs, 125*, 109–156.

Tzuriel, D. (Ed.) (1999c). *Mediated learning experience: Theory, research, and applications.* Haifa: Ach Press, Oranim College, and the International Center for Enhancement of Learning Potential (in Hebrew).

Tzuriel, D. (2000a). The Seria-Think instrument: A novel measure for assessment and intervention in seriational-computational domain. *School Psychology International, 20*, 173–190.

Tzuriel, D. (2000b). *Prediction of expressive language processing by conceptual and perceptual analogies before and after training among kindergarten children.* Unpublished paper, School of Education, Bar-Ilan University, Ramat Gan, Israel.

Tzuriel, D. (2000c). Dynamic assessment of young children: Educational and intervention perspectives. *Educational Psychology Review, 12*, 385–435.

Tzuriel, D. (2000d). The Cognitive Modifiability Battery (CMB)—Assessment and Intervention: Development of a dynamic assessment instrument. In C. S. Lidz & J. Elliott (Eds.), *Dynamic assessment: Prevailing models and applications.* (pp. 375–406). Greenwich, CT: JAI Press.

Tzuriel, D. (2001a). Dynamic assessment of learning potential. In J. J. W. Andrews, H. L. Janzen, & D. H. Saklofske (Eds.), *Ability, achievement, and behavior assessment: A practical handbook* (pp. 451–497). Orlando, FL: Academic Press.

Tzuriel, D. (2001b, June). *Prediction of Auditory Associations and Expressive Language Processing by Pre- and Post-Teaching Scores of Conceptual and Perceptual Analogies.* Paper presented at the 8th Conference of the International Association for Cognitive Education, Jyvaskyla, Finland.

Tzuriel, D., & Alfassi, M. (1994). Cognitive and motivational modifiability as a function of Instrumental Enrichment (IE) program. *Special Services in the Schools, 8*, 91–28.

Tzuriel, D., & Baruch, T. (1995). *The Frame Test of Cognitive Modifiability: Reliability and validity of a novel dynamic assessment test.* Unpublished manuscript, School of Education, Bar-Ilan University, Ramat Gan, Israel.

Tzuriel, D., & Caspi, N. (1992). Dynamic assessment of cognitive modifiability in deaf and hearing preschool children. *Journal of Special Education, 26*, 235–252.

Tzuriel, D., & Eiboshitz, Y. (1992). A structured program for visual motor integration (SP-VMI) for preschool children. *Learning and Individual Differences, 4*, 104–123.

Tzuriel, D., & Eiboshitz, Y. (1999). *The effectiveness of a structural program for enhancement of visual-motor integration, reading and math in kindergarten.* Unpublished manuscript, School of Education, Bar-Ilan University, Ramat Gan, Israel.

Tzuriel, D., & Eran, Z. (1990). Inferential cognitive modifiability as a function of mother-child mediated learning experience (MLE) interactions among Kibbutz young children. *International Journal of Cognitive Education and Mediated Learning, 1*, 103–117.

Tzuriel, D., & Ernst, H. (1990). Mediated learning experience and structural cognitive modifiability: Testing of distal and proximal factors by structural equation model. *International Journal of Cognitive Education and Mediated Learning, 1*, 119–135.

Tzuriel, D., & Feuerstein, R. (1992). Dynamic group assessment for prescriptive teaching: Differential effect of treatment. In H. C. Haywood & D. Tzuriel (Eds.), *Interactive assessment* (pp. 187–206). Berlin: Springer-Verlag.

Tzuriel, D., & Galinka, E. (2000). *The Children's Conceptual and Perceptual Analogies Modifiability (CCPAM) test—Instruction manual.* School of Education, Bar-Ilan University, Ramat Gan, Israel.

Tzuriel, D., & Galinka, E. (2001, June). *Effects of Teaching of Conceptual and Perceptual Analogies on Analogical Cognitive Modifiability among 4- and 5-years old Kindergarten Children.* Paper presented at the 8th Conference of the International Association for Cognitive Education, Jyvaskyla, Finland.

Tzuriel, D., & Gerafy, O. (1998). *Changes in teachers' attitudes and mediational teaching as a function of dynamic assessment training.* Unpublished manuscript, School of Education, Bar-Ilan University, Ramat Gan, Israel.

Tzuriel, D., & Hatzir, A. (1999, June). *The effects of mediational strategies of fathers and mothers and amount of time they spent with their young children on children's cognitive modifiability.* Paper presented at the 7th International Conference of the International Association for Cognitive Education (IACE), Calgary, Canada.

Tzuriel, D., & Haywood, H. C. (1992). The development of interactive-dynamic approaches for assessment of learning potential. In H. C. Haywood & D. Tzuriel (Eds.), *Interactive assessment* (pp. 3–37). Berlin: Springer-Verlag.

Tzuriel, D., Kaniel, S., Kanner, A., & Haywood, H. C. (1999). The effectiveness of Bright Start Program in kindergarten on transfer abilities and academic achievements. *Early Childhood Research Quarterly, 14,* 111–141.

Tzuriel, D., Kaniel, S., & Yehudai, M. (1994, July). *Mediated learning experience (MLE) interactions among Ethiopian immigrant and Israeli-born mothers.* Paper presented at the 12th International Congress of the International Association for Cross-Cultural Psychology, Pamplona, Spain.

Tzuriel, D., Kaniel, S., Zeliger, M., Friedman, A., & Haywood, H. C. (1998). Effects of the Bright Start program in kindergarten on use of mediated learning strategies and children's cognitive modifiability. *Child Development and Care, 143,* 1–20.

Tzuriel, D., & Kaufman, R. (1999). Mediated learning and cognitive modifiability: Dynamic assessment of young Ethiopian immigrants in Israel. *Journal of Cross-Cultural Psychology, 30,* 364–385.

Tzuriel, D., & Klein, P. S. (1983). Learning skills and types of temperament as discriminants between intrinsically and extrinsically motivated children. *Psychological Reports, 53,* 59–69.

Tzuriel, D., & Klein, P. S. (1985). Analogical thinking modifiability in disadvantaged, regular, special education, and mentally retarded children. *Journal of Abnormal Child Psychology, 13,* 539–552.

Tzuriel, D., & Klein, P. S. (1986). Innovations in assessment of young children's cognitive modifiability. In E. Chiger (Ed.), *Special education and social handicap.* (pp. 151–162). London: Freund.

Tzuriel, D., & Klein, P. S. (1987). Assessing the young child: Children's analogical thinking modifiability. In C. S. Lidz (Ed.), *Dynamic assessment* (pp. 268–282). New York: Guilford Press.

Tzuriel, D., & Klein, P. S. (1990). *The Children's Analogical Thinking Modifiability (CATM) test—Instruction manual.* School of Education, Bar-Ilan University, Ramat Gan, Israel.

Tzuriel, D. & Samuels, M. T. (2000). Dynamic assessment of learning potential: Inter-rater reliability of deficient cognitive functions, type of mediation, and non-intellective factors. *Journal of Cognitive Education and Psychology, 1,* 41–64.

Tzuriel, D., Samuels, M. T., & Feuerstein, R. (1988). Non-intellectual factors in dynamic assessment. In R. M. Gupta & P. Coxhead (Eds.), *Cultural diversity and learning efficiency: Recent developments in assessment* (pp. 141–163). London: NFER–Nelson.

Tzuriel, D., & Schanck, T. (July 1994). *Assessment of learning potential and reflectivity -impulsivity dimension.* Paper presented at the 23rd International Congress of Applied Psychology, Madrid, Spain.

Tzuriel, D., & Shamir, A. (2001). Computer-assisted dynamic assessment of seriational thinking. *Journal of Computer Assisted Learning.*

Tzuriel, D., & Weiss, S. (1998a). Cognitive modifiability as a function of mother-child mediated learning interactions, mother's acceptance-rejection, and child's personality. *Early Childhood and Parenting, 7,* 79–99.

Tzuriel, D. & Weiss, S. (1998b). *Prediction of children's cognitive modifiability by specific mediated learning strategies in mother–child interactions.* Unpublished manuscript. School of Education, Bar-Ilan University, Ramat Gan, Israel.

Tzuriel, D., & Weitz, A. (1998). *Mother-child mediated learning experience (MLE) strategies and children's cognitive modifiability among very low birth weight (VLBW) and normally born weight (NBW) children.* Unpublished manuscript, School of Education, Bar-Ilan University, Ramat Gan, Israel.

Tzuriel, D., Kaniel, S., & Yehudai, M. (1994, July). *Mediated learning experience (MLE) interactions among Ethiopian immigrant and Israeli-born mothers.* Paper presented at 12th International Congress of the International Association for Cross-Cultural Psychology, Pamplona, Spain.

Utley, C. A., Haywood, H. C., & Masters, J. C. (1992). Policy implications of psychological assessment of minority children. In H. C. Haywood & D. Tzuriel (Eds.), *Interactive assessment* (pp. 445–469). Berlin: Springer-Verlag.

Valsiner, J. (1984). Construction of the zone of proximal development in adult–child joint interaction: The socialization of meals. In B. Rogoff & J. V. Wertsch (Eds.), *Children's learning in the 'zone of proximal development': New directions in child development* (Vol. 23, pp. 65–76). San Francisco: Jossey–Bass.

Valsiner, J. (1987). *Culture and the development of children's action.* New York: Wiley.

van der Veer, R., & Valsiner, J. (1993). *A quest for synthesis: Life and work of Lev Vygotsky.* London: Routledge.

van Geert, P. (1994). Vygotskian dynamics of development, *Human Development, 37,* 346–365.

Vaught, S. R., & Haywood, H. C. (1990). Interjudge agreement in dynamic assessment: Two instruments from the Learning Potential Assessment Device. *The Thinking Teacher, 5,* 1–6, 11–13.

Verster, J. M. (1973). *Test administrators manual for deductive reasoning test.* Johannesburg: National Institute for Personnel Research.

Vibbert, M., & Bornstein, M. (1989). Specific associations between domains of mother–child interactions and toddler referential language and pretense play. *Infant Behavior and Development, 12,* 163–184.

Vygotsky, L. S. (1956). *Izbrannye psikhologicheskie issledovaniya [Selected psychological investigations].* Moscow: Izdatel'stvo Akademii Pedagogicheskikh Nauk.

Vygotsky, L. S. (1978). *Mind in society.* Cambridge, MA: Harvard University Press.

Vygotsky, L. S. (1981). The genesis of higher mental functions. In J. V. Wertsch (Ed.), *The concept of activity in Soviet psychology* (pp. 144–188). Armonk, NY: Sharpe.

Wachs, T. D. (1992). *The nature of nurture.* Newbury Park, CA: Sage.

Wachs, T. D., Bishry, Z., Sobhy, A., McCabe, G., Galal, O., & Shaheen, F. (1993). *Relation of rearing environment to adaptive behavior of Egyptian toddlers. Child Development, 64,* 586–604.

Wachs, T. D., & Gruen, G. (1982). *Early experience and human development.* New York: Plenum Press.

Wachs, T. D., & Plomin, R. (1991). *Conceptualization and measurement of organism-environment interaction.* Washington, DC: American Psychological Association.

Warnez, J. (1991). Implementation of the CCYC in a therapeutic center. *The Thinking Teacher, 6,* 7–9.

Waters, J., & Stringer, P. (1997). The Bunny Bag: A dynamic approach to the assessment of preschool children. *Educational and Child Psychology, 14,* 33–45.

Wechsler, D. (1991). *Manual for the Wechsler Intelligence test for Children—III.* New York: The Psychological Corporation.

Weikart, D. P., & Schweinhart, L. J. (1997). High/Scope Perry preschool program. In G. W. Albee & T. P. Gullota (Eds.), *Primary prevention works: Issues in children's and families' lives* (Vol. 6, pp. 146–166). Newbury Park, CA: Sage.

Wertsch, J. V. (1984). The zone of proximal development: Some conceptual issues. In B. Rogoff & J. V. Wertsch (Eds.), *Children's learning in the 'zone of proximal development': New directions in child development* (Vol. 23, pp. 7–18). San Francisco: Jossey-Bass.

Wertsch, J. V. (1985). *Culture, communication and cognition: Vygotskian perspectives.* London: Cambridge University Press.

Wertsch, J. V., & Tulviste, P. (1992). L. S. Vygotsky and contemporary developmental psychology. *Developmental Psychology, 28*, 548–557.

Wiedl, K. H. (1984). Lerntests: nur Forschungsmittel und Forschungsgegenstand? [Learning tests: Means and subject of research only?]. *Zeitschrift fur Entwicklungspsychologie und Pädagagische Psychologie, 16*, 245–281.

Wood, D. J. (1989). Social interaction as tutoring. In M. H. Bornstein & J. S. Bruner (Eds.), *Interaction in human development* (pp. 59–80). Hillsdale, NJ: Lawrence Erlbaum.

Wood, D. J., Bruner, J., & Ross, G. (1976). The role of tutoring in problem solving. *Journal of Child Psychology and Psychiatry, 17*, 89–100.

Yarrow, L. J., Rubenstein, J. L., & Pedersen, F. R. (1975). *Infant and environment.* New York: Wiley.

Zambrana-Ortiz, N. J., & Lidz, C. S. (1995). The relationship between Puerto-Rican mothers' and fathers' mediated learning experiences and the competence of their preschool children. *Journal of Cognitive Education, 4*, 17–32.

Zigler, E., Abelson, W. D., & Seitz, V. (1973). Motivational factors in the performance of economically disadvantaged children on the Peabody Picture Vocabulary Test. *Child Development, 44*, 294–303.

Zigler, E., & Butterfield, E. C. (1968). Motivational aspects of changes in IQ test performance of culturally deprived nursery school children. *Child Development, 39*, 1–14.

Zilber, D. (2001, June). *Readiness for Math in Kindergarten and its Relation to Conceptual and Perceptual Analogical Thinking.* Paper presented at the 8th Conference of the International Association for Cognitive Education, Jyvaskyla, Finland.

Index